JES

". . . and thou shalt call his name Jesus: *for he shall save his people from their sins."*
Matthew 1:21

An anonymous author made this striking comparison. "Socrates taught for 40 years, Plato for 50, Aristotle for 40, and Jesus for only 3. Yet the influence of Christ's 3-year ministry infinitely transcends the impact left by the combined 130 years of teaching from these men who were among the greatest philosophers of all Antiquity.

"He painted no pictures, yet some of the finest paintings of Raphael, Michelangelo, and Leonardo da Vinci received their inspirations from Him. Jesus wrote no poetry, but Dante, Milton, and scores of the world's greatest poets were inspired by Him.

"He composed no music, still Haydn, Handel, Beethoven, Bach, and Mendelssohn reached their highest perfection of melody in the hymns, symphonies, and oratorios they composed in His praise. Every sphere of human greatness has been enriched by this humble Carpenter of Nazareth.

"His unique contribution to the race of men is the salvation of the soul! Philosophy could not accomplish that. Not art. Not literature. Nor music. Only Jesus Christ can break the enslaving chains of sin and Satan. He alone can speak peace to the human heart, strengthen the weak, and give life to those who are spiritually dead."

Please let me introduce you to Jesus. He has been my personal friend for nearly 40 years. He loves you, and you'll find Him very easy to love, too.

Bob Gass

The Best of The Word *for* Today

Bob Gass

Bridge-Logos *Publishers*

Gainesville, Florida 32614 USA

Unless otherwise indicated, the Scripture quotations in this publication are from the New King James Version. Copyright 1979, 1980, 1982, Thomas Nelson, Inc., Publishers. Used by permission.

Scripture quotations marked (AMP) are taken from the Amplified Bible, Old Testament, Copyright 1965, 1987 by The Zondervan Corporation. The Amplified New Testament, Copyright 1954, 1958, 1987 by The Lockman Foundation. Used by permission.

Scripture quotations marked NASB are from the New American Standared Bible. Copyright 1960, 1962, 1963, 1968, 1971, 1972, 1973, 1975, 1977 by the Lockman Foundation. Used by permission.

Scripture quotations marked TLB are from The Living Bible. Copyright 1971 by Tyndale House Publishers, Wheaton, IL. Used by permission.

Scripture quotations marked NIV are taken from the Holy Bible: New International Version. Copyright 1973, 1978, 1984 by the International Bible Society. Used by permission of Zondervan Bible Publishers.

Scripture quotations marked TM are taken from The Message. Copyrighted 1996 by NavPress Publishing Group. Used by permission.

The Best of the Word for Today
by Bob Gass
International Standard Book Number: 0-88270-731-0
Library of Congress Card Catalog Number: 96-78633
Copyrighted 1996 by Bob Gass
Reprinted 2000

Published by:
Bridge-Logos *Publishers*
P.O. Box 141630
Gainesville, FL 32614, USA
http://www.bridgelogos.com

Dedication

To my wife, Debby, who typed her wee fingers to the bone, and without whom this book would not be in your hands. You're a gift lady!

To my mother, whose love and prayers molded me into a man of God. I miss you! We'll have much to talk about when I get home.

To my friend and pastor, Bishop Earl Paulk, who walked with me through the worst moments of my life—and never let go.

To Pastor Sarah Utterbach, whose insights have enriched the pages of this book more times than I could count.

To my sister, Ruth, whose love for poetry showed me the value of a verse well chosen.

To Dr. Mike Murdock, always a friend and an inspiration!

To Sherman Owens, whose writings have given me so much.

To Dr. James McConnell, my first mentor and role model for ministry.

To Gordon Magee, my spiritual father, "Your gift lives in me and so many others!"

And to all the others, too many to mention by name, thank you! I couldn't have done it without you.

Preface

Bob Gass is my friend and mentor. Bob is not afraid to admit to his mistakes, but the test of the mettle in this man is his singular desire to put the Word of God into practice.

The Word for Today has proved to be so popular that we have had to print nearly a million quarterly booklets. This book contains the very best of those daily Bible readings.

They contain much that has been learned during a lifetime's work serving the Lord. I trust that what Bob has written here will strengthen your relationship with Jesus and provoke you to go "scurrying" to your Bible to check out what God is saying to you today!

Gareth Littler
Managing Director
United Christian Broadcasters
Europe

Acknowledgments

Paul said, "Give attention to reading." To read is to grow and I have experienced personal growth and inspiration from the writings and teachings of the following ministries. I recommend them highly: Rick Joyner, Frances Frangapane, T.D. Jakes, Malcolm Smith, Judson Cornwall, Bob Yandian, Sarah Utterbach, John Mason, Bishop Earl Paulk, Joyce Meyers, Mike Murdock, and Sherman Owens.

These are "quality" ministries and their thoughts have enriched many of the days in this devotional. I am grateful to them.

A NEW BEGINNING

* * *

He who was seated on the throne said, "I am making everything new!"
Revelation 21:5 (NIV)

Everybody needs a new beginning. After Jonah failed and ran from the call of God, we read, "The word of the Lord came to Jonah a *second time*" (Jonah 3:1). He's the God of the second chance! (And a third, if you need it.) When David failed so badly, he discovered there was "a fountain opened to the house of David for sin and uncleanness" (Zechariah 13:1). The good news is *you can start again!* You can close the door on last year with all its pain and failure. The only place it can live is *in your memory.* The only power it can have over you is *the power you give it.* Paul says, "Forgetting those things which are behind, and reaching forth unto those things which are before" (Philippians 3:13).

If you're making resolutions, *start small*! Don't set yourself up for failure by saying "I'll pray *two* hours every day." My wife tells me the gym she goes to is *full* during the first week of January but almost empty by Easter. The ones who are still there will make it through the rest of the year. Staying fit isn't something you do short term, it's a daily habit and a way of life—and it's the same spiritually.

* * *

You don't need new rules. What you need is a new relationship with God. So why don't you make *that* your number one resolution for this year?

A JUMP START FOR COLD MORNINGS

* * *

Strengthen me according to Your word.
Psalm 119:28 (NKJV)

When I started writing devotionals, I hoped I could say something every day that would bless everybody, and be just what they needed. I was wrong. The Bible tells us the people heard *John* but they followed *Jesus.* My assignment is to nudge you closer to Him. Getting into this devotional will help you, but getting into His Word and into His presence, will *change* you and transform you into His image. (See 2 Corinthians 3:18.)

The only question that really matters is, *Do you want to grow?* My friend Sherman Owens says, "Growth comes through either the pain of discipline or the pain of regret. Discipline weighs an ounce, regret weighs a ton." Make your choice. You weren't born qualified, you become qualified—so make a commitment to read, meditate, and live in the Word. Solomon says, "A wise man will hear and increase learning" (Proverbs 1:5, NKJV).

The word for today is a *jump start for cold mornings.* It gives you an entry point into the Word and into fellowship with Him—then He'll do the rest. God gave Joshua the formula for quality living: "This Book of the Law shall not depart out of thy *mouth*; but thou shalt *meditate* therein day and night, that thou mayest *observe to do according to all that is written* therein: for then thou shalt make thy way prosperous, and then thou shalt have good success" (Joshua 1:8).

* * *

The answer is at your fingertips—use it!

STAY ON THE BATTLEFIELD

* * *

At the time when kings go forth to battle,
. . . David tarried still at Jerusalem.

2 Samuel 11:1

David didn't get into trouble until he left the battlefield! When he stopped fighting, he suffered his greatest defeat. Your protection depends on being in the right place. Stay at your post—don't give the enemy an inch or he'll take a mile. Keep your sword drawn and your shield high. Of all the armor Paul speaks of in Ephesians 6, there's none for your *back*. If you think fighting is tough, wait till you see what happens when you *stop fighting*.

We read, "He saw a woman washing herself; and the woman was very beautiful to look upon." Even though she was someone's wife and David knew the consequences he "sent messengers and took her; and she lay with him" (2 Samuel 11:1-4). Before it was over, David committed murder in a vain attempt to cover up his sin, a baby was born and died, David's name was dragged through the mud and, saddest of all, there was given "great occasion to the enemies of the LORD to blaspheme" (2 Samuel 12:14).

You need a goal so noble and a cause so great that you wouldn't dream of endangering it by laying down your sword and leaving the battlefield.

* * *

Child of God, stay on the battlefield—it's the only *safe* place to be.

TOO MUCH TO LOSE

* * *

Then Jesus said unto him, . . . take up the cross, and follow me. And he was sad at that saying, and went away grieved: for he had great possessions.

Mark 10:21-22

This man really *wanted* to follow Jesus, but he had too much to lose. He could have been another John or Mark, but that's the *last* we ever hear about him, because he had become accustomed to a life of privilege and couldn't live with less.

Imagine him years later as an old man. His grandson climbs up on his lap and says, "Granddad, who was the greatest man you ever met?" Without hesitating, he replies, "Jesus!" "What made Him so great" the child asks? He replies, "Son, there's never been anyone like Him. He healed the sick, and even raised the dead. I saw Him do it!" The little fellow says, "Granddad, did He ever talk to you?" "Yes," He replies. The child asks, "Well, Granddad, what did He say to you?" Looking at the child he says, "He asked me to follow Him." Earnest eyes look up at the old man and ask, *"Did you do it, Granddad, did you follow Him?"*

Fighting back tears of regret,he sets the little fellow down and walks out into the garden of his luxurious home with the words ringing in his ears, "Did you do it Granddad, did you follow Him?"

* * *

When your life is over, will you be able to look back with joy and say, "I followed Jesus"? What else matters?

STAY FOCUSED

* * *

Do not turn aside to the right or to the left. Walk in all the way that the LORD your God has commanded you, so that you may live and prosper and prolong your days in the land that you will possess.

Deuteronomy 5:32 (NIV)

The way to kill a man with a great dream is to give him another one! The devil's strategy is to get you *spread out so thin* that you become *mediocre* in everything and *excellent* in nothing. Paul's strategy for life can be summed up in one line, "I am bringing all my energies to bear on this *one* thing" (Philippians 3:13 ,TLB). *Did you know that a dove has no peripheral vision?* It cannot see right or left—only straight ahead. What a picture! The dove is a symbol of the Holy Spirit, and the Holy Spirit will *focus* you on your purpose and aim you toward your destiny. Most things in life fail for one reason—broken focus! Don't let it happen to you. Don't get distracted by lesser things no matter how loud or how long they call to you. Isaiah said, "Therefore have I set my face like a flint and I know I shall not be put to shame" (Isaiah 50:7, NIV).

One of Satan's favorite tricks is to get you to say "yes" to too many things. Because something is *good* does not mean it is *right for you*. There comes a time when your "plate is full" doing what God has told you to do, and you've got to learn to say "no" to even the best of ideas.

* * *

Child of God, start learning to say *no* to lesser things so that you can say *yes* to the things that matter most—the things God has called *you* to do.

GOD HAS A PURPOSE FOR YOUR LIFE

* * *

Ye have not chosen me, but I have chosen you.

John 15:16

It doesn't take a lot of people to bring about change. In fact, too many people can get in the way. Gideon chose 32,000 men to fight, but God only needed 300. He doesn't care how many can be *counted*—He only cares how many can be *counted on*! The truth is, your life could be messed up because too many people are telling you what to do. Don't listen to them. Get down before God and ask *Him* to speak to you. He'll give you the word you need.

God doesn't need a crowd—He just needs someone who will listen and obey. If He wants to start a nation, He'll give hope and vision to an Abraham. If He wants to bring down an Egyptian Pharaoh, He'll reach into the bulrushes and pull out a Moses. When He wants a lineage for His Son, He'll go to the *Red Light District* and find a Rahab. He's just looking for a willing heart!

Ethel Waters loved to say, "My God don't sponsor no flops!" Her grammar was slightly off, but her theology was right on. Don't spend your life trying to be *ordinary.* Don't try to fit somebody else's expectations. *God has an agenda just for you!*

* * *

The reason God has brought you through so much is because He has a higher plan and purpose for your life. Get into His presence today and ask Him all about it.

THE RIVER OF REVIVAL

* * *

And I saw water . . . the temple . . . water that was ankle deep . . . water that was knee deep . . . water that was up to the waist . . . now it was a river, deep enough to swim in.

Ezekiel 47: 1-9 (NIV)

Ezekiel saw a river, and everywhere it flowed, it brought *life!* Take a moment and read the first 12 verses, *it's prophetic concerning what God is doing in our day.*

Note, it started in the oldest religious institution on earth—the temple. Look at this river of revival: first it was ankle deep, then knee deep, then waist deep, and, ultimately "rivers to swim in", and "something he couldn't get over." That's what I want—something I can't get over! Do you know what I mean? I've noticed that in this latest move of God, pastors—thousands of them—dry, weary, barren, and desperate for the river of God, are coming to see, hear, and drink. Some even *swim!* Then they take it back home to their thirsty congregations. *You only need one qualification—you must be thirsty!*

Note, this river will not flow into a "swamp" (Ezekiel 47:11), for a swamp will control it and, ultimately, kill it. Note also that this river brought *fruit* (character), and *food* (the Word), and *healing* (verse12) wherever it went. Today, the thirst you feel within you is born of God, and I believe it's leading you to that river. God said, "I will pour water on him that is thirsty, and floods upon the dry ground" (Isaiah 44:3).

* * *

If you're thirsty and dry, lift your hands toward the sky, it's beginning to rain!

KINDNESS AFOREHAND

* * *

There came a woman having an alabaster box of ointment; very precious . . . and poured it on his head.

Mark 14:3

Don't keep the alabaster box of your love sealed up until your friends are dead! Break it open now, pour it out and fill their lives with joy while you can. Those words of kindness you've thought of saying a thousand times—say them now while their ears can hear them and their hearts can still be touched. Those flowers you keep meaning to send—do it this week and brighten their home *before they leave it!*

It's amazing! The crowd in the house saw her do it, argued about it, and *missed the whole point.* That very night following this woman's act of devotion, Judas would go out and set the wheels in motion that would lead Jesus to the cross. Somehow she sensed that time and opportunity were running out. If she was *ever* going to show Him her love, this was it! Listen to what Jesus said: "She came aforehand to anoint my body" (Mark 14:8). There it is—*kindness aforehand.*

Joseph of Arimathea brought 100 lbs. of precious ointment to anoint Jesus after He was dead, but not a word of praise is spoken about his "post-mortem" kindness. She brought only *1 lb.* of ointment and poured it on Him—*while He was still living*—and Jesus said, "Wherever the gospel is preached throughout the world, what she has done will also be told in memory of her" (Mark 14:9 NIV). Are you getting the message?

* * *

If my friends have any alabaster boxes laid away for me, I would rather they bring them out *now.*

WALKING THROUGH THE FIRE

* * *

The one who called you is completely dependable. If He said it, He'll do it!

1 Thessalonians 5:24 (TM)

Did you hear that? *If He said it, He'll do it!* He's completely dependable. No matter *what* you're going through today, you can count on Him to be with you—and when *He's* with you, you can be sure He'll *bring you through.*

Remember the three Hebrew children? They refused to bow to the king's idols, so he threw them into a furnace heated seven times over. Maybe you feel like you're walking through the fire and it's seven times worse than anything you've ever experienced. But look what happened. When the king looked into the fire, he said, "Did not we cast *three* men bound into the midst of the fire? Lo, I see *four* men loose, walking in the midst of the fire, and they have no hurt; and the form of the fourth is like the Son of God" (Daniel 3:24-25). In the midst of the furnace the three Hebrew children were *"loose,"* they had "*no hurt,*" and they were "*walking with the Son of God.*" Today, if He allows you to go through the fire, He'll be with you; it won't hurt you; *and the very thing the enemy meant to destroy you, will set you free.* The One who called you is *completely dependable.*

* * *

Also, *you* are not the only consideration here. Like the Hebrew children, your faith in the fire will touch the lives of *others* and turn them to God.

YOUR ATTITUDE DETERMINES EVERYTHING

* * *

My servant Caleb has a different attitude, and has wholeheartedly followed me.

Numbers 14:24 (Berk)

Caleb went against the crowd and against popular opinion. While the majority thought the giants were too big and God's people were too small, Caleb never doubted God for a minute. The *miracles* proved that nothing was too big for God to handle. The *manna* proved He cared and *every need* would be supplied. So, with a God like this, how can you fail?

Listen: "Caleb stilled the people before Moses, and said, Let us go up at once, and possess it; for we are well able to overcome it" (Numbers 13:20). What an attitude! If only they'd listened. But no; their negative attitude landed them in the wilderness—for 40 years! *Doubt and unbelief will* always *lead you into the wilderness. Grumbling and complaining will fill your life with barrenness.* John Mason says, "It's your *attitude* that determines your *altitude.* You'll *never* rise any higher than it." Caleb had a *different attitude* and look at the results he got: "Hebron therefore became the inheritance of Caleb, because that he wholly followed the LORD God of Israel" (Joshua 14:13).

* * *

How's *your* attitude and your outlook today?

GO FOR THE GOLD!

* * *

I'm running hard for the finish line. I'm giving it everything I've got. No sloppy living for me. I'm staying alert and in top condition.

1 Corinthians 9:26 (TM)

I live in Atlanta, the city where they held the 1996 Olympics. You should have seen this place. Three billion dollars worth of new construction, half a million visitors, and thousands of athletes and their trainers from all over the world competing for Olympic Gold. No hour was too early to rise; no distance too great to run; no sacrifice too great in order to win.

Listen to how Paul describes it: "You've all been to the stadium to see the athletes run. Everyone runs; one wins! *Run to win!* (1 Corinthians 9:25, paraphrase). Mom, use *today to sow the seeds of Christian character* into the lives of your children. Sir, *strive for excellence,* whether you sweep streets or build skyscrapers. *Reach out in love* and touch someone with kindness, expecting nothing in return, and be assured that *every* thought, *every* word and *every* deed, will be rewarded at the end of the race. Don't let *anything* keep you from reaching the finish line.

Paul said, "I'm not going to be caught napping; telling everyone else about it, and then missing out myself" (1 Corinthians 9:27, paraphrase). Come on, child of God. This calls for discipline! It calls for endurance! It calls you to sacrifice lesser things in order to win a crown of glory.

* * *

The word for you today is, *"Go for the gold!"*

LOOK FOR THE BEST IN OTHERS

* * *

Be careful not to stir up discontent.
1 Corinthians 10:9 (TM)

Have you ever been around someone who loved to *stir things up*? It may seem harmless to us, but *God* has a different view of it. Twenty-three-thousand of God's people died in one day because they murmured against Moses, the manna, the direction God was leading them, and all sorts of things. Never had a people been more protected, privileged, or prospered, but you couldn't tell it by what they were saying. These *murmurers* never made it into the Promised Land. *Murmurers* never *do!*

Do you know which church Paul was speaking to when he wrote, "I have confidence in you?" The Corinthians. Amazing! Some of them got drunk at communion, tolerated fornication, doubted the resurrection, and these were only a *few* of their problems. One man told me, "I read the Book of Corinthians just to get encouraged. I know at least I'm not doing *that* badly." But along comes Paul and says, "I have confidence in you." "You're full of faith." "You come behind in no gift." He focuses on the *positive*; he builds on their *strength*. *A mature Christian always focuses on the strengths and good things in others.*

So, today, look for the best in others. Listen: "You'll do best by filling your minds and meditating on . . . the best, not the worst; the beautiful, not the ugly; things to praise, not things to curse" (Philippians 4:8, TM).

* * *

When you look for the good in others today—you'll find it!

GOD WANTS TO BLESS YOUR WORK

* * *

Put God in charge of your work, and what you've planned will take place.

Proverbs 16:3

God wants to be *included* in *all* your plans, *consulted* in *all* your decisions, and *honored* in *every area* of your life. If you do, what you plan will prosper and what you plant will produce fruit.

If you've been taught that He is only interested in church matters, or the spiritual side of your life then listen: "In *all* thy ways acknowledge Him, and He shall direct thy paths" (Proverbs 3:6). Did you hear that? *All* thy ways!

Moses told the people, "Remember the LORD thy God: for it is he that giveth thee power (ability, insights, ideas, and skill) to get wealth" (Deuteronomy 8:18). *Imagine having one of God's ideas for your business, your career, or your life!* God has ideas nobody has ever thought of. Imagine, the God who gave Edison "incandescent light," and showed Fleming how to turn a piece of molding bread into the miracle of "penicillin," being *your* God, *your* source, *your* Father, and He wants to talk to you, *if you'll just take time to listen.*

* * *

Have you talked with Him *today*?

11TH HOUR REAPERS

* * *

I will give unto this last even as unto thee.

Matthew 20:14

It's going to take an *11th hour crew* to reap the *11th hour harvest. The previous generation of reapers struggle to understand them.*

Recently I spent two days listening to contemporary Christian music, including *Christian Rock* and *Rap*. The guitars wailed, the bass throbbed, the drums pounded, and they sounded like they were screaming the words. I got a headache. Later, when someone read them to me, the words were solidly scriptural and Christ exalting. What does this mean? It means it's going to take a redeemed generation of their *peers*, who understand and speak their language, to gather this final harvest.

The 11th hour reapers grew up in a generation where guns go to school, and drugs are available on every corner. Half of them come from single parent families, and others sought for companionship and worth in a gang. Their mentors and heroes had blue cropped-off hair, multiple earrings, and wore leather. But the 11th hour reapers know how to *gather in this harvest*. So to us who are part of another generation, let's withhold criticism and *pray for a heart of love. God is visiting them, just like He did us*. We have only to rejoice in the harvest and remember the promise, "I will give unto this last, even as unto thee" (Matthew 20:14).

* * *

Read Matthew 20 and think about it.

IT RUBS OFF

* * *

His face glowed from being in the presence of God.

Exodus 34:29 (TLB)

You can only talk convincingly about the God you know—the one *you've* spent time with. Any other God belongs in a theology book, and you'll have a hard time selling Him. When Moses came down the mountain, his face shone. He had been in God's presence and when you've been there *it shows.* It shows in the way you look, the way you walk and talk, the way you treat your family, the way you spend your money, and the way you respond to hurting people. *It rubs off!*

Paul Cain says, *"Most of us are as close to God as we want to be."* Think about it. "Draw nigh to God, and he will draw nigh to you" (James 4:8). How could you possibly be the same when you've been with Him? He transforms everything He touches. Listen: "He that *dwelleth* in the secret place of the Most High shall *abide* under the shadow of the Almighty" (Psalm 91:1). He didn't say "visit" or "drop in if you have time," He said "*dwell.*" Take up residence. Move in and set up house. It's all got to do with your *desire.* David said, "One thing have I desired of the LORD, that will I seek after" (Psalm 27:4).

* * *

Today, make up your mind to rearrange things in your life so that you can spend more time in His presence. If you do, it will show, because it rubs off!

IN THE PRESENCE OF MINE ENEMIES

* * *

Thou preparest a table before me in the presence of mine enemies: thou anointest my head with oil; my cup runneth over.

Psalm 23:5

When does God make your cup overflow? In the presence of your enemies. *When does God anoint your head with oil?* In the presence of your enemies. *When do you need goodness and mercy the most?* In the presence of your enemies. *When do you need the rod and staff of His comfort and protection?* In the presence of your enemies. Can you see this? The very fact that you've made it this far proves His goodness and mercy have been with you *all*—not just *some,* but *all*—the days of your life.

You may say, "But I'm still struggling." Wonderful; *struggle is proof that you refuse to surrender, and that you haven't been conquered.* As long as you hold that position, God can do something for you. He can send His Spirit; He can send His Word; He can send friends who've been where you are and who are strong where you're weak. If you're teachable, you're reachable. Just keep an open heart and listen. His promise to you today is, "Thou preparest a table before me in the presence of mine enemies. Thou anointest my head with oil, my cup runneth over. Surely goodness and mercy shall follow me *all the days of my life*" (Psalm 23:5-6).

* * *

Today is one of those days.

THE BENEFITS OF PRAYER

* * *

Men ought always to pray and not to faint.

Luke 18:1

The devil will do anything to keep you from praying. You'll be too tired, too busy, too depressed—it's endless. There's a reason: in prayer I *get real.* When I'm alone with God, the pretense is gone, for He knows my heart. There I repent of attitudes and actions that don't seem to bother me at other times. Prayer keeps me honest. Have you found it to be that way?

In prayer, God speaks to me. No, it's not an audible voice, but it's unmistakably *His voice* speaking to the deepest part of my consciousness. Sometimes it's just *a word.* Isaiah says, "Morning by morning He . . . gives me *a word*" (Isaiah 50:4, paraphrase). If God talked to men and women all through the Bible, then shouldn't we expect Him to speak to us, too?

In prayer, He teaches me to be thankful. "With *thanksgiving* let your requests be made known" (Philippians 4:6). Van Crouch says, "If *you were Jesus, wouldn't you like to be* thanked *before you get* involved?"

* * *

Today, take some time out and get alone with God in prayer. You'll be glad you did.

DON'T QUIT—JUST KEEP PLAYING

* * *

My grace is sufficient for thee: for my strength is made perfect in your weakness.

2 Corinthians 12:9

I heard a story the other day about a mom who wanted to encourage her little boy to keep practicing the piano, so she took him to hear Paderewski play. They sat near the front, and the boy was fascinated by the big grand piano on the stage. While his mother was talking to a friend, she didn't notice her son slip away. As the house lights dimmed, and the spotlight hit the piano, she gasped as she saw her son on the piano bench, playing "Twinkle, Twinkle Little Star." Before she could get to him, Paderewski walked over to the keyboard and sat down beside the boy. *"Don't quit, keep playing,"* he whispered. Then he reached down with his left hand and began filling in the bass part, and with his right arm he reached around the other side encircling the child and added a running obligato. Together the old master and the child brought the crowd to its feet.

Child of God, no matter how ill equipped you may feel today, the Master has a word for you: "*Don't quit, keep playing.*" No matter what you're doing today; raising those children, running that business, pastoring that church, or just trying to be a better Christian; whatever it is you're doing, *don't quit, keep playing,* and He will add whatever is needed to turn your efforts into a masterpiece.

* * *

Remember, His grace is sufficient for thee.

FREE TO "KEEP QUIET"

* * *

Self-control means controlling your tongue. A quick retort can ruin everything.
Proverbs 13:3 (TLB)

Don't let the need to *rescue* someone push you into answering before you have heard the whole story, and before you have taken time to pray about it. I'm amazed how differently I feel about something just a few hours or a few days, and in some cases a few years later. Hindsight truly is 20/20.

Pride says, "Don't just stand there, *say* something!" Wisdom says, "Don't just say something, *stand* there!" Quietly ask God for insight. One word from *Him* can turn things around in a hurry. In this age of instant tea and instant potatoes we look for *instant answers*. When tragedy strikes, not only do we get the news immediately, but within minutes experts appear on television to tell us *why* it all happened. But sometimes wisdom is *silence.*

Jesus had the power to summon 12 legions of angels to defend Him, yet, "He opened not His mouth." Pilate did all the talking. Jesus just stood there quietly, for *He* was not on trial, Pilate was, and the religious system's men were. Jesus knew His destiny and, most of all, He knew His Father intimately.

* * *

When you know God, you can face *anything* with confidence—and yet be free to keep quiet. What a wonderful place for you to be today.

MINDING YOUR OWN BUSINESS

* * *

Peter asked Jesus, "What about him, Lord?" Jesus replied, "What is that to you? You follow me."

John 21:20-22 (TLB)

Anytime you share something that tears someone else down, it sends a message that doesn't compliment you either. It says, "If you'll tell *me* about *them*, wouldn't you also tell *them* about *me* if the circumstances were different?"

And what about the harvest law? Listen: *"Whatsoever* a man soweth, that shall he also reap" (Galatians 6:7). Did you hear that? *"Whatsoever"*—that includes criticism, gossip, or slander. Even when it's couched in terms like, "I know he's a wonderful brother, *but* . . ." Since words are seeds, what kind of a harvest will *you* reap on the words you spoke today? Paul says, "Let your conversation be gracious" (Colossians 4:6, TLB).

Recently, when I criticized someone, God said to me, "Have you prayed for them?" I was instantly ashamed, for I was willing to talk to everybody *but God* about them. Then God's Spirit spoke again and said something that greatly helped me, *"If you could have heard them praying yesterday, pouring out their heart, asking for help in those very areas of weakness that* you *were talking about, then maybe you could see them through eyes of compassion. Their battle may be different from yours, but their heart cry is the same."*

* * *

When we're tempted to get into other people's business, we need to hear again the words of Jesus to Peter, "What is that to you? You follow me."

A DISCERNING HEART

* * *

Give therefore thy servant an understanding heart.
1 Kings 3:5-9

God guides us by *revelation* and by *relationships*. That means you need *discernment* about the people who come into your life. For example, when trouble hits your life, you'll discover who your friends really are. You can't lose a *real* friend, for the Word says, "A friend loveth at all times, and a brother is born for adversity" (Proverbs 17:17). But a lot of us get hurt by discovering that some people weren't true friends at all.

A friend recently went through some difficulties. When he reached out to a pastor he thought would stand by him, the man said, "I'm sorry you're going through this, and I'll pray for you, but it would hurt me to be seen with you at the moment. People might think I was being *soft on sin.*" How sad, but would you have acted differently?

Discernment is *not* for judging *people*. It's for discerning *their spirit*. Have you ever been around someone with a critical spirit? A competitive spirit? A controlling spirit? Jesus once said to His disciples, "Ye know not what manner of spirit ye are of" (Luke 9:55). Amazing! Even the disciples couldn't discern the spirit that was at work in their own ranks. Can you?

* * *

Today, ask God for a discerning heart. He'll give you one.

HUNGRY FOR GOD

* * *

O God, thou art my God; early will I seek thee: my soul thirsteth for thee.

Psalm 63:1

I know what David was talking about and I'm sure you do, too. Talk about "lifestyles of the rich and famous." He had the world's most beautiful women, but *sex* could not fill the void. If *fame* could satisfy, he was in a class of his own. If *looks* could do it, he was an Old Testament version of Sean Connery. But you can eat lobster thermidor every night and own resort homes in paradise and still have an emptiness in your heart as big as the Grand Canyon. *You see, there's a God-shaped blank inside of you.* He made you that way.

Ever since Adam walked with God, there has been a longing—sometimes it feels like a *primal scream*—for God's presence in our lives. David speaks for all of us, "My soul thirsteth for thee, my flesh longeth for thee in a dry and thirsty land, where no water is" (Psalm 63:1). He's saying, "I've seen man's best and it's fleeting." It's a seat on the board, a trophy from the field of athletics, or a crowd applauding, then it's all gone and the emptiness is still there.

There's only one place to go, and that's to *Him*. Listen to the rest of the Psalm, "Because thy lovingkindness is better than life, my lips shall praise thee. Thus will I bless thee while I live" (Psalm 63:3-4).

* * *

Today, let your hunger lead you into His presence.

WHEN YOU'RE FULL YOU ACT DIFFERENTLY

* * *

Be not drunk with wine . . . but be filled with the Spirit.

Ephesians 5:18

Billy Graham tells of a pastor who got drunk and the church board asked him to resign. He said he would if *they* would resign also. When they asked him why, he said, "Because *I* failed the first part of the verse, *'Be not drunk with wine,'* but *you* failed the second part, *'be filled with the Spirit.'*" I wonder how many of us could pass such a test? I wonder how many choir members would still be singing in the choir next Sunday, or how many deacons would still be serving on the board?

Paul says, "If the Spirit of him that raised up Jesus from the dead dwell in you, he that raised up Christ from the dead shall also quicken your mortal bodies" (Romans 8:11). There are two words you need to look at here. First, "if." A lot of people who are saved are not necessarily *filled* with the Spirit. The second word is "dwell." Maybe you were *once* filled, but other things have entered your life and the oil has run low, or run out.

* * *

All you have to do is go to Him today and ask Him to fill you again with His Spirit. He'll do it! Don't live another day without it.

DARE TO BE DIFFERENT

* * *

Do not conform any longer to the pattern of this world, but be transformed by the renewing of your mind.

Romans 12:2 (NIV)

If a million people do the wrong thing—that still doesn't make it right! Righteousness is *never* dependent upon or the opinions of others. Listen: "To you it is commanded, O people, nations, and languages, . . . fall down and worship the golden image, . . . that the king hath set up" (Daniel 3:4-5). Everybody in Babylon was doing it, and it meant death if you didn't. But neither peer pressure nor threat could move the three Hebrew children: "Our God whom we serve is able to deliver us from the burning fiery furnace, . . . *But if not*, be it known unto thee, O king, that we will not serve thy gods" (Daniel 3:17-18). *That's not stubbornness, it's integrity!*

If there's nothing different about your life, maybe it's time to reevaluate yourself. Peter says you are a "royal priesthood, an holy nation, a peculiar people" (1 Peter 2:9). You're called to be "one of a kind!"

Forget about having "a consensus of opinion" before you make a move. In every battle in the Bible God was on the side of the underdog. *Don't let people who have no vision vote on yours!* Listen to God! Walk with God! Do only what *He* tells you to do. When Luther was told, "The whole world is against you," he replied, "Then I'm against the whole world".

* * *

That's why he made a difference; *how about you?*

THE UNHEARD CRY

* * *

There met him out of the tombs a man with an unclean spirit.

Mark 5:2

Jesus heard a cry nobody else heard. It came from a place nobody else wanted to go. And it came from a man nobody else wanted anything to do with. *And when Jesus really lives in your heart, you'll hear that cry, too. It will touch your spirit.*

He was a madman who lived in a graveyard, and his appearance was enough to make any normal person avoid him. But something deep inside him longed to be free, and it *reached out and touched* the Spirit that was in Jesus. To get to him, Jesus had to go through a storm. He had to overcome the objections of His disciples who probably said, "Why risk it? He's not worth it."

Child of God, if you want to follow Jesus, then you'll have to open your heart to a cry that nobody else is listening to. You can't listen to the crowd *around* you, you've got to listen to the Spirit *within* you; *He'll* tell you where to go. *He'll* tell you who to minister to. You can't be put off by their *lifestyle* or their *appearance.* All that matters is getting them to Jesus.

* * *

Just get them to Him today, and He'll take care of the rest.

WHEN YOU CAN'T UNDERSTAND—TRUST!

* * *

The secret things belong unto the LORD our God.

Deuteronomy 29:29

I received this letter from a missionary couple who lost their 14 year old son. They wrote, *"Last summer, our younger son, aged 14, went down with a very severe strain of meningitis. Many prayed for his healing, but we lost him. Our hearts are broken. We cannot understand why God would send or allow us such a sorrow or burden to carry. Can you help us?"*

One thing is sure, *God is too good to do wrong and too wise to make a mistake.* When we have to know all the details, we're walking by *sight*, but when we can trust Him in the dark, we're walking by *faith.*

"Without faith it is impossible to please God" (Hebrews 11:6). Note that it doesn't say, "without understanding." When we walk by faith we don't necessarily gain *understanding*, but rather *acceptance. Confidence in God* is God's *highest purpose* for our lives. When we can trust and accept without questioning, we move into a dimension of greater peace and intimacy with Him.

Someone is probably watching you as you walk through this storm to see how your faith works, and if your relationship with God will sustain you. It will!

* * *

These days of questioning and grieving will pass; soon you will say like Job, "When I am tried I shall come forth as gold." (See Job 23:10.) ***My prayers are with you today.***

THEN JESUS COMES

* * *

And they went out and found the man sitting at the feet of Jesus, clothed, and in his right mind.

Luke 8:35 (Paraphrase)

The man in the tombs was bound by demons, filled with fear, and separated from his family. Society said he was *hopeless*. That's when Jesus loves to step in—when all hope is gone. When human wisdom says, "It can't be done," *then Jesus comes!* Look at this man now, "clothed, and in his right mind."

But the world couldn't handle him like this. So they asked Jesus to go back to where He came from. The world hasn't changed much. When *you* meet Jesus and they see you "clothed, and in your right mind," they won't know what to do with *you* either. Have they noticed the difference yet? If none of your old friends are *shaken up*, you're not doing something right. "If any man be in Christ, he is a *new* creature" (2 Corinthians 5:17).

This man wanted to join Jesus and His disciples, but Jesus said "No." Not everybody is called to full-time ministry. But we've *all* have been called to do one thing: "Return to thine own house, and show how great things God hath done unto thee" (Luke 8:39). *The* first *place you need to start today is among the people you love and live with.* Tell *them* how great Jesus is. Tell *them* what He's done for you. Tell *them* what He can do for them.

* * *

Don't put if off until tomorrow, do it today.

WAITING FOR JESUS

* * *

And . . . when Jesus was returned, the people gladly received him: for they were all waiting for him.

Luke 8:39-40

That's what your friends and loved ones are doing today—*waiting for Jesus.* Don't leave Him in church or confine Him to your Sunday activities. The miracles Jesus and the apostles did were not done in church; they did them *on their way* to wherever they were going. *With them it wasn't an event—it was a lifestyle.* The very shadow of Peter touching the sick as he walked by would bring healing. (See Acts 5:15.)

Today, we try to reproduce it in *a controlled environment,* and look at the results. If all our churches were filled tomorrow, they would hold *less than 10% of the people.* Something's got to happen! We've got to start praying for boldness and the compassion to take the gospel to the neighborhood, instead of trying to bring the neighborhood to us. They've been to church, and most of them didn't like it because they didn't see Jesus there. And they're still waiting for Him!

* * *

Introduce Him today to somebody you love. They'll be *eternally* grateful.

PATIENCE IS THE BRIDGE

* * *

For ye have need of patience, that, after ye have done the will of God, ye might receive the promise.

Hebrews 10:36

Recently, Sarah Utterbach said to me, "Patience is the bridge that carries you from the will of God to the promises of God. If you do the will of God on this side, the promises are waiting for you on the other side; but *patience is the bridge that gets you from one side to the other!* The key is—*bridges comes in different lengths!*" What insight! *Only God knows the length of your bridge.* Sometimes you'll get to the promise in just a few steps, and other times it may feel as if you'll never get there. If that's where you are today, there are two questions you need to answer:

First, have you done the will of God yet? What has He spoken to your heart? What has He revealed to you in His Word? Be honest with yourself, for you only receive the promise *after* you've done the will of God. *Next, are you walking patiently and confidently before the Lord in this matter?* You may ask, "How does patience walk?" Look at Abraham; even though he was 100 when God told him he'd be a father, we read, "He considered not his own body." Did you hear that? Don't even *consider* your limitations, they are nothing to God. Abraham "strengthened in his faith, and kept giving glory to God" (Romans 4:18-21). Stay in the Word!

* * *

Keep strengthening your faith daily and, whatever you do, *keep giving glory to God for what He's going to do.*

LISTENING PRAYER

* * *

Be still, and know that I am God.

Psalm 46:10

Jesus did a lot of praying. On more than one occasion He prayed all night, yet *few* of His words were recorded. *Could it be that He did more listening than talking?* And when His prayer was recorded, what was it? "Father, . . . not my will, but thine, be done" (Luke 22:42).

When Jesus prayed He surrendered totally to the will of God. From then on He believed He would automatically be given two things that we all keep asking for: *direction* and *the ability to deal with things*.

Thank God for the revelation of *who we are in Christ,* and *our authority as believers* before God and before men. But recently, God's been letting me know that there's *more* to prayer than to "come boldly unto the throne" (Hebrews 4:16). That kind of praying is about what *you* want, but this kind is about what *He* wants, and since He sees the whole picture clearly, and since He designed the plan, don't you think it's time to get quiet before Him so that He can *tell* us all about it?

* * *

The word for you today is, *be still and let God be God in your life.*

IT'S A DAILY WALK

* * *

Noah walked with God.
Genesis 6:9

To *walk with God* means that we stay yielded to His Word and attentive to His presence. Though we do not see Him, we know Him. We have found our security in *Him;* not in people, places, or things—But in *Him alone!*

The name Noah means *rest.* Noah not only knew his mission in life, but He also knew His *source.* When you know *that*, you don't have to worry any more. Step-by-step, day-by-day, Noah lived in God's presence. Now, knowing God deeply doesn't happen quickly; it takes *time.* Time spent with Him on the mountain and in the valley; time with Him in joy and in adversity. *Time will test the quality of your relationship with Jesus.* Prisons, shipwrecks, betrayals, beatings, hunger, and disappointment didn't shake Paul's confidence in God. Listen: "None of these things move me" (Acts 20:24).

Another man who walked with God was Enoch. Listen again: "Enoch walked with God: and he was not; for God took Him" (Genesis 5:24). *Every day* he rose and sought the Lord, walking with Him and seeking to please Him in all that he did. Their relationship was *intimate.* Listen to this: "He obtained the witness that before his being taken up he was *pleasing to God*" (Hebrews 11:5, NASB). *Imagine living in such a way that you have a "witness" in your spirit that God is truly pleased with you.*

* * *

Not only is such a life possible, but it can be yours starting *today.*

ARE YOU READY TODAY?

* * *

Behold, I am here, Lord.

Acts 9:10

Ananias was just a disciple, but when Saul of Tarsus needed to be saved, he was *ready* for the job. Imagine it; he led the apostle Paul to Jesus, and then prayed for him to receive his sight. Before Paul left that house, he was filled with the Holy Spirit and called to the ministry. What a testimony Ananias had!

If the Lord had a job to do today, would He know where to find you? Would you be ready?

If God nudged you today about speaking to someone who is hurting, could you handle it? Could you respond like Ananias and say, "Behold, I am here, Lord?" Do you realize who Saul of Tarsus was? He had a death warrant for every Christian in town, including Ananias. Little wonder Ananias said, "Lord, I have heard by many of this man, how much evil he hath done" (Acts 9:13). Isn't it wonderful: *God doesn't consult your past to determine your future.* Don't ever write somebody off because of what they've been through. Hannah said, "He . . . lifteth up the beggar from the dunghill, to set [him] among princes" (1 Samuel 2:8).

* * *

Don't try to get ready—live ready and God will use you every day.

THE CALL OF GOD

* * *

Before I formed thee in the belly I knew thee; . . . and I ordained thee a prophet unto the nations.

Jeremiah 1:5

Think of it—before Jeremiah was born, God already saw him ministering to nations.

This is when discernment is so important. You don't *decide* your calling—you *discern* it. Have you discerned yours yet? If you haven't, then get into God's presence today and stay there until He reveals it to you.

Listen to what Jeremiah told God, "Ah, Lord GOD! behold, I cannot" (Jeremiah 1:6). Is that what you've been saying? I cannot—I'm too young. I'm too poor. I don't have the training. I'm the wrong nationality. I'm too old. I don't have the right connections. The first thing God did was to change what was coming out of Jeremiah's mouth: "Say not." Did you hear that child of God?—"Say not." If you keep contradicting what God says, you're pulling the plug on everything He wants to do for you. Listen to God's Word to Jeremiah, and to you, "Be not afraid of their faces: for I am with thee to deliver thee, saith the LORD. . . . Behold, I have put My words in thy mouth . . . . I will hasten My word to perform it" (Jeremiah 1:8-9, 12). When God guides, He provides. Don't listen to the wrong voices.

* * *

Today, start listening to the Word of God; receive it by faith; step out and obey it; for the promise to you today is, "I am with thee." What more do you need?

PERFECT LOVE

* * *

His perfect love for us eliminates all dread . . . If we are afraid, it . . . shows that we are not fully convinced that He really loves us.

1 John 4:18 (TLB)

God couldn't love you any more than He does right now! Take a moment and let that sink in!

You say "What does God's love look like?" Look at the Cross. If you were the only person who needed forgiveness, He'd have gone to the Cross for you. You say, "What does God's love cost me?" It comes with *no strings attached.* You couldn't do anything to deserve it—so when you fail, you don't forfeit it. He'll never stop loving you. (See Romans 8:38-39.)

John says that since God's love is the only "perfect" love, it casts out all your fear. What are you afraid of today? Afraid you won't get something you need, or you'll lose something you already have? You need to ask God to give you a fresh understanding of how much He loves you.

We're attracted to people who love us and show it, so why is it so difficult for us to go to God in prayer or spend time in His presence? It's because we need a fresh revelation of His love. Listen to Paul: "I pray that you'll be able to take in the extravagant dimensions of Christ's love. Reach out and experience the breadth. Test its length. Plumb the depths. Rise to the heights. Live in the fullness of God" (Ephesians 3:18-19, TM).

* * *

May God help you to experience that measure of His love today.

THE ORPHAN HEART

* * *

God's Spirit touches our spirit and confirms who we really are.

Romans 8:16 (TM)

Do you have an orphan heart? It's a heart that needs everybody to love it. Ten thousand people may, but that's not enough—it will always focus on the one who doesn't and obsess over them. Have you ever held arguments in your mind with people who criticized you, or worse, snubbed you? That's the orphan heart, and no amount of human love can ever meet its need.

But there's something that can: the Spirit of adoption. Listen: "Ye have received the Spirit of adoption, whereby we cry, "Abba, Father" (Romans 8:15). *The Message* says, "God's Spirit confirms who we really are" (Romans 8:16). That's what the Spirit of God wants to do for you today; let you know who you really are. You're God's child! You're an heir to all He owns! You're protected day and night by His love! You're directed step-by-step by His Spirit! You're given favor even in the midst of adversity! You're His!

Adoption is an act of premeditated love. It says, "Before you saw Me, I saw you. I adopted you. I gave you My name, My nature, My family, and My inheritance. Now you can call Me "Abba," which literally means, "My Daddy." How wonderful!

* * *

You can run to God today, curl up into His arms, and say to Him, "My Daddy" What a picture!

PATIENCE IS THE BRIDGE

* * *

For ye have need of patience, that, after ye have done the will of God, ye might receive the promise.

Hebrews 10:36

Patience is the bridge that carries you from the will of God, to the promises of God. If you do the will of God on this side, the promises are waiting for you on the other side; but the patience is the bridge that *gets you from one side to the other!* The key is—*bridges come in different lengths! Only God knows the length of your bridge!* Sometimes you'll get to the promise in just a few steps, and other times it may feel like "you'll never get there." Maybe that's where you are today.

If so, there are two questions you need to answer. *First, have you done the will of God yet?* Be honest with yourself, for you only receive the promise *after* you've done the will of God. *Next, are you walking patiently and confidently before the Lord in this matter?* You may ask, "How does patience walk? How does it act?" Look at Abraham; even though he was 100 years old when God told him he was to be a father, we read, "He considered not his own body." Did you hear that? Don't even *consider* your limitations, they mean nothing to God. Abraham waited 20 years before Isaac was born, but he "*was strong in faith, giving glory to God"* (Romans 4:18-21). Stay in the Word! Keep strengthening your faith daily, and whatever you do, *keep giving glory to God for what He is going to do.*

* * *

Stand on the Word, and when the promise arrives, make sure you're still at the right address.

JUST WHAT YOU NEED TO HEAR

* * *

A word in season to him that is weary.

Isaiah 50:4

When I started writing the quarterly edition of *The Word For Today*, it was read by a few thousand people. Today its circulation is just over 500,000 and growing, but its *purpose*. Each day I ask God for "just the right Word at just the right time for those who may be struggling and trying to get through another day." Isaiah said, "The Lord GOD hath given me the tongue of the learned, that I should know how to speak a word in season to him that is weary: ". . . *morning by morning, he wakeneth mine ear to hear*" (Isaiah 50:4).

Are there those you love but you don't know what to say to them anymore? Child of God, you can't give them what you don't have. You have to receive "a word in season" before you can give it to others. Until you do, let them know you care, you're praying, and you're available. But it's the *Word* that makes the difference. Listen: "He sent His Word, and healed them" (Psalm 107:20). "Now are you clean through the Word" (John 15:3). "These things have I spoken unto you, that my joy might remain in you" (John 15:11). It's all in the Word.

* * *

Something special happens when you fall on your knees, open your heart, and cry from the depths of your being, "Father, I need a word from You today." Do it, and see what happens.

FRIENDS

* * *

I have called you friends; for all things that I have heard of my Father I have made known unto you.

John 15:15

If Jesus walked into your house today He'd probably say, "Hello, My friend!" What a privilege! It means, "My door is always open to you. There's nothing you can't talk to Me about and I'll never betray you. I'll always listen, and if you're restless and can't sleep, I'll sit up with you. I'll go with you wherever you go—and our friendship isn't subject to human limitations. You can be comforting a crying child, working at a computer screen, or driving a bus and your spirit can be fellowshipping with Me."

Jesus will always be there when you need Him. It's His nature to be faithful. Flesh will fail you, even well-intentioned flesh, but not Jesus. Listen: "I will not leave you comfortless: I will come to you" (John 14:18). The precious Holy Spirit that is living in you right now is how Jesus keeps His promise never to leave you.

But remember, His friendship depends upon your obedience to Him. Jesus said, "Ye are my friends, if you do whatsoever I command you" (John 15:14). The Holy Spirit is pictured in the Bible as a dove. When a dove comes back to its nest, it is so sensitive that if it finds *one thing out of place* it will not land. Are you getting the message?

* * *

Always make Jesus feel at home and always protect that friendship, for it's the most wonderful relationship you've got.

AN ANTI-GOSSIP PACT

* * *

He who is trustworthy and faithful in spirit keeps the matter hidden.

Proverbs 11:13 (Paraphrase)

In 1752, a group of Methodist men, including John Wesley, signed a covenant that every man agreed to hang on his study wall. The six articles of this agreement were as follows:

That we will not listen or willingly inquire after ill concerning one another;

That if we do hear any ill of each other, we will not believe it;

That as soon as possible we will communicate what we hear by speaking or writing to the person concerned;

That until we have done this, we will not write or speak a syllable of it to any other person;

That neither will we mention it, after we have done this, to any other person;

That we will not make any exception to any of these rules unless we think ourselves absolutely obliged, and then only in conference.

Always remember, the person who says to you, "Don't tell this to a soul," has probably told all the souls they know. Confront them in love about what they're doing and don't carry it a step further.

* * *

Don't you think as Christians we owe this to one another?

THE BUSINESS OF LOVING OTHERS

* * *

For I have given you an example, that ye should do as I have done to you.

John 13:15

Armand Hammer, the great humanitarian and chairman of Occidental Petroleum, tells the following story:

> My father had become a prominent and greatly loved figure in the area. . . . It was an almost ecstatic experience for me to ride with him when he went on his doctor's rounds. Patients at their doors greeted him with such warmth that waves of pride would surge in me to find myself the son of such a father, a man so obviously good, so obviously deserving of the affection he received.
>
> He could have made himself many times richer, however, if he had insisted on collecting all his bills; or if he could have restrained himself from giving money away; but then he would not have been the man he was. I have seen, in his office, drawers full of unpaid bills for which he refused to demand payment because he knew the difficult circumstances of the patients. And I heard innumerable stories from patients about his leaving money behind to pay for the prescriptions he had written when he visited people who were too poor to eat, let alone pay the doctor.

* * *

What a wonderful legacy to leave your child—the *business* of loving and giving to others. Today, you'll have opportunities to show God's love; don't miss one of them.

HE'S WATCHING OVER YOU TODAY

* * *

Let Him have your worries and cares, for He is always thinking about you and watching everything that concerns you.

1 Peter 5:7 (TLB)

What a source of strength! Not only is He watching over you, but He's watching over those you love, including the ones you've been so worried about lately. God's love and care followed the Prodigal Son all the way to the hog pen and brought him safely home again. When others give up, He doesn't! Every day for 40 years, God fed the Israelites, clothed them, protected them, and directed every step they took. He never missed one day! Listen: "Thou shalt remember all the way which the LORD thy God led thee" (Deuteronomy 8:2). What a God!

Do you remember the poem *Footsteps*? First there were two sets of footprints, then there was only one set. When the Lord was asked, "Why? Didn't you promise you'd never leave me?" He answered, "Yes, My child. The two sets of footprints were the times when we walked together side by side. But when you saw only one set of footprints; *they were not yours, they were Mine. Those were the times when you didn't have the strength to go on—so I carried you.*"

* * *

Child of God, you're not here today because you're lucky, you're here because you're blessed! Take a moment and begin to praise Him—He's worthy of it.

AN ATTITUDE OF GRATITUDE

* * *

Freely ye have received, freely give.

Matthew 10:8

The Bible teaches *sowing* in order to *reap*, or giving for a desired result. In salvation, you gave your heart to Jesus expecting something in return—eternal life. And He didn't disappoint you. It also says about Jesus, "Who for the joy that was set before Him endured the cross, despising the shame, and is set down at the right hand of the throne of God" (Hebrews 12:2). He looked beyond the Cross to the throne; that was His reward.

But there's another way of looking at it. *Today instead of giving to get, why don't you give because of what you've already received?* If God never did one more thing for you, wouldn't it take eternity to praise Him for the love He has already shown you? Do you remember what your life was like before you met Jesus? Those habits that bound you? The awful emptiness you could never fill? Where would the road you were on have ended?

In those times when I'm tempted to pass judgment on someone, I pray, "God help me to be quiet, look up, and remember with David, 'He brought me up also out of an horrible pit, out of the miry clay, and set my feet upon a rock, and established my goings. And He hath put a new song in my mouth, even praise unto our God'" (Psalm 40:2-3).

* * *

Today, ask God to help you to have an attitude of gratitude, and then go out into your day rejoicing.

A WARNING FOR THOSE IN CHRISTIAN SERVICE

* * *

And him only shalt thou serve.

Luke 4:8

A minister I'd once known and worked with died of AIDS. He was one of the most requested guests on Christian television, and was used of God to work miracles. But success led him to believe he could bend the rules and get away with it—and for a while he did. But the termites of self-indulgence were eating away at his foundations. First he lapsed into alcoholism, and then perversion. Sadly, only a handful of people attended the funeral of this man who once ministered to multitudes. I wondered, "Why didn't someone reach out to him while there was still time?" I understand several tried to, but out of the fear of losing his ministry, he denied everything and denounced them. He valued his lifestyle more than life. He became more concerned about his reputation than his relationship with God.

When I heard about it, I felt two things. First, great sadness, for he died almost friendless and alone. Second, a sense of warning: *The most dangerous lies are not the ones we tell others, they're the ones we tell ourselves and finish up believing.* If you find yourself constantly maneuvering for recognition and competing for position in the kingdom, don't walk—run to the Cross and repent.

* * *

Cry out to the One who "made Himself of no reputation," and ask Him to help you love Him instead of His work, and seek Him instead of success.

IMPORTUNITY

* * *

Many tried to hush him up, but he yelled all the louder; and Jesus stopped in His tracks!

Mark 10:46 (TM)

His *deliverance* meant more to blind Bartimaeus than his dignity, and *seeing* meant more to him than looking good. If what you've done thus far hasn't worked, at least be willing to try something different. *Don't give up until you get God's attention.*

Most of the crowd that day would have been happy to see Bartimaeus sit blind and begging by that highway for the rest of his life. Note the words, "Many tried to hush him up." You'll have to overcome some of those same voices to get to Jesus. Like the sincere Christian who'll tell you that "the day of miracles has passed." Please understand that there never was a day of miracles. There's only a God of miracles and He never changes.

Others who love you and feel protective over you will try to lower your expectations to keep you from reaching out and being disappointed. Some will even say, "You got yourself into this mess, so don't expect God to get you out of it." Don't listen to those voices.

Zacchaeus climbed up a tree to get to Jesus. Others raised the roof. Child of God, if you can think—then pray! If you can still breathe—then call on His name! As long as you're living, keep reaching for Him!

* * *

My friend, Ron Dryden, in Oklahoma City, has a sign on his desk with only one word: "IMPORTUNITY." Never! Never! Never give up!

LOVE AND ANSWERED PRAYER

* * *

Giving honour unto your wife . . . that your prayers be not hindered.

1 Peter 3:7

I wonder why we hear so little about the last part of this verse? When preachers talk about hindrances to prayer they usually talk about things like lack of faith, disobedience, or unforgiveness. But Peter says a big one is *how you treat your partner*. Not only do our petitions end up in the unanswered prayer department of heaven, but they end up as unopened mail.

I have a wonderful wife; she's everything I could ever ask for. But, like anyone else, when she gets tired, she gets touchy. Now knowing this, you'd think that when she says something that bothers me I would just let it pass. But not me—I'm human—I'm Irish—and sometimes I'm carnal. So I *straighten her out*. Have you ever done that? Usually the issue is so insignificant that a few hours later neither of you can even remember it, yet it generates a lot of heat at the time.

Listen: "Love suffers long and is kind" (1 Corinthians 13:4, NKJV). Sometimes I wonder why God put this stuff into the Bible, for it's *hard* to live. So I apologize to my wife and ask God to help me do it better *next time.* That makes for a happy home.

* * *

I'm also doing it for another reason: "That [my] prayers be not hindered."

NO ONE HAS THE RIGHT TO DO LESS THAN THEIR BEST

* * *

Whatever your hand finds to do, do it with all your might.

Ecclesiastes 9:10 (NIV)

The area I live in recently had the lowest voter turnout in Atlanta, Georgia. That may not seem significant, until you start listening to some of the people around here complaining. Do we really have the right to complain about what we permit?

We march against abortion, but how about providing a home for that girl who went wrong? We've had a lot of attention on the plight of the elderly who have to choose between prescriptions to keep them healthy or food to keep them alive. So many live in despair and loneliness, but have you visited any of them? James says that pure religion will cause us to reach out to those who hurt. (See James 1:27.)

When Jesus told the rich young ruler how much it would cost to follow Him, "He went away sorrowful," wishing it could have been easier (Matthew 19:22). Salvation may be free, but discipleship will cost you everything you've got. It's literally signing your name to the bottom of the check and saying, "Lord, You fill in the amount."

* * *

Remember yesterday? There's not a thing you can do about it, except learn from it and go out today asking God to give you the grace to make it count for Him.

PERFECT PEACE

* * *

Thou wilt keep him in perfect peace, whose mind is stayed on thee: because he trusteth in thee.

Isaiah 26:3

A friend, Sarah Utterbach, called today with another great insight. She was singing the little chorus, "He is our peace who has broken down the middle wall," when suddenly it dawned on her that *He can't be your peace until He first becomes your focus.* Think about it! Did you notice the words, "Whose mind is *stayed* on thee?" An athlete has only one thing in mind—the prize. Paul says that as we focus on Jesus, we're changed into His very image and likeness. (See 2 Corinthians 3:18.) For us the only questions that matter are: "Where is He in all of this? What does He want me to do?"

The disciples failed to see Him in the worst storm of their lives and yet He was right there beside them. Mark says, "And about the fourth watch of the night He cometh unto them, walking upon the sea, and would have passed by them" (Mark 6:48). He was in control of their circumstances. He was watching over them every moment. He was right there beside them, but they almost missed Him. Sound familiar? Don't leave Him in church. Don't confine Him to your morning devotions.

* * *

Today, look for Him constantly in every storm and every circumstance of your life, for when your eyes are on Him, His peace will flood your soul.

HOW TO TREAT ONE ANOTHER

* * *

Make a clean break with all cutting, backbiting, profane talk. Be gentle with one another, sensitive; forgive one another as quickly and thoroughly as God in Christ forgave you.

Ephesians 4:31-32 (TM)

G. LeTourneau, an outstanding Christian businessman, made a fortune manufacturing large earth moving equipment. He made a scraper known as "Model G." One day someone asked one of his salesmen what the "G" stood for. The man, who was quick-witted, replied, "I'll tell you, the "G" stands for gossip, because this machine can move a lot of dirt and move it fast." *The trouble with gossip is not so much that it is spoken as an intended lie, but that it is heard as if it were the absolute truth.*

Abraham Lincoln had a favorite riddle he used to put to people: "If a man were to call the tail of a dog a leg, how many legs would the dog have?" The usual reply was "five." "Wrong!" Lincoln would say with his wry smile. "The dog still has four legs. Calling the tail a leg doesn't make it one."

Just because a story may have been repeated many times by so-called reliable sources doesn't necessarily make it true. *And if it is true, it should be put under the Blood and not into your conversation.*

* * *

Ask God today to help you talk like a Christian.

PLEAD YOUR CASE

* * *

Put me in remembrance: let us plead together: declare thou, that thou mayest be justified.

Isaiah 43:26

Pleading is not begging. *We have been authorized to bring before God that which He has already promised and plead our case.* As a child of God, you have direct access to your Father.

In the years I pastored and my children were growing up, things could get pretty hectic. A staff, a budget, schedules—there never seemed to be enough hours in the day. But I left clear instructions to my staff: "Any time my children call, put them through immediately."

That's the deal God has made with you today. You can use His Name. You can use His Word. You can have His Holy Spirit to comfort you, guide you, and instruct you every step of the way. What an arrangement! *That means your confidence is intact even if you're under attack.*

* * *

Today, stand on His Word and begin to plead your case, for He promised, "If ye shall ask any thing in my name, I will do it" (John 14:12). What a privilege!

THINGS THAT NEVER CHANGE

* * *

Remove not the old landmark.

Proverbs 23:10

Thank God for "Big Ben." It has kept us on time for generations. Thank God for the compass that always points toward the magnetic north—without it no one would be able to get anywhere. Thank God for "seedtime and harvest," for the Word says, "While the earth remaineth, seedtime and harvest . . . shall not cease" (Genesis 8:22). That reassures me that the seeds I've sown will produce a harvest.

Last night on the news, some people were trying to stop the sale of a hot selling video that is protected under the "Freedom of Speech Act." The video shows how to assassinate someone in a professional manner. Dear God! I never thought I'd get this old this fast. But today I thank God for the values that don't change, and principles that are *still* the only guarantee of the "more abundant" life that Jesus talked about. (See John 10:10.)

Prayer *still* changes things, and more importantly it changes me. Bible reading *still* strengthens and gives me peace and joy like nothing else I know. Most of all I'm glad He said, "I am the LORD, I change not" (Malachi 3:6). *What He was He still is. What He said, He still says. What He did, He can still do today.*

* * *

I'm so glad He's the unchanging One, aren't you?

THE OPEN DOOR POLICY

* * *

Behold, I have set before thee an open door, and no man can shut it.

Revelation 3:8

God guides us in many ways, and one of them is what I call the "open door" policy. I'm stubborn and it's taken me a long time to learn not to keep knocking on doors that are closed, but instead to walk through the ones He has opened. Are you like that? My friend, Mike Murdock, says, "*Don't stay where you're tolerated, go where you're celebrated.*" God says no man can close the door, so if it's closed, He may have a hand in it and you need to pay attention.

The mighty Mississippi is two miles wide at one point, but so narrow at another that you can jump across it. Now when you walk through a door things may look small in the beginning, but as you remain faithful and keep walking, you'll discover that you're connected to something deeper, wider, and bigger than you ever conceived.

Years ago, I thought my life was over, but today I have more joy and a greater purpose than ever. *When God closes one door, He opens another.* Walking through it can be fearful, especially when you don't know what's on the other side. But it shouldn't be so with us, for Jesus said, *"He goes on ahead of them, and his sheep follow him because they know his voice"* (John 10:4, NIV).

* * *

Child of God, when you walk through this door, He'll be waiting there for you. So don't be afraid.

FAITH OR FEAR?

* * *

According to your faith be it unto you.

Matthew 9:29

One day, two blind men came to Jesus to receive their sight, and He said to them, "'Believe ye that I am able to do this?' They said unto him, 'Yea, Lord.' Then touched he their eyes, saying, 'According to your faith be it unto you.' And their eyes were opened" (Matthew 9:28-30). Faith is a force like gravity or electricity, but it needs something to *flow through*, an object to *flow to*, and a *point of contact*. For the child of God, Jesus is the object of our faith—He's the healer. Prayer and the *laying on of hands* can be our point of contact. (See Mark 16:18.)

Then why are so many of God's people sick? One reason is *fear*. The Bible speaks of people who "Through fear of death were all their lifetime subject to bondage" (Hebrews 2:15). Fear can release a chain reaction of negative forces that will destroy your health. It's a form of faith, but it's *faith in the worst, not in the best.*

Never allow your symptoms to determine the state of your health. Don't spend time comparing your condition to that of somebody who died. And whatever you do, *don't speak words that reinforce your problem—it's a trespasser!* It has no legal right to stay, for the Word says, "By whose stripes ye were healed" (1 Peter 2:24).

* * *

Today, the Lord wants to touch you, so reach out to Him in faith.

THINGS I'VE NOTICED ABOUT JESUS

* * *

This is my beloved Son, in whom I am well pleased.

Matthew 3:17

Jesus didn't care about His reputation, or He wouldn't have eaten dinner with Zacchaeus. Tax collectors were despised Jews who worked for the Romans and extorted taxes from their own people. But Jesus wasn't concerned with what people thought of Zacchaeus, for He sees us not as we *are*, but as we *will be* when He gets through with us. After he met Jesus, Zacchaeus was so changed that he said, "If I have taken any thing from any man . . . I restore him fourfold" (Luke 19:8). That's what is called being "radically saved."

I've noticed, too, that Jesus always "went to bat" for losers, like the woman caught in the act of adultery. He listened to her self-righteous judges and then wiped them out with one phrase, "He that is without sin among you, let him first cast a stone at her" (John 8:7). To fully appreciate this story, you have to know what's it's like to be lifted by Christ from your own gutter. Listen: "Neither do I condemn thee: go, and sin no more" (John 8:11). Is He serious? This woman could no more stop sinning than you could lift yourself up by your own bootstraps. Ah, but what He meant was, "*Go, and because you've met Me, you'll never have to go back to your old life anymore.*"

* * *

He's the "Lifting Christ," and He can lift you today from where you are. Just reach for Him.

SO YOU PLANNED TO GO TO SPAIN?

* * *

Whensoever I take my journey into

Spain, I will come to you.

Romans 15:24

When things don't seem to work out the way you plan, God is still at work. Paul planned to go to Spain; it was certainly a good idea, but God had a better one and Paul landed in prison. It was there he wrote his prison Epistles—words that would last far beyond his short lifetime, and touch multitudes more than the small group of believers who were waiting for him in Spain. Listen, child of God: "In his heart a man plans his course, but the LORD determines his steps" (Proverbs 16:9, NIV). Sometimes your disappointments are His appointments.

Two of my friends recently walked through this very experience. They loved one another dearly and planned to get married. They had even made reservations for a honeymoon in the Bahamas. But, God spoke and told them they were not to get married. It hurt! They cried for days, but they knew that it was God who closes a lesser door to open a greater one.

David said, "You . . . scheduled each day of my life before I began to breathe" (Psalm 139:16, TLB). Have you asked Him about the schedule? Have you submitted your plans to Him and asked Him to direct your steps?

* * *

Spain may look good to you, but what does *He* want for your life?

WHEN THE PUPIL IS READY, THE TEACHER WILL COME

* * *

They took him aside and explained to him the way of God more accurately.
Acts 18:26 (NKJV)

God is not unwilling to give. The problem is, we are not always willing to receive. You would imagine we would be glad to have someone show us a better way, but it doesn't seem to work that way for a lot of us. A lady told me, "My husband will drive miles in the wrong direction before he'll stop and ask somebody for help." Sound familiar? It takes humility to say, "I don't know, I need help," and that's the kind of man Apollos was.

He was a powerful preacher, but he was working with limited revelation. Priscilla and Acquilla went to hear him preach, and seeing his potential they took him aside and "expounded unto him the way of God more perfectly" (Acts 18:26, KJV). Afterwards, he had a powerful ministry.

There's a lesson here for us. Today we have "the Word people," "the Kingdom people," "the Toronto blessing" people, etc. But wouldn't it be something if we were to go and hear some wonderful ministries who *don't* see eye-to-eye with us but have a real heart for God?—to befriend them; to encourage them; and, when God opens the door, to share with them "the way of the Lord more perfectly."

* * *

God has a lot of people like Apollos out there, who may not be persuaded by the force of our arguments but they could be by the power of our love. What do you think?

THE COMPARISON TRAP

* * *

Where envying and strife is, there is confusion and every evil work.

James 3:16

Competitive jealousy has been around since Cain killed Abel. It caused Jesus' disciples to quarrel over who would be greatest in the Kingdom. (See Mark 10:35-41.) Only when you understand the nature of this cunning spirit, can you free yourself from it. *When I'm comparing myself with others, I'm not pursuing God's plan for my life or listening to what God's telling me.*

This spirit will trap you into comparing yourself unfavorably with others, and then criticizing them in the hope that you can make yourself feel better by cutting them down. Instead of concentrating on "the edifying of the body of Christ" (Ephesians 4:12), we strive to outdo each other.

It's not God's will for you to get caught in this trap. Listen: "God . . . hath quickened us *together* with Christ . . . and made us sit *together* in heavenly places in Christ Jesus" (Ephesians 2:4-6). Through Jesus we have equal rights and equal access to the throne of God.

* * *

You don't have to compete with anyone. You don't have to strive for position, favor, power, or influence—because right now all these things belong to you in Jesus Christ.

IN THE MIDDLE

* * *

O LORD, revive thy work in the midst of the years.

Habakkuk 3:2

We all need to pray, "O LORD, revive thy work," but we also need to remember that He'll only revive *His* work—He may let *yours* die. It's happened to me and it's painful. Jesus said, "Every branch in me that beareth not fruit he taketh away" (John 15:2). If you could even blame the devil it wouldn't feel so bad, but when God takes it away, that's rough.

Now, the trouble is always in the middle of the years. Beginnings are exciting, and endings are wonderful—for the crown is in sight and you're almost home. But the challenge is how to stay on fire *in the middle* of the years.

It's in *the middle* of the marathon that you need your second wind. Thank God for Sunday's blessings, but it's in *the middle* of the week that I need another touch of His presence. The hardest place to be is in *the middle* of the battle, with no end in sight.

* * *

Take courage, child of God, and take some time out today to get into His presence and cry like the prophet, "O LORD, revive thy work in the midst of the years." And start with me!

A PLACE FOR THE HURTING

* * *

There I will . . . transform her Valley of Troubles into a Door of Hope.

Hosea 2:15 (TLB)

When your brother or sister falls, what do they need from you? *First, they need a place of anonymity.* A place where it's safe to be honest—where no one points accusing fingers and says, "How could you have done such a thing?" Peter says, "Love will cover a multitude of sins" (1 Peter 4:8, NKJV). Note, love doesn't spread—it covers.

Next, they need a place of mercy. The God of the Old Testament built cities of refuge where offenders could run to safety. In the New Testament, Jesus lifted the fallen woman and restored Peter after his painful chapter of denial. Think of it, if you can't find mercy in the family of God, where are you going to find it?

Finally, they need a place of hope. In Hosea 2:15, God said He would open a Door of Hope in the Valley of Trouble (Achor). *Achor* was where Achan was stoned to death for disobeying God. If you're going through a time of trouble today—even if it's your own fault—remember, God has not abandoned you. It's those He loves who experience His correcting hand. But He's not through blessing you. He's going to bring you out stronger than you were when you went in.

* * *

Today, He's opening a door of hope for you in your valley of trouble.

WATCH WHAT YOU SAY!

***

This book of the law shall not
depart out of thy mouth
Joshua 1:8

Your tongue is one of the greatest gifts God has placed at your command so use it wisely! The Bible says, "Life and death are in the power of the tongue." Strong words—yet so often we don't stop and think, *before* we speak, or consider the effect our words will have.

Have you ever used words like, *"I can't handle this"* or, *"This will never change?"* I know I have! Your words don't just affect those around you they affect God. *Faith-talk* is what he responds to. What you *say* about your situation affects what you believe, and what you believe determines what you'll receive from God.

Are you talking about your *expectations*, or are you still rehearsing *past experiences?* Listen, "Out of the same mouth come praise and cursing. My brothers, this should not be" (Jas 3:10 NIV). It's so easy to slip from speaking *faith* to speaking *fear.*

***

Make a decision today to guard your words carefully, and remember others may not speak words of faith to you today—*so practice speaking them to yourself! (By Debby Gass)*

KEEP BELIEVING GOD

* * *

Now faith is being sure of what we hope for and certain of what we do not see.

Hebrews 11:1 (NIV)

Keep exercising your faith in little *things, and when the big tests come, it will be strong enough to take you over the top*. Real faith knows the promises and stands on them regardless. Listen: "For everyone that useth milk is unskillful in the word"(Hebrews 5:13). How skillful are you in the Word? Have you found the promises that deal with your circumstances? Are you standing on them? When you've prayed do you conclude that if you don't "feel something" your prayers didn't work? If the symptoms don't change immediately do you doubt and say, "Well, I guess God isn't going to heal me?" *Never speak words that make the devil think he's winning*. He can't read your mind, but he can hear your words!

When Jesus touched the blind man and asked him what he could see, he replied, "I see men as trees walking"(Mark 8:23-25). Did the man give up? Did Jesus quit in discouragement? No, He laid hands on him again, and this time, he was completely healed. There's a lesson here for you today—don't give up! Keep going back to the source! Keep praying and believing and standing on the Word! Some answers come quickly and some slowly but your *fixed position* is to keep believing God. Faith is not an impulse, it's an attitude—it's not an event, it's a walk.

* * *

So keep walking by faith day-by-day—"sure of what you hope for and certain of what you do not see!"

SPIRIT-LED PEOPLE

* * *

To be carnally minded is death; but to be spiritually minded is life and peace.

Romans 8:6

Casey Treat says, *"When your mind agrees with your spirit, you're spiritually minded; but when your mind agrees with your flesh, you're carnally minded."* That's why you need to read the Word daily. Listen: "A good man out of the good treasure of his heart bringeth forth good things" (Matthew 12:35). First you have to get it into your heart, *then* you can bring it forth. *Anything you can conceive you can bring forth.* That's why the enemy will do everything he can to keep you out of the Word.

Have you ever changed a baby's diaper? As you know, before you put on the *new* you have to take off the *old* or you'll have problems. Paul tells us to *"put off your old self, which is being corrupted . . . put on the new self, created to be like God"* (Ephesians 4:22,24, NIV).

He calls this being "renewed in the spirit of your mind" (verse 23). As long as the Prodigal Son had a "hog-pen mentality," he was dead to his father's blessings and his rightful place as a son and an heir. But when he remembered, repented, and renewed his mind, things turned around for him. *And it's the same for you.*

* * *

As a spirit-led person, you need to renew your mind every day and *today* is one of those days—so get started!

WHEN YOU NO LONGER *NEED GOD*

* * *

As long as he sought the LORD, God made him to prosper.

2 Chronicles 26:5

Uzziah was a *Lincoln* or a *Churchill* when it came to leadership. Listen to his accomplishments: He defeated *all* the enemies of Israel; created an army of 307,000 elite troops; developed state of the art warfare; built towers and reservoirs; and developed agriculture and cattle farming so that Israel became the envy of the world. All this happened "*as long as he sought the Lord.*"

But then it all changed. Listen again: "But when he was strong, his heart was lifted up to his destruction" (2 Chronicles 26:16). Child of God, learn this lesson well. *It's okay to possess things so long as things don't possess you.* You don't own anything—you're just the administrator of God's estate and the executor of His will. So long as you pursue God, His blessings will pursue you.

It's when the pressure is off that we stop seeking God. Now we don't *need* Him like we once did. *Things* become more important to us than Him. We get so busy building homes, buying cars, and bringing up families, that before we know it, *He's pushed aside.*

Do you remember when you had such a hunger for Him? You couldn't wait to get to His house. You couldn't wait to read His Word. You talked about Him constantly. But now that fire has become a smoldering ash.

* * *

***Today,* He's calling you back to your first love—back to the place you once knew.**

A GOD-ALTERED PERSPECTIVE

* * *

Rejoice in the Lord always.

Philippians 4:4 (NIV)

Paul was in prison when he wrote, "Rejoice in the Lord alway." *Around* him was the cruelty of men, but *within* him was the Kingdom of God. How is such joy possible? Paul gives us the key: "We look not at the things which are seen, but at the things which are not seen: for the things which are seen are temporal; but the things which are not seen are eternal" (2 Corinthians 4:18). *Child of God, there are things we see that the world doesn't.*

Paul was saying, "You can lock me up, but you can't keep me in. Outside these bars Caesar rules, but in here, Jesus is Lord, and when my assignment is complete, I'm out of here. Go ahead, take your best shot. Beat me, imprison me, behead me, but one second after the ax falls I'll be more alive than I am now." *There's nothing you can do to a man like that. He's beyond your reach.*

Paul was saying, "This is the best it will ever be for you, but you ought to see where I'm going."

"For we know that if our earthly house of this tabernacle were dissolved, we have a building of God, an house not made with hands, eternal in the heavens" (2 Corinthians 5:1). That's a God-altered perspective.

* * *

Praise Him today, not because of what you *feel,* but because of what you *know* and you'll have a joy that transcends anything that comes against you.

FRAIL BUT NOT DISQUALIFIED

* * *

We have not an high priest which cannot be touched with the feeling of our infirmities.

Hebrews 4:15

The word "infirmities" is in the plural, meaning we all have several. Yet many of us struggle to admit to the presence of even one. T. D. Jakes says, "We have carefully hidden our struggles and paraded only our victories, but the whole country is falling asleep at the parade." For God's sake, and a dying world's sake, will somebody *please get real!*

The Greek word for infirmities is *malady* or *frailty*. All of us have some malady or frailty that incapacitates us to the degree that we need His mercies newly bestowed on us every morning. David succeeded on the battlefield, but failed in the bedroom, yet no man was more used of God. This should encourage you today, for God's not only sympathetic, He also uses people like you and me who are affected by the same stimuli and struggles as David

Paul spelled it out clearly, "We also are men of like passions with you" (Acts 14:15). Only a fool would refuse to lift a diamond out of a drain and God is no fool. The church has thrown away thousands of valuable diamonds by denying her wounded soldiers a chance to return to active service.

* * *

If *God* is able to sympathize with our weaknesses, shouldn't we be willing to do *at least* that much for each other?

WE CAN'T LOSE

* * *

I want to report to you, friends, that my imprisonment has had the opposite of its intended effect. Instead of being squelched, the message has actually prospered.

Philippians 1:12 (TM)

When I read the words, "My imprisonment has had the opposite of its intended effect," I shouted for joy! And that's not all, listen: "Not only that but most of the Christians here have become far more sure of themselves in the faith than ever, speaking out fearlessly about God" (Philippians 1:14, TM). The devil's plan backfired. He thought that by locking Paul up, he could shut him up; but, instead, he starting writing books that would change the world. He thought imprisoning him would intimidate all the other Christians in town; but, instead, it ignited them.

And to make matters worse, they changed his guard every few hours and chained him to another two Roman soldiers. That's what's called *a captive audience*. Every few hours, two new converts would leave, and two new prospects would arrive, until there were "saints in the household of Caesar" (Philippians 4:22). Finally, they decided that the only thing to do was to kill Paul. Kill *what*? They could destroy the shell, but they couldn't lay a finger on the treasure. Listen again: "They didn't shut me up; they gave me a pulpit. Alive, I'm Christ's messenger; dead, I'm His bounty. Life versus even more life. I can't lose" (Philippians 1:23, TM).

* * *

Rejoice, child of God, we're on the winning side today. We just can't lose!

INCREASE YOUR FAITH

* * *

What is faith? It is the confident assurance that something we want is going to happen.

Hebrews 11:1 (TLB)

The best definition of faith I've ever heard is, *acting on what you believe.*

You may *say* you believe the Word, but are you *acting* on it? If not, all you have is a *belief.* You can *believe* that God is real and yet never have a personal relationship with Him. You can *believe* the Bible is the Word of God, yet never see one of its promises fulfilled in your life.

When Jesus walked on the Sea of Galilee, eleven of the disciples believed it was Him but they all *remained* in the boat. Peter, however, stepped out and began walking toward Jesus. That's faith.

Listen: "So then faith comes [continually] by hearing [continually], and hearing by the Word of God" (Romans 10:17). You say, "I heard that years ago." Maybe you did, but you have to hear it *over and over again,* for that's how faith grows.

A woman touched the hem of Jesus' garment and was healed. Jesus gave credit for the miracle to *her faith;* listen: "Thy faith hath made thee whole" (Mark 5:34). The Bible says, "Without faith it is impossible to please Him [God]" (Hebrews 11:6). I didn't get into *"faith"* because I wanted money, or healing, or things; I got into faith to please my Father. That's the highest motive and one that truly honors Him.

* * *

Today, get into the Word and start building your faith.

GOD CAN DO SO MUCH WITH SO LITTLE

* * *

She hath done what she could.

Mark 14:8

Edmund Burke says, "*Nobody ever made a greater mistake than he who did nothing, because he could only do little!*" It's one of the best-kept secrets—God can do so much with so little!

Last night in church I met a "genuine hero." She's a grandmother who has already raised one family, and all of them but one became great successes. Sadly, that one became a drug addict and abandoned her 4 children. Into the gap, with a huge heart of love, stepped this grandmother. Alone, at 68 years old, she's raising her daughter's children. Every time the church doors are open, she has them there. They're in school making "straight A's." She's wise enough to know she can't do it by herself, so she has solicited God's help on the project! David said that those who are *planted* in the house of God, shall "*flourish*" (Psalm 92:13). She keeps the light burning and the door open, praying for the day when her prodigal will return, but, until then, she's molding another generation for God. *You'll meet her some day—when heaven gives out its highest awards.* She's like the little woman of whom Jesus said, "She hath done what she could."

* * *

The question is, have you?

YOU'RE STILL HIS

* * *

When I was still in my mother's womb, he chose and called me.

Galatians 1:15 (TM)

Satan is terrified of those who have been called by God. He'll set traps and initiate attacks to keep you from discovering and fulfilling your destiny. Don't waste your time being terrified of him—he's terrified of *you*. Listen: "The God of peace will soon crush Satan under your feet" (Romans 16:20, NIV). Your struggle is just an indication of *who* you are and *what* your worth is to God. Satan doesn't attack a retreating army, he joins them. You have value in the kingdom of God. Never forget that!

He'll do whatever he can today to destroy *your confidence in God* and blind you to how great, how powerful, and how mighty your God is. He wants to sabotage your success because you were created to *win*, not to lose. This morning I read something wonderful, and I believe God wants me to share it with you. Listen:

> *I pray that your hearts will be flooded with light, so that you can see something of the future He has called you to share. I pray that you will begin to understand how incredibly great His power is to help those who believe Him. It is the same mighty power that raised Christ from the dead and seated Him in a place of honor at God's right hand in heaven.*
>
> Ephesians 1:18-22 (TLB)

* * *

Today, that power is yours—*use it.*

PHARAOH, YOU CAN'T HAVE WHAT BELONGS TO GOD

* * *

Let my people go, that they may serve me.

Exodus 8:1

The *same* God who said to Pharaoh, "Let *my* people go," is saying again, "Pharaoh, you've got something that belongs to *me*. You've picked a fight you can't win. I'm going to set this child of mine free, and there's *nothing* you can do about it."

For too long, Pharaoh has contaminated your mind and caused you to think that you're a zero, a reject, a nothing. That's a lie! God doesn't check your bank account, your nationality, your education, or your talent to see if He can use you. God will use you *in spite* of your broken home, *in spite* of your broken health, and *in spite* of your broken dreams. *Don't let Pharaoh have your first-born!* Don't let him have your inheritance. Don't let him have your future. Don't let him keep you in Egypt another day.

Turn to God and watch what He'll do on your behalf. He'll bring Pharaoh down! He'll open the Red Sea and make a way out for you. *Who do you think brought you this far?* Just because you couldn't see Him, didn't mean He wasn't watching over you.

* * *

Child of God, I have a word from *Him* for *you*: "Do not be afraid. Stand firm and you will see the deliverance the LORD will bring you today. The Egyptians you see today you will never see again" (Exodus 14:13-14, NIV).

RESTING

* * *

There remains therefore a rest for the people of God.
Hebrews 4:9 (NKJV)

If the devil can't drive you into carnality, He'll be just as happy to drive you into exhaustion. He tried it with Moses. No man ever had so much trouble with a congregation as Moses had with the congregation of Israel in the wilderness. When he complained to God, God told him, in effect, "I never told you to do it all by yourself. It's *My* work and they're *My* people and I'm well able to take care of them."

God's got some players who act like they're the whole team. D. L. Moody once said, "You can either do the work of ten men, or get ten men to do the work." It's called delegation. Our church pews are filled with spectators and "frozen assets." Paul said the responsibility of those who minister is "the perfecting of the saints, for the work of the ministry" (Ephesians 4:12). Are you being trained and equipped to minister to others? Are you discipling and training anyone else? Give these questions some serious thought because you *will* be answerable to God for this.

The Lord told Moses, "My presence shall go with thee, and I will give thee *rest*" (Exodus 33:14). *There is no burnout in the will of God.* There is, however, in the will of the flesh. But in God's will there is only rest and peace.

* * *

Today, ask Him to help you enter that place of rest.

A MORE EXCELLENT WAY—LOVE

* * *

And yet I will show you a still more excellent way—one that is better by far and the highest of them all, love.
1 Corinthians 12:31 (AMP)

God doesn't measure you by your gifts—men do that. God measures you by your *love*. Sadly, I've met some gifted ministers whom God used to work miracles or deliver riveting sermons, but as I got to know them I was disappointed. They loved *crowds*, but they didn't seem to love *people*. That's a trap any of us can fall into, and today I prayed, "Lord, please help me to love people like You do."

Now here's the standard by which we are all measured:

> Love is very patient and kind, never jealous or envious, never boastful or proud, never haughty or selfish or rude. Love does not demand its own way. It is not irritable or touchy. It does not hold grudges and will hardly even notice when others do it wrong. It is never glad about injustice, but rejoices whenever truth wins out.
>
> If you love someone you will be loyal to him no matter what the cost. You will *always* believe in him, *always* expect the best of him and *always* stand your ground in defending him.
>
> 1 Corinthians 13:4-7 (TLB)

* * *

What an assignment! When everything else fails, remember, "*Love never fails.*"

KEEP THE CHANNEL OPEN

* * *

Blessed are the pure in heart: for they shall see God.

Matthew 5:8

In his book, *Naked and Not Ashamed,* T. D. Jakes says, "When a man crawls naked onto the operating table before the surgeon, he is neither boastful nor embarrassed, for he understands that his exposed condition is a necessity of their relationship. Whether the doctor finds good or evil, what is there is there, and the man's comfort lies in the conviction that the surgeon possesses the wherewithal to restore order and to bring healing to those areas that are sick." What insight!

When Jesus said, "Blessed are the *pure* in heart," He was using the Greek word *katheros* from which we derive *catherise.* It's how doctors cleanse impurities or remove blockages from the body. What a picture! You must *show* Him what is clogging the flow of His life to you so He can cleanse you and keep you acceptable before Him. He can't purify what you *hide* in secret corners. Listen to the hymn:

> Lord Jesus, I long to be perfectly whole;
> I want thee forever to live in my soul.
> Break down every idol, cast out every foe;
> Now wash me and I shall be whiter than snow.

* * *

Your record was swept clean at Calvary, but your heart must be cleansed day by day.

STAYING ON TRACK

* * *

He's the one who will keep you on track.

Proverbs 3:6 (TM)

I recently had a real *off day*. A friend asked, "What is God saying to you in all of this? After all, He's not the author of confusion." (Don't you hate it when friends call you to accountability on an *off day*?) I was miserable because I *knew* the answer but I didn't *like* it. Now, we can shorten the process, but since I'm stubborn, I took the long route. Finally, my wife said, "You've completely lost your serenity and you need to *do* something about it."

All those great promises came flooding back, "Thou wilt keep him in perfect peace, whose mind is stayed on thee" (Isaiah 26:3). Or how about this one, "Let not your heart be troubled, neither let it be afraid" (John 14:27). Now if I don't have the peace He's promised, it's not His fault.

Finally, I asked Him to forgive me for my lousy *attitude* and *lack of trust in Him*. I'd made others my source, and when they didn't *act* the way I wanted them to, I tried to force the issue. Since people can't make *me* do what they want, why would I think I could make them to do what *I* want? At last I took all the pieces and threw them at the feet of Jesus and asked Him to sort it all out. He did! Guess what? I'm back on track again.

* * *

Is there a message in this for you today?

IT WASN'T THAT HE DIDN'T KNOW, IT WAS JUST THAT HE DIDN'T CARE

* * *

The Pharisee . . . said to himself, "If this man was the prophet I thought he was, he would have known what kind of woman this is."

Luke 7:39 (TM)

She was a prostitute and everybody seemed to know it except Jesus. As He ate with some clergymen, she washed His feet with her tears and dried them with her hair. One preacher commented, *If He was a real prophet, He'd know what kind of woman this is.* They had been with Jesus, but they didn't know Him at all. They had heard His words, but they didn't know His heart. He knew all about this woman. It wasn't that He didn't *know*—it was that He just didn't *care.* How wonderful!

Your past doesn't matter to Him! Jesus said concerning the Prodigal Son, "When he was yet a great way off, his father saw him, and had compassion, and ran, and fell on his neck, and kissed him . . . and said to his servants . . . my son was dead, and is alive again; he was lost, and is found. And they began to be merry" (Luke 15:20-24).

We *all* have a past—but the *blood of Jesus* cleanses us from *all* sin. (See 1 John 1:7.) Come just as you are. Once you've met Him, you'll never be the same. Listen to what Jesus said concerning this woman: "Her sins, which are many, are forgiven" (Luke 7:47).

* * *

Today, He's saying those same words to you.

REAL FRIENDSHIP

* * *

A man that hath friends must show himself friendly.

Proverbs 18.:24

If you can count your real friends on one hand—you're blessed! Solomon says, if you *want* a real friend, then *be* one. So how do you do that? Listen: "As iron sharpens iron, so one man sharpens another" (Proverbs 27:17, NIV). Sometimes that means telling someone *things they don't want to hear*, but if your friendship can't handle the truth, then it has little value. All of us have faults and a friend will risk telling you the truth to help you deal with them. The Word says: "A friend loveth at *all* times" (Proverbs 17:17). Paul spoke with gratitude about who stood by him when he was in trouble and visited him in prison.

Jim Bakker told me that when he got out of prison one of the first people to befriend him was Franklin Graham, the son of Billy Graham. Franklin provided him with a home and a car and a guarantee that he'd be there for him. That Sunday, Franklin's mother, Ruth, took Jim to church, sat him in the family pew beside her, and introduced him to all their friends. Afterwards she took him home to join the family for dinner. It moved Jim deeply because many who sought his favor and friendship in the days of his fame ran for cover when trouble hit him.

* * *

Today, instead of asking God to *give* you a friend, why don't you ask Him to *make* you one.

IT'S TIME FOR THE WORD TO BECOME FLESH

* * *

And the Word was made flesh, and dwelt among us, and we beheld . . .

John 1:14

Jesus didn't just *have* a sermon, He *was* the sermon. He didn't just talk about love; He fed the hungry, ministered to the sick, and lifted the fallen. It wasn't just "a Sunday thing"—they saw "the Word made flesh" seven days a week and in *every* circumstance of His life.

He taught forgiveness by forgiving those who ripped the flesh from His back and nailed Him to the Cross. He called Matthew the tax collector and told him to bring his *pen* with him, because He wanted him to write a book. How wonderful! The fact that John's nets were empty and his business was failing, didn't mean a thing to Jesus, for with Him every loser is a potential winner. They all got the same instructions: "Follow Me."

Talk about spiritual warfare—one fourth of His ministry was spent confronting the devil and evicting his demons. He prayed before dawn and often all night. Think of it: *He did—but we don't!* And doesn't it show up in the results?

It's time to get your theology off the drawing board. The Word has got to become flesh in your home, on your job, and in every area of your life.

* * *

It's a *show me* world out there, and they don't want to see *you*, they want to see *Jesus*.

POURED FROM VESSEL INTO VESSEL

* * *

Moab has been at ease . . . he hath . . . not been emptied from vessel to vessel.

Jeremiah 48:11

The finest wine was perfected by being "poured from vessel to vessel." Each vessel served a different purpose. The goal was to one day be set on the king's table and poured out in his service. What a picture of your Christian life—*poured from experience into experience.* One of those vessels was called, "The vessel of pressure and testing." When the lid was clamped on, the pressure would build and they'd put it in a dark basement and often leave it there for years. As the pressure kept working, it produced purity and maturity that is found only in the best wines. Does this sound like where you've been lately?

What you've been *taught* must be *tested* or it has no real value. Before you move from the natural to the supernatural, you'll have to face the wind and the waves. Some lessons can only be learned in the storm. When you tell God you want to grow, don't be surprised if He tells you to get into the boat. That's how you develop real faith and confidence in God. That's how you get to know He's bigger than anything you'll ever face, and when He tells you to go over to the other side, no power can keep you from getting there.

* * *

Today, if you find yourself being poured from vessel to vessel, *rejoice*, it means you're getting closer to the King's table.

DOING WHAT YOU'RE SUPPOSED TO DO

* * *

When ye shall have done all those things which are commanded you, say, We are unprofitable servants: we have done that which was our duty to do.

Luke 17:10

Has God ever surfaced in you things you never knew were there. It happened to me recently. I got angry and took my frustration out on the wrong person. It usually happens to me for two reasons: I'm afraid I'm not going to *get* something I need, or I'm going to *lose* something I've got. All my fears seem to fall into those two categories.

Afterwards, I felt rotten. Here I am writing a devotional and telling others they should be loving, patient, and kind, and I act like a spoiled child who can't get his own way. So I apologized and felt much better. Then a voice said, "That was *big* of you—you're really something." No sooner had I heard it, than *another* voice said, *"You're still an unprofitable servant."* Wow—what an ego deflator! No trumpet volley, no parades, no words of praise. Listen to these words again: "When you've done everything expected of you, be matter of fact and say, 'The work is done, what we were told to do, we did" (Luke 17:10, TM).

* * *

The songwriter puts it into perspective with these words:

Take up thy cross and follow me,
I hear my blessed Savior call.
How can I make a lesser sacrifice,
When Jesus gave His all?

DON'T COME DOWN

* * *

I am doing a great work and I cannot come down.

Nehemiah 6:3 (NASB)

Satan will use anything he can to bring you down! Nehemiah was told to remove the rubbish, rebuild the walls, restore the temple, and reclaim the people of God—the same assignment that *we've been given* today! The enemy tried threats, diplomacy, and fifth columns, but Nehemiah stood firm and said, "I am doing a great work, and I cannot come down." That's the word for you today—*don't come down!*

When they ask you to explain what you're doing, or to defend yourself, *don't come down!* When faint hearts say, "Couldn't we compromise and just get along with them," *don't come down*! When human wisdom says, "It's not a good time to move forward, perhaps we should wait," *don't come down*! When doubt and fear say, "The job is too big and God is too small," *don't come down*! Take your sword in one hand and your mortarboard in the other, and whether you have to build or battle, *stay up there* and keep doing the job God has called you to do.

If you even *think* of coming down, you've sent a signal to the enemy that his strategy is working. You've stepped down to the level of your accuser and the work God gave you to do is put on hold.

* * *

Child of God, stay up there and before you know it, the wall will be built, the enemy will be beaten, and God will be glorified in your life.

WHATEVER IT COSTS—IT'S WORTH IT

* * *

The sufferings of this present time are not worthy to be compared with the glory which shall be revealed in us.

Romans 8:18

This morning I was reading about Paul's calling. It's *different* from much of what I'm hearing today. Listen: "He is a chosen vessel unto me, to bear My name before Gentiles, and kings, and the children of Israel: For I will show him how great things he must *suffer* for my name's sake" (Acts 9:15-16). What's this? *Suffer* great things for My name? I thought I was signing up to be prospered, not pulverized. Think again. The blessing of God doesn't *exempt* you from attack, it equips you to handle it. His grace is what carries you through it. Paul spent all but seven years of his ministry in prison.

Where did you get the idea that it's fun being a Christian? Now you can have joy in jail and fellowship in suffering, but if you're any threat to the devil then get ready for attack, because it's coming. The important part is not what's going on *around* you, it's what is going on *within* you. Listen: "What we suffer now, is nothing compared to the glory He will give us later" (Romans 8:28, TLB).

* * *

Rejoice, you're part of an army that's destined to *win*, and a kingdom that's going to *prevail.*

GRACIOUS WORDS

* * *

The words of a wise man's mouth are gracious.

Ecclesiastes 10:12

Sometimes gifted people and busy people can be harsh or unkind without meaning to be. They live by a schedule and they get upset when others fail to respect it. But not Jesus. He had the most important job in the world and yet He stopped for children and spent time with them. Sometimes the only people who seem to matter to us are those who contribute to our goals. *That's not ambition, that's selfishness!*

Jesus had many opportunities to ingratiate Himself with the rich and powerful, and He did have friends among them, but mostly He gave Himself to common folks. He was so secure in His identity and clear in His purpose, that He spent time lifting losers like Mary Magdalene, out of whom He cast seven devils.

The law of kindness governed His words, and He taught this law to His disciples. Listen: "Love your enemies, bless them that curse you, do good to them that hate you, and pray for them which despitefully use you" (Matthew 5:44). When I read those words, my heart cries, "Help!" I fall *so far short* of this goal. Jesus didn't berate Peter when he failed—he restored him and made him a leader in the Church. He didn't degrade Thomas for doubting, He strengthened him.

* * *

Before you go anywhere today, take a few moments and ask God to help you stay cool under fire, and be *gracious* to those you meet.

THE GENTLENESS OF JESUS

* * *

A bruised reed shall he not break, and the smoking flax shall he not quench.

Isaiah 42:3

I love to talk about Jesus, and I find myself increasingly wanting to be around others who love to talk about Him. It's a growing hunger that's becoming an obsession. Today, I saw another wonderful thing about Him; Isaiah says, "A bruised reed shall He not break, and the smoking flax shall He not quench." Can you think of *anything* more worthless than a bruised reed that men have trampled on? Jesus will not walk *by* it and He will not walk *on* it, He'll stop and gently *strengthen* it in the broken places and then He'll *straighten* it up so it can grow again.

Can you picture *anything* more useless than a smoking flax that once burned brightly. But watch how Jesus works—He carefully pours fresh oil into the empty lamp and then gently blows on the flax until it burns again.

I don't know about you, but I've been that bruised reed and that smoking flax, and when I couldn't even reach up, He reached down and lifted me from hopelessness and despair. He made me strong in the broken places and fanned the smouldering flax into a flame of love.

* * *

And He did it for *you,* too, didn't He? Why don't you take a few moments today and just tell Him how much you love Him.

REBUILDING TRUST

* * *

Love . . . always trusts, always hopes,
always perseveres.
1 Corinthians 13:6-7 (NIV)

Has your trust been violated? Have you become distrustful and started having questions in areas you never did before? Sometimes you can't receive the love you need, because your wounded spirit says, "Nobody will ever do that to me again." *The real damage is not what you went through, but what you're left with—terrible doubt.* When the woman at the well met Jesus, she didn't know He was *different* from the men she had known before. He had to take down her defenses or she'd have missed the greatest experience of her life.

Now Jesus is "the same *yesterday*, today and forever" (Hebrews 13:8). *You can't go back, but He can.* He can heal those wounded areas, and *break* the chains that bind you to memory. Listen: "The former things shall not be remembered, nor come into mind" (Isaiah 65:17). You don't have to wait until you get to heaven to experience this, He can do that for you *now* but you'll never experience what He's promised until you learn to *trust* again. *Trust God. Trust* the people He sends to bless you. Sure, you'll be disappointed, don't look for perfect treatment from imperfect people. *You'll get lots of practice forgiving—that's the Christian life.*

* * *

Ask Him today to help you take down the wall of fear so you can trust again, and live again.

THE "I ONLY" SYNDROME

* * *

And I, even I only, am left; and they seek my life, to take it away.

1 Kings 19:10

Elijah was convinced he was the only man of God left in the world. Imagine it—the *only* ministry still preaching righteousness and standing up to Jezebel and her corrupt religious system. God soon disillusioned him, "I have left me seven thousand in Israel, all the knees which have not bowed unto Baal" (1 Kings 19:18). What a humbling revelation. You may be a great quarterback, but you're not the whole team. *God has others.*

Sometimes leaders fall into the trap of *turf guarding.* From there it's only a short step to believing that *"our church is the only place where God is moving—so if you're mature and love the truth, you'll walk and worship with us."* Elijah *really believed* he was the only standard-bearer of truth in the land, and when that happens to us, we become *critical of others.* Usually we say, "They're not very deep, or they're not very spiritual, or what have they ever done for God anyway?" When someone else has had an experience that's different from ours, we diminish it and then dismiss it. Check your heart, child of God—Jesus said, "By this shall all men know that ye are my disciples, if ye have love one to another" (John 13:35).

* * *

Today, ask God for the grace to first recognize His work in others, and then reach out to them in His love.

YOUR TIME HAS COME

* * *

None of my words will be delayed any longer.

Ezekiel 12:28 (NIV)

One translation says, "All delay has ended; I will do it *now.*" Rejoice, child of God, your delivery date has come. The waiting is over. God is about to answer your prayer.

When Peter was imprisoned, the Church began praying around the clock. It worked. The angel of the Lord came and delivered him to *the very door* where they were praying. But when they heard Peter was at the door they said, "It couldn't be." When it was confirmed they said, "It must be an angel." Finally, when they *saw* him it says, "They were astonished" (Acts 12:13-16). They were praying—but not believing. *They were locked into a posture of asking—but not expecting.* Maybe that's where you are—expecting little or nothing. Today, God is saying to you, "The answer is knocking at your door, go and open it."

Don't wait until the walls fall—shout *now.* When praise fills your mouth, expectation will fill your heart and God will move on your behalf. When God gives you a word—*act on it!* Before their prison doors opened, Paul and Silas filled the place with praise, for that produces a climate that faith can grow in. So start praising Him now for what He is about to do.

* * *

His word to you today is, "All delay has ended, I will do it now!"

HOW TO HAVE A RELATIONSHIP WITH GOD

* * *

I can of mine own self do nothing: as I hear, I judge.

John 5:30

Jesus spent 3 ½ years showing us how to build a relationship with God. He didn't respond to the *need*, He only responded to the *Father*. Listen to these words: "I don't do a solitary thing on my own; I listen: then I decide" (John 5:30, TM). The King James version says, "As I hear, I judge." What a way to live. When you hear from God, *people* can no longer control you or set your agenda. *Unmet needs* can no longer discourage you, for you're listening to one voice only—*His.*

Jesus spent whole nights in prayer, and often rose before dawn to pray. What was He doing? Making *deposits* early in the morning so that He could make *withdrawals* all day long.

Listen again: "For the Father loves the Son, and shows Him all things that He Himself does" (John 5:20, NKJV). You don't reveal yourself to just *anyone*—only to those with whom you're *intimate*. Child of God, power flows from intimacy. Wisdom flows from intimacy. Authority flows from knowing you've been with God.

The Bible tells us that Jesus called the disciples to be *with* Him, and then He sent them out *from* Him. Don't try to go out for Him, until you've first spent time with Him.

* * *

Don't try to build a ministry until you've first built a relationship, and if that means rearranging your priorities, *then start doing it today.*

HE'S THE ONLY ONE WHO CAN DO IT FOR YOU

* * *

And the Lord will guide you continually,
and satisfy you with all good things,
and keep you healthy too.
Isaiah 58:11 (TLB)

No political party can do this for you. No insurance policy can give you such coverage. Look what He promised. First, *He'll help you make all the right decisions.* Next, He'll keep you *healthy.* Then He'll satisfy you with all *good* things. The problem is, most of the time we don't *know* what's good for us—a good husband or a good wife—no husband or no wife? *It's better to want what you don't have, than to have what you don't want.* God told Jeremiah that the plans He had for him were *good.* (See Jeremiah 29:11.)

But who are these good things for? You may be surprised. They are for those who don't criticize or gossip. God said, "Then you will call, and the LORD will answer; you will cry for help, and he will say: 'Here am I. If you do away with the yoke of oppression, *with the pointing finger and malicious talk,* and if you spend yourselves in behalf of the hungry and satisfy the needs of the oppressed, then your light will rise in the darkness, and your night will become like the noonday' " (Isaiah 58:9, NIV).

* * *

These promises are for those who *love God* and *love people*—that means they're for *you.* Take a few moments today and ask yourself, "Am I living by these principles?"

HEALING WORDS

* * *

Pleasant words are . . . sweet to the mind and healing to the body.

Proverbs 16:24 (AMP)

A young minister was delivering his first sermon, and some of his colleagues came to hear him. When he quoted something, one whispered, "*That's Spurgeon.*" When he quoted something else, another said, "*That's Calvin.*" Finally, the young preacher lost his cool and said, "Would you mind being quiet." Whereupon one of elder ministers said, "*That's himself!*" It makes you smile, but it makes you think. Today, I prayed, "Lord, when I speak, let them hear You—not me, and help me to speak healing words."

Getting something off your chest may make *you* feel better, but if you harm someone else, you've made the problem worse. Jesus said you'll give account for the words you speak. (See Matthew 12:36.) If we really believed that, we would pray more and say less.

One of the loveliest pictures in the Bible is Joseph meeting his brothers after they'd sold him into slavery. Now he has the power to "even the score." But not a word of resentment comes out of his mouth. Listen: "Ye thought evil against me; but God meant it unto good . . . Now therefore fear yet not: I will nourish you, and your little ones. And he comforted them, and spake kindly unto them" (Genesis 50:20-21). What an example!

* * *

Today, ask God to give you not just the spirit of Joseph, but also his gracious words.

YOU DON'T FALL *FROM* GRACE, YOU FALL *INTO* IT

* * *

Whosoever of you are justified by the law; ye are fallen from grace.

Galatians 5:4

When I was young, *falling from grace* was like a huge *net* that caught everybody for every shortcoming. Then when I had to deal with my teenage sexuality, I went through terrible condemnation. How could someone who wanted to be pure have such unclean thoughts? Some who read this will understand, and others will think such things should not be aired in public. But we shouldn't be afraid to discuss what God wasn't afraid to create. In those days I thought, "If anybody has fallen from grace, it's *me*."

Then I discovered something wonderful. When you lose your way or fall flat on your face, you don't fall *from* grace, you fall *into* it. Listen: "The blood of Jesus Christ his Son cleanseth us from all sin" (1 John 1:7). What a relief! The expression "fallen from grace" is aimed at people who think their *works* will get them to heaven. But the truth is, the harder you work at it the further you push yourself away from God. *Trying* will not get you into heaven, *trusting* will. Paul says, "By grace are you saved through faith; and that not of yourselves: it is the gift of God" (Ephesians 2:8).

* * *

This doesn't mean God's love will let you *off*, it simply means His love will never let you *go*. What an assurance!

THE MINISTRY OF WORRYING

* * *

Be anxious for nothing.
Philippians 4:6 (NKJV)

Some of us have been trained to worry by parents who weren't there when we needed them. Others were trained by religious systems that had no power, so they said, "God doesn't do that anymore." And some were told that once God saved us the *rest* was up to *us*. So we work hard and worry *a lot.*

The hardest people to deal with are those who feel called to *the ministry* of *worrying*. Malcolm Smith says, "I once had an old aunt who showed up every Christmas, and always seemed to know when we were in trouble. Her stock phrase was, "Well, *I can't really help, but I'll worry for you.*" Worry has become such a way of life for some of us that we worry if we're not worried about something.

Today, I came across a wonderful translation of Philippians 4:6 in *The Message*—it may be just what you need:

> Instead of worrying, pray! Let petitions and praises shape your worries into prayers, letting God know your concerns. Before you know it, a sense of God's wholeness, everything coming together for good, will come and settle you down. It's wonderful what happens when Christ displaces worry at the center of your life.

* * *

Read that again. Paul's not saying, "Don't look at the problem," he's saying, "Let Christ displace worry at the center of your life." It's the only way to live.

SOMETIMES *MORE* ISN'T BETTER

* * *

If riches increase, set not your heart upon them.

Psalm 62:10

Don't get me wrong, I believe God longs to bless you, and that includes every area of your life. But when you get more, you get more responsibility, more pressure, more insurance, more wear and tear, and more bogged down by the very thing that was supposed to be such a blessing. Can I ask you something? When you had *less,* did you have more time to read the Word and more time to pray? The danger comes when the *things* we have consume so much of our time that we've little or nothing left for *Him*. Even ministers fight this. *It's a lot easier to get involved with the work of the Lord, than it is to get involved with the Lord of the work.*

Did you think that new home or that new car would satisfy you? Shouldn't any joy that costs that much, last a little longer? The Bible says, "Let us lay aside every weight" (Hebrews 12:2). Lighten up for the race. This is always a tough call because it's not a *right* or *wrong* issue, it's about what *drains* you and *diverts* you from being all that you were meant to be. Paul says, "I bring all my energies to bear on this one thing . . . to reach the end of the race and receive the prize" (Philippians 3:13-14, TLB).

* * *

The question you need to think about today is, "*Where* am I putting most of my energies?"

UNDER CONSTRUCTION

* * *

For we are his workmanship, created in Christ Jesus unto good works.

Ephesians 2:10

The way to live in defeat is to keep giving in to thoughts that lead you down the wrong road. *Anything you stop feeding will die.* God wants to create in you a new mentality that will enable you to rise above your impulses. Paul says, "Let this mind be in you, which was also in Christ Jesus: Who, being in the form of God, thought it not robbery to be equal with God: But made himself of no reputation" (Philippians 2:5-7). Jesus didn't suffer from *low self-esteem,* because He knew who He was, and He never allowed the opinions of others to change that. When you have healthy thoughts about your own identity, it frees you from the need to impress others. Their opinions simply don't matter anymore.

Most of us come to the Lord as "damaged goods." No matter who you meet, once you get to know them you realize we *all* have our battlegrounds. Even the people you thought had it *all together* have a twisted board here, a loose nail there, or even a squeaky frame. But the good news is, *He's still working on you.* We come to Him as condemned buildings, and He reopens, restores, and renews us, and makes us His habitation.

* * *

Can you imagine what you'll be like when He's through with you?—changed into His very image from "glory to glory."

GIVE IT ALL TO HIM

* * *

Cast all your anxiety on Him because He cares for you.

1 Peter 5:7 (NIV)

Perhaps you've done all you can and things aren't getting any better. That's a frightening place to be, but spiritually speaking, *you're on the threshold of a miracle.* Don't beg and plead with God, He's your *Father.* Jesus said, "Your Heavenly Father knoweth that ye have need of all these things" (Matthew 6:32). *He knows what you need.*

Hannah Whitehall Smith tells of a man in a horse and wagon who saw a stranger struggling under a heavy load. He stopped and offered him a ride. As they rode along together, he noticed that the stranger kept carrying the huge sack on his back. So he said, "Why don't you set it down?" The stranger replied, "*Oh no, it's good of you to carry me but I couldn't expect you to carry my burden, too.*" Now you may smile, but is that when you've been doing?

Listen to this promise: "I will be your God throughout *all* your lifetime, yes, even when your hair is white with age. I made you and I will care for you" (Isaiah 46:4, TLB). And if you need more assurance, listen: "The eternal God is thy refuge, and underneath are the everlasting arms" (Deuteronomy 33:27).

* * *

When you stop *taking* those cares back, Satan will stop *bringing* them back. Now that you know this, start acting on it.

WHEN YOU'RE WAITING!

* * *

Wait on the LORD, and keep His way, and

He shall exalt thee.

Psalm 37:34

Waiting time is not wasted time! David was called by God to be Israel's next king—but he's in a cave hiding in fear for his life and wondering, "Where is God in all this?" So the question arises, *how do you behave in a cave?* What do you do in a waiting period?

First, David encouraged himself in the LORD. (See 1 Samuel 30:6.) He *reminded* himself of God's faithfulness, and you should too. God told Moses to put the rod and the manna into the Ark of the Covenant, as a *reminder* to His people of His great faithfulness. Abraham built seven altars during his life as *memorials* to God's goodness. Start remembering!

Next, David thought of Joseph's experience. Listen: "Until God's time finally came—how God tested his patience!" (Psalm 105:19, TLB). David learned from Joseph; who are you learning from?

When Potiphar threw Joseph into prison, he didn't lie there thinking, "This is the break I've been waiting for." No, waiting can be rough. That's why you have to fill *your* cave with *praise.* Make your waiting room a worship room! It will help you hold on a little longer. Stay shut in with God, and when the time is right He'll come and get you.

* * *

If God did it for David and for Joseph, He will work it out for you too—if you'll only wait.

MORE ABOUT WAITING

* * *

Wait on the LORD: be of good courage.

Psalm 27:14

Waiting is not my favorite word. When I hear it I usually ask, "Why?" How about you? I'm part of the leadership of a ministry in Britain called *United Christian Broadcasters*. It was founded by an outstanding Christian network in New Zealand called *Radio Rhema*. God has worked miracles and we are now live on satellite across Europe. In addition, we have a network of 15 Christian stations in Ireland. We're now building the first national Christian radio network in Britain.

Now, when you work with governments you get lots of practice waiting. Sometimes I call Gareth Littler, who leads the ministry, and ask, "What's happening?" If nothing's happening, or if it's not happening fast enough, I'll say, "Can't we *do* something?" Those who know me well call me a "driver" or "project person."

But even though I struggle with it, I know that *everything God does is connected to a schedule.* Furthermore, *everything that makes a difference starts in obscurity.* The birthing process requires waiting. Impatience will deliver something too weak to handle the assignment. You must stay connected to the umbilical cord of the Word and the Spirit so that you can be born healthy!

* * *

So the word for you today is, "Wait on the LORD, be of good courage."

LEARNING TO BE ALONE

* * *

He departed again into a mountain himself alone.
John 6:15

If you can't be alone, you'll have nothing to give when you're with others. You'll say much but it will mean little, because the well is empty. Any Christian who ever said anything worth remembering, first learned to spend time alone with God. Paul said, "I conferred not with flesh and blood" (Galatians 1:16). The assignment God gave him was so big it called for three years alone in the Arabian desert. If you're going to build a relationship, catch a vision, or get clear directions for your life, you *must* spend time alone with God. If you don't hear from *Him*, you'll have nothing to give to *them*.

T. D. Jakes tells of his grandmother who picked cotton, fought her way through slavery, earned a degree, and finally taught in college. He said, "She had learned how to be alone without being lonely. She had learned how to rely on her own thoughts, motivate her own smiles, and find serenity and confidence within herself as she communed with her God. She looked beyond the visible and rejoiced in the invisible; she looked out the window and saw *far* down the road."

How about you? Do you have a dream or a goal that looks impossible? You may have to *hold* it or *hide* it, but you'll definitely have to *water* it, and that only happens when you get alone with God.

* * *

When you take care of the source *within*, you'll never be subject to the things *without*.

FOUR SEASONS

* * *

Come before winter.

2 Timothy 4:21

Spring speaks of *youth*, summer of *manhood*, autumn of *old age,* and winter of *death* and the judgment beyond. And the word to you today is, "Come before winter." Mark Twain said, "Some folks get bothered about the Scriptures they *don't* understand, but it's the ones I *do* understand that bother me." Here's a Scripture that would bother me greatly if I didn't know Jesus, "It is appointed unto men once to die, but after this the judgment" (Hebrews 9:27).

A legend from the streets of Baghdad tells of a wealthy merchant who sent his servant to the market to buy goods. The servant returned empty-handed and frightened, and said he had just met Death and she made "a threatening gesture toward me." He borrowed the fastest horse from his master's stable and left Baghdad to flee to Samaria, believing death would never find him there. That afternoon the master himself met Death in the marketplace and said to her, "Why did you frighten my servant? Why did you make that threatening gesture toward him?" Death answered, "Sir, you're mistaken, that was nothing but an expression of surprise. I did not expect to see your servant in Baghdad, *for I have an appointment with him this evening in Samaria.*"

* * *

All of us have an appointment in Samaria. The question is not, "Is it coming?" The question is, "Will *you* be ready when it arrives?"

GUARD YOUR THOUGHTS

* * *

Anyone who looks at a woman lustfully has already committed adultery with her in his heart.

Matthew 5:28 (NIV)

The real temptation is to entertain certain thoughts in the privacy of your own mind. After all, who knows what you're thinking? Why be concerned? Because *you will ultimately become whatever you meditate upon.* The Bible says, "As [a man] thinketh in his heart, so is he" (Proverbs 23:7). When Satan wants to tear down your character, he doesn't start with an *act*, he starts with a *thought.*

He'll plant seeds in the form of thoughts. These thoughts aren't yours just because they come to mind. They *become* yours when you allow them to move in and rearrange the furniture.

A thought left to ramble in your mind can attach itself to the pain of the past, and feed on it until it grows like a virus. The stronger it gets, the weaker you become, until all your strength has been drained. Don't let that happen. Listen: *"You'll do best by filling your minds and meditating on things true, noble, reputable, authentic, compelling, gracious, the best* and not the *worst*" (Philippians 4:8, TM).

* * *

Now that you know this, start putting it into practice.

THERE'S NO NEED TO HIDE

* * *

Everything is uncovered and laid bare before the eyes of him to whom we must give account.
Hebrews 4:13 (NIV)

God knows your every thought! You can't lie to Him, for He knows you inside out. Just be honest and say, "Father, this is what I'm being tempted with, help me! Cleanse me and give me strength. Thank you for loving me in spite of all You know about me. Forgive me for judging others. If it were not for Your mercy, I would be guilty of the very things for which I have condemned them. Help me to be more like Jesus."

The book of Hebrews doesn't stop by telling us God *sees* and *knows* everything about us. Listen: "For we have not an high priest which cannot be touched with the feeling of our infirmities" (Hebrews 4:15). Great news! You have a high priest and He has provided forgiveness for *all* your sins.

Today, if you're feeling frustrated by your failures and discouraged over your defeats, listen: He can be touched with the feeling of your infirmities. He's been to your point of despair. He's faced the tempter in every area—*and defeated him*. All He asks is an *invitation* to come in and cleanse your heart and mind.

* * *

You don't have to hide anymore—He's waiting to forgive and restore you. All you have to do is ask Him.

HE WON'T GIVE UP ON YOU

* * *

So shall my word be that goeth forth out of my mouth: it shall not return unto me void, but it shall accomplish that which I please

Isaiah 55:11

The reason I keep urging you to get into God's Word is that *the more you hear His thoughts, the more you start thinking like Him!* Peter became so dependent upon the words of Jesus, that when others walked away he said, "Lord, to whom shall we go? thou hast the words of eternal life" (John 6:68). Job said that he considered God's words to be more necessary than food. (See Job 23:12.) It's through the Word that God speaks to you, comforts you, counsels you, and deals with your problems.

God's Word will accomplish what He sends it to do. He won't stop in the middle of the job and He won't give up on you. He'll keep hammering until the foundation is secure and the building is strong. And the wonderful thing is that *no one will ever get to know that you were in such terrible shape.* He'll cover you with His precious blood even while He works on you. Think of it: you're covered while you're being changed into His image. In a world void of commitment, isn't it comforting to know that *God won't give up on you?*

* * *

If anybody ought to praise the Lord, it should be you.

THE KING AND I

* * *

I will surely show thee kindness for Jonathan thy father's sake.

2 Samuel 9:7

Mephibosheth, Jonathan's son, was lame because he was dropped when he was a baby. Year's later, King David, who had a covenant with his father, redeemed him and gave him a place at the king's table. What a story—lifted from the fall, saved because of another, and made a child of the king. Sounds like your testimony and mine, doesn't it?

But there's a problem in his *thinking*. Although he's been redeemed, he stlll sees himself as *worthless*. Listen: "And he bowed himself, and said, What is thy servant, that thou shouldest look upon such a dead dog as I am?" (2 Samuel 9:8). He thought of himself as a dead dog, so he lay on the floor like one. His feet were not only lame, his *thinking* was.

The word of the Lord to you today is: "You've been on the floor long enough. It's time for a resurrection and it must start in your thinking. Just because you've been treated like a dog, doesn't make you one. Get up off the floor and take your seat at the King's table—for He has made you worthy. You have a right to be at His table. Not because of your goodness, but because of *His grace!"*

* * *

Let God heal your thoughts so that you'll be able to enjoy what He is doing in your life right now.

DEVOTED

* * *

I will love thee, O LORD, my strength.

Psalm 18:1

It's easy to get distracted and grow cold. That's a battle you'll fight constantly. Listen: "For the sinful nature desires what is contrary to the Spirit, and the Spirit what is contrary to the sinful nature. They are in conflict with each other" (Galatians 5:17, NIV). Every day you'll have to make a decision. If you don't, the flesh will decide for you and you'll finish up asking, "How did I *ever* get here?" And the answer is, "Because you never decided not to!"

When two people are devoted to each other, they don't mind sacrificing for their dream. Their relationship may come under attack, but it only draws them closer. Temptation may try to lure them away, but they find strength in each other's arms. To them, giving is not a *discipline*, it's a *delight*. David cried, "Lord, how I love you! For you have done such tremendous things for me" (Psalm 18:1, TLB).

* * *

You see, when you really love Him it's easier to *obey* Him, *serve* Him, and *follow* Him.

GROUNDED AND STEADY

* * *

Stay grounded and steady . . . constantly tuned to the message.

Colossians 1:23 (TM)

We live in an entertainment-based society and we've brought it into the church. Great emphasis is placed on *feeling good.* One pastor told me, "People have had a hard week, and when they come to God's house they should have a good time." In a sense that's true. David said, "In thy presence is fulness of joy" (Psalm 16:11). But when there's a cancer, do you tell the patient or just keep him feeling good until his condition is hopeless?

Jeremiah was told "to root out, and to pull down, . . . to build, and to plant" (Jeremiah 1:10). Now building and planting are more enjoyable than *rooting out* and *pulling down,* and definitely draw bigger crowds, *but what if the patient dies?*

Let's read carefully what Paul told Timothy: *"You're going to find that there will be times when people will have no stomach for solid teaching, but will fill up on spiritual junk food—catchy opinions that tickle their fancy. They'll turn their backs on truth and chase mirages. But you—keep your eye on what you're doing*" (2 Timothy 4:2-5 ,TM).

* * *

As we get closer to the coming of Christ, the only thing that will sustain you is knowing His Word, and drawing on your relationship with Him.

JOHN AND JUDAS

* * *

And Jesus said unto him, "Friend."

Matthew 26:50

God's purposes in your life are tied to relationships—and not always enjoyable ones. But God can turn your rejection into direction. Sometimes He opens doors, other times He closes them. Personally, I'm grateful for some of the doors He has closed, for had I been allowed to walk through them, I would have been destroyed. But that doesn't mean people can just walk in and destroy God's plan for your life. Their access to your future is limited by the shield of His divine purpose and protection. What a comfort! God can still hang Haman on the gallows he built for you. (See Esther 7:10.) Paul said the purposes of God for him included, "False brethren" (2 Corinthians 11:26). The pain *they* caused him made the shipwrecks look easy.

As you look back, you realize it was *persecution* that taught you *perseverance,* and *rejection* that taught you *forgiveness*. They produced Christian character. *It's much easier to forgive the actions of men when you understand the purposes of God.* The challenge is to sit at the table with John *and* Judas and love them equally, even when you know each one's agenda. We all want a friend like John who'll love us, or Peter who'll fight for us. Peter's misguided love would have stopped Jesus from going to the cross, but through Judas He reached His goal.

* * *

That's why Jesus kissed him and called him, "Friend." Think about it!

TO THINE OWN SELF BE TRUE

* * *

Blessed is the man who perseveres under trial, because when he has stood the test, he will receive the crown of life.

James 1:12 (NIV)

When you violate your own values, you stop enjoying your own company. When you talk one way and *live* another, you become somebody you can't respect, and it's hard to be alone with a person like that. Everybody deals with temptation, and if you don't learn how to handle it, it will run over you like a steamroller. For example, cheating the tax man is one of the more *acceptable* transgressions in the kingdom. But how do you *feel* afterwards? If you save on your taxes but lose your integrity, what have you gained? Does money mean *that* much to you?

And what about Joseph? Potiphar's wife was beautiful, she was lonely, and she was available. She didn't try to entice Joseph just once, she did it for months. But Joseph didn't consult his *flesh—he consulted his spirit. He didn't ask, "Can I get away with it?" He asked, "Can I live with it afterwards?"* The house you're building today is the one you're going to live in tomorrow, and every time you say no to sin and yes to God, you add one more brick to the wall of character.

* * *

Ask God today to bring into your life people who draw you closer to Him, for when you think about it, you're only going to get one shot at the goal. Don't miss it.

HINDSIGHT

* * *

This I recall to my mind, therefore have I hope.

Lamentations 3:21

When Jacob was facing the crisis of his life, God visited him, but he didn't realize it until later. Listen: "Surely the LORD is in this place; and I knew it not" (Genesis 28:16). *Sometimes you can't see God's hand until you look back.*

When Jeremiah wrote *Lamentations,* he was going through tough times. Listen: "All peace and prosperity have long since gone . . . I have forgotten what enjoyment is" (Lamentations 3:17, TLB). I'm glad that men of God not only experienced real life, but recorded it so we wouldn't feel *terminally unique*. They not only shared the problem, they also shared the solution. Listen again: "This I recall to my mind, therefore have I hope." Go ahead, start recalling. Do you remember when Jesus stood on the bow of your ship and spoke peace to the storm that terrified you? When you think of what He's brought you *through,* and what He's kept you *from,* it's only by His grace that you've made it!

Here's the word for you today: "It is of the LORD'S mercies that we are not consumed, because his compassions fail not. They are new every morning: great is thy faithfulness" (Lamentations 3:22-23). This morning you woke in His arms, surrounded by His love. *Nothing* can get at you without first coming through Him.

* * *

Today, He'll forgive you, lift you, strengthen you—and before you reach bedtime, you'll look back and say, "Great is thy faithfulness."

THE BUSINESS OF JUDGING

* * *

They are God's servants, not yours. They are responsible to Him, not to you.

Romans 14:4 (TLB)

When you have strong personal convictions, you can easily become judgmental and not know it. The other day, I heard that a man who had been discredited by the church for personal failure, had been *used by God* miraculously. As a result, a whole family had been saved and two churches established. I just preached in one of them to a congregation of 500 people. Amazing! Afterwards I prayed, "Dear God, help me to leave the business of judging to You!" Paul asks us, "Who art thou that judgest another man's servant?" (Romans 14:4, KJV). *Who made it your business, anyway?*

Abraham, the friend of God, gave his wife away and *lied* to save his neck. Peter, one of the leaders of the Church, was *a racist,* and Paul had to confront him on it. God recorded this to let us know that, given the right circumstances, *not one of us is so holy or strong that we wouldn't do the same thing. We* all *need His grace.*

Until you breathe your last breath, keep sowing seeds of mercy, for Jesus said, "Blessed are the merciful, for they shall obtain mercy" (Matthew 5:7).

* * *

Ask God today to help you move from the judgment seat to the mercy seat. Ask Him for a heart of love.

EXERCISING DISCERNMENT

* * *

But strong meat belongeth to them . . .
who by reason of use have their senses
exercised to discern both good and evil.
Hebrews 5:14

When God wants to bless you, He'll send a person. When Satan wants to bother you, he'll also send somebody. That's why you need *discernment*. The world calls it "a gut feeling" or an "intuition," but the Bible calls it *the discerning of spirits.* Not just evil spirits—*all* sorts of spirits. When someone comes into your life, they bring their spirit. Have you ever been around someone with a *controlling spirit*? Or a *resentful spirit?* Even the business world tries to screen out those with the *right* abilities but the *wrong* attitudes by using "Personality Profile Testing."

Now discernment is something you have to *exercise.* You need to give it a daily workout. The reason children need protection is because they lack discernment. Predators and pedophiles feed on that ignorance, and so does the devil. If you are to have mature discernment, you must move from milk to meat, the strong meat of the Word.

Like a knife that's sharpened on a well-oiled stone, so your sense of discernment will be sharpened as you *live in the Word* and *stay filled with His Spirit.*

* * *

When both are active in you, you'll not only discern what is at work in others, but you'll have the wisdom to deal with it.

THE INGREDIENTS OF AN ANOINTED LIFE

* * *

Take . . . pure myrrh . . . it shall be an holy anointing oil.

Exodus 30:23,25

What a picture of the anointed life! The first ingredient in the anointing oil was *myrrh,* which speaks of *change.* It was used to anoint the living and embalm the dead—*before the birth of the new we experience the death of the old.* Before Elisha received the double portion, he had to break his plough. That wasn't easy, for it put food on his table and gave him an identity as a farmer. But if you want to become a prophet, you have to break your plough. Moses was the meekest man on earth. (See Numbers 12:3.) How did that happen? *Forty years in the wilderness will do it every time.*

What makes change so difficult is *the opinions of others.* What will they say? Most denominations never make it beyond the point of their greatest revelation. They celebrate it, institutionalize it, and stop it. To backslide you don't have to go back, you only have to stay in the same place while God moves on. Solomon says, "The path of the just is as the shining light, that shineth more and more unto the perfect day" (Proverbs 4:18). *You'll never become what you're called to be by remaining what you are.*

* * *

God has words you've never heard, places you've never been, joys you've never experienced. All He asks you to do is open your heart and let Him lead you today.

BOLDNESS

* * *

Take . . . sweet cinnamon . . . it shall be an holy anointing oil.

Exodus 30:23,25

The second ingredient in the anointing oil was *cinnamon*. It came from a root system so strong that it would uproot anything that hindered it. What a picture of *boldness.* When is the *last* time you did something for God for the *first* time? You can choose to sit in the boat or get out and walk on the water.

Listen again: "With great power gave the apostles witness of the resurrection of the Lord Jesus: and great grace was upon them all" (Acts 4:33). A friend of mine was traveling on a plane and there was one seat left—the one beside him. A lady asked him, "Is that seat saved?" He replied, "No, but I am, please sit down and I'll tell you about it." Before they reached their destination, she had given her life to Christ. Every day opportunities are coming toward you, *but you've got to have boldness.*

A teenager once said to me, "I'm just a loser, and I come from a family of losers." I said, "No way! In the act of procreation, over a *million* seeds were released, but only one of them made it—*you*. So, any way you look at it, *you're one in a million."* You may smile, but the truth is you were born to win.

* * *

You were created for a high purpose, so ask God to give you the second ingredient in a truly anointed life—boldness!

COMPASSION

* * *

Take . . . sweet calamus . . . it shall be an holy anointing oil.

Exodus 30:23,25

The third ingredient in the anointing oil was *calamus*. From it we get *calamine lotion*, which is used to comfort and heal. What a picture of *compassion!* Listen: "When He saw the multitudes, He was *moved* with compassion" (Matthew 9:36). The Good Samaritan didn't just look, feel bad, and walk away. Jesus said, "When he saw him, he had compassion on him, And went to him" (Luke 10:33-34). General Booth once said, "How can you convince a man of the love of God when his feet are perishing in the cold?"

Compassion took me to Romania 19 times to feed, clothe, and care for the tiniest victims of Communism's failure the children. Many had AIDS, Hepatitis B, and parasites. There were holes in the orphanage roof, and when it rained, water would pour in on the children. We found a large church just down the street, but when we asked them to get involved, they refused. So we went to work and put on a new roof, poured concrete driveways, put in playing fields, replaced hundreds of urine-soaked beds and mattresses, and started sending 40-ton trucks filled with food and relief.

Compassion costs—but it also brings God's blessing: "Blessed is he that considereth the poor: the LORD will deliver him in time of trouble" (Psalm 41:1).

* * *

Today, God is giving you a choice—get involved, or walk by on the other side. What will your decision be?

INNER CLEANSING

* * *

Take . . . cassia . . . it shall be an holy anointing oil.

Exodus 30:24, 25

The fourth ingredient in the anointing oil was *cassia*, and it was used as a laxative for *inner cleansing*. The problem is not just that we sin, but that we try to hide it, defend it, or rationalize it away. A man told me, "Maybe I do sin, but I'm no worse than anyone else." I said, "Sir, you're measuring by the wrong standard."

When my son was little, he hated the evening ritual of getting bathed. One night he said, "Pop, give me a break!" I said, "What do you have in mind?" He smiled and said, *"Couldn't you just dust me off a little?"* Most of us do the same thing. Instead of repenting, we go to church for a light religious dusting. But it doesn't work. Sin is a heart condition.

Most of us know about David's sin, but have you ever read his prayer of repentance? Listen: "Against thee, thee only, have I sinned, and done this evil in thy sight . . . Purge me with hyssop, and I shall be clean: wash me, and I shall be whiter than snow" (Psalm 51:4, 7). God heard David, forgave him, and totally restored him. His greatest psalms were written *after* his failure, and his greatest days were lived after this prayer.

* * *

Yours can be, too. But to be anointed, you must have a clean heart.

IT'S TIME TO MOVE ON

* * *

How long wilt thou mourn for Saul, . . . fill thine horn with oil, and go . . . for I have provided.

1 Samuel 16:1

Samuel was still mourning the loss of King Saul. So God visited him and told him it was time to move on. There's another step beyond death, and that's *burial*. It separates the living from the dead and the past from the future. Some of us get through it faster than others and some *never* do. *They talk only of the past, because they stopped living years ago.*

Anytime you discuss the past as if it were the present, it's because you've let the past *steal* the present from you. Don't do it! Rise up and take it back. Listen again to God's word to Samuel: "Go . . . for I have provided." Did you hear that, child of God? He's provided everything you need to start again.

Here's your choice: you can keep lamenting what *nobody* can change, or you can live in the present and plan for the future. God says "I have provided." There are friends who *want* to be part of your life the moment you decide to live again. Don't keep reliving events that are dead and gone. Stop arguing with people who aren't listening.

* * *

Take *all* your time, *all* your love, and *all* your energy, and give it to your future, for *it's time to move on.*

WHEN MOSES DIES

* * *

As I was with Moses, so I will be with thee.

Joshua 1:5

Stop thinking God will use anybody but you, or bless others more than you. Moses spoke for God, stood up to Pharaoh, and worked miracles—but he died. *There's some things you'll never know until Moses dies.* Joshua wanted to know if God would be with him too. God said, "I will." What faithfulness! People will enter and people will leave your life. Circumstances will change overnight. Life will hit you like a tornado and you'll struggle to get back up and wonder if you can go on. But through your tears you'll hear Him saying, "As I was with Moses, so I will be with you."

Listen to Jesus: "The stone which the builders *rejected,* the same is become the *head* of the corner: this is the Lord's doing, and it is marvelous in our eyes" (Matthew 21:42). Imagine—the *rejection* of men can be "the Lord's doing." He'll take what is painful and make it "marvelous in our eyes." Are you grieving over something —as though you have no God to *direct* it and no grace to *correct* it? You need to see it from *His* perspective! When you do, you may well see that *the worst possible thing that could have happened to you* was the Lord's doing, and it will suddenly look marvelous in your eyes.

* * *

Rejoice child of God, be strong, for *He is with you.*

ARE YOU READY?

* * *

Behold, I will do a new thing; now it shall spring forth.

Isaiah 43:19

If God says He's going to bless you, then ignore the circumstances and believe the God who cannot lie. You're too important to God to be destroyed by a situation that was only meant to give you *character* and *direction*. It was the grace of God that enabled you to survive and make it through. God proved that He can bring you out of the fire without even the smell of smoke, and out of the lions den without so much as a bite mark. If you want to know what God can *do* for you, look at what He's already *done* for you—and start praising Him.

And that's not all. Listen: "Behold I will do a *new* thing; now it shall *spring forth.*" After feeling like you've waited forever, God will suddenly move. If you're not ready you'll miss Him.

When the Church was born we read, "*Suddenly* there came a sound from heaven as of a rushing mighty wind, and it filled all the house where they were sitting" (Acts 2:2). When God decided to bring Paul and Silas out of prison we read, "And *suddenly* there was a great earthquake . . . and immediately all the doors were opened" (Acts 16:26). Are you ready for God to move *suddenly?* Are you ready for the doors to open?

* * *

The word to you today is, "I will do a new thing; now it shall spring forth."

CHRISTIAN LIFE ISN'T NATURAL, IT'S SPIRITUAL

* * *

But we have this treasure in earthen vessels, that the excellency of the power may be of God, and not of us.

2 Corinthians 4:7

The love of God I knew as a young Christian was based on *performance*, like a merit system. If I did well, He loved me—if I failed, He didn't. What a roller coaster! To make matters worse, there were those testimonies from people who lived in unending bliss. They never had a Monday morning—at least, never one I heard about. I thought they woke up swinging from rafters, never had a down day, terrorized the devil, and heard from heaven regularly. Meanwhile, I soldiered on. Sometimes I felt ashamed, most times I felt insecure, and all the time I felt like something was missing. Even though I was a babe in Christ, I always felt like I should be further along. Sound familiar?

Then I read, "I don't mean to say I am perfect. I haven't learned all I should even yet, but I keep working toward that day when I will finally be all that Christ saved me for and wants me to be" (Philippians 3:12, TLB). The mighty apostle Paul said that! Today, I understand that the Christian life isn't *natural,* it's *spiritual*! It isn't natural to "do good to them that hate you" (Matthew 5:44). Forgiveness isn't natural at all, *and without God it can't be done.*

* * *

It's enough to drive you into the arms of Jesus—and that's the way He planned it.

THE NEW BIRTH PRODUCES A NEW BATTLE

* * *

Now there was long war between the house of Saul and the house of David: but David waxed stronger and stronger, and the house of Saul waxed weaker and weaker.

2 Samuel 3:1

Paul represents the *flesh* and David represents the *spirit*; and the war between them lasted a *long* time. It takes *faith* and *patience* to produce in any of us the nature of Christ. Today, in *The Message,* I read a remarkable statement by Paul: *"I decide to do good but I really don't do it; I decide not to do bad, but then I do it anyway. My decisions such as they are don't result in actions."* Now if that sounds familiar, listen to what he says next: *"I've tried everything, and nothing helps. I'm at the end of my rope! Is there no one who can do anything for me? The answer, thank God, is that Jesus Christ can and does."* (See Romans 7:17-25.) The answer is to feed David and starve Saul. You've *got* to move closer to Jesus.

Paul says, "My little children, of whom I travail in birth again until Christ be *formed* in you" (Galatians 4:19). Only God knows the process it will take for the Christ who *saved* you to be *formed* in you. That's when you begin to *resemble* your Father.

* * *

This only happens as the house of Saul grows weaker, and the house of David grows stronger in our lives.

CHARACTER CLASS AND CHRISTIANITY

* * *

He will sift out everything without solid foundations so that only unshakeable things will be left.

Hebrews 12:27 (TLB)

The Lord often uses trials to realign us, and storms to attack everything in us that can be shaken. Everybody God uses goes through experiences that cause them to let go of the *temporal* and take hold of the *eternal.* Some of them wake up in hospital rooms with monitors beeping in their ears and discover that the things they thought were so important mean nothing at all. Others discover it when the person they thought was *everything* just walks away and leaves them. Job went through it—one day he had everything, the next day nothing. His health was a shambles, his children dead, and his marriage a joke. At times like that you discover what it means by "things which cannot be shaken"—things that are worth living for.

Things like *character, class,* and *Christianity. Character* is not what you *know*, it's what you *are. Class* doesn't show in what you have, it shows in the way you *act*, and even more in the way you *react. Christianity* is not a culture, it's a way of life. It's seeking to be *Christ-like*—not just to keep rules or impress people but *to please Him.* That's why Paul calls it "the high calling of God in Christ Jesus."

* * *

Child of God, when the sun rises tomorrow you'll have *one day less* to live, so *give your life* to the things that cannot be shaken.

HAVE YOU BEEN SPECIFIC?

* * *

Let your requests be made known unto God.

Philippians 4:6

Too often we talk to everybody about our problem except *the One who can really* do *something about it.* God says, "Let your requests be *made known unto [Me]*." Have you done that today? Have you talked to God about the *specific* things you're so concerned over? If you'll be specific with Him, He'll be specific with you. Jesus said, "*Whatever* you ask for in prayer, believe that you have received it, and it will be yours" (Mark 11:24, NIV). How do you think you would act if you knew for sure that your prayer had already been answered? Wouldn't you praise the Lord? Wouldn't you speak confidently?

Perhaps you're having difficulty believing. Then the word for you today is, "If two of you on earth agree about anything you ask for, it will be done for you" (Matthew 18:19, NIV). Join your faith to the faith of others—multiply your impact before the throne. Unite and get results. When someone asks you to pray for them, take it seriously. Don't just promise to pray—do it! The Bible is about *us,* not *you*! We are told to pray for one another, encourage one another, and bear one another's burdens.

* * *

Today, get into God's presence and "let your requests be made known." The door is open—He's inviting you to come.

DON'T GO UNTIL HE SENDS YOU

* * *

I waited patiently for the LORD; and he inclined unto me.

Psalm 40:1

Don't jump the starter's gun or you'll be disqualified from the race. Don't come out until God has finished working on you or you won't be ready for the job.

There's never been a day like this. Listen: "Woe to the earth and the sea, because the devil has gone down to you! He is filled with fury, because he knows that his time is short" (Revelation 12:12, NIV). Forces have been released that no previous generation ever faced, and if we're not strong and well-equipped, we won't be able to cope with them, much less conquer them.

How long did it take to prepare Ananias to lead Saul of Tarsus to Christ? And after he did it, he was never heard of again. He was born for a purpose and when it was completed, he disappeared. That's hard on the ego. We want to be *permanent*. We want to be *featured.* But John the Baptist said, "*He* must increase, but *I* must decrease" (John 3:30).

In the wilderness, Moses learned *reverence* and *dependence* and built a *relationship with God* that would sustain him for the rest of his life. Child of God, *stop looking for a door out of your wilderness.*

* * *

If you don't stay where He has you *today*, you won't make any difference where He sends you *tomorrow*.

SET FREE!

* * *

Go, sell the oil, and pay thy debt, and live thou and thy children of the rest.

2 Kings 4:7

In Old Testament days, if you couldn't pay your bills, your creditor came and took your children and made them work off the debt. In 2 Kings 4, the widow of a prophet was in that position. But she turned to a man of God—and that's always a wise move. If you can hear from a *man of God,* you can hear from *God.* (See John 13:20.)

The prophet asked her, in effect, "What have you got?" (See 2 Kings 4:2.) *God always uses what you've got to create what you need.* All she had was a little pot of oil, but no matter how little it seems when you put it into *His* hands, it multiplies. Remember this principle: *When what you have isn't enough to be a harvest, make it a seed!* Don't eat it. Don't keep it. Sow it and start a harvest. The woman was instructed to borrow all the empty vessels she could and *"pour out."* That's the key—*pour out!* Find something outside yourself, something bigger than you, and pour your time, your life, and your resources into it. The oil from her little pot kept pouring until her debt was paid and her children were redeemed. This shows you the character of God, and that *never* changes. Today, God wants to lift your burden, cancel your debts, and set you free to live.

* * *

Why don't you take a few moments and talk to Him about it. He'll tell you what to do.

HOW BADLY DO YOU WANT IT?

* * *

Let us throw off everything that hinders.

Hebrews 12:1 (NIV)

You'll start getting well when getting well is what matters most to you. Let your desperation drive you beyond concern over the opinions of others. As long as you're conscious of *people* and not conscious enough of *God*, you'll never get what you need.

When Hannah, mother of Samuel, prayed in the temple, there was so much locked up in her that when she began to empty herself out, Eli thought she was *drunk.* (See 1 Samuel 1:13.) God is raising up people who will confound us—radical Christians. They might even look drunk, like those on the day of Pentecost, but they're hungry for God. They'll raise the roof to get to Jesus. They'll interrupt your carefully laid plans and cry like blind Bartimaeus, "Jesus, thou son of David, have mercy on me" (Mark 10:47). *When you're blind, all that matters is receiving your sight.*

Child of God, when it looks like there's no way out for you—start shouting! *You have been chosen for a miracle.* Faith is born in the storm and conceived in the incubator of impossibility. Don't panic. Don't quit. Don't stop short of the prize. The greater the conflict, the greater the conquest. You can't even get toothpaste out of a tube without squeezing. There's something *good* inside you and God wants to get it out.

* * *

The question you need to answer today is, *how badly do I want it?*

INTERCESSION OR ACCUSATION?

* * *

Then you shall call, and the LORD will answer; . . . "If you take away the yoke from your midst, The pointing of the finger, and speaking wickedness."
Isaiah 58:9 (NASB)

Has your healing failed to come? Do troubles follow you more than blessings? Are your prayers seldom answered? The reason for this could be that we have a *yoke* in our lives called, *"The pointing of the finger, and speaking wickedness."* God promised through Isaiah that our lives would change radically, *when we remove this yoke!*

There are two ministries that go on continually before the throne of God. One is *intercession,* the other is *accusation.* Jesus lives to intercede for His people, and if you abide in Him you will intercede for them too. (See Hebrews 7:25.) On the other side, Satan is "the accuser of our brethren" (Revelation 12:10). When you give him access to your life, you'll become increasingly *critical* of others. You've *got* to make a choice about which of these ministries will be yours. You may ask *how* Satan could continually accuse the saints before God, if he's been thrown out of heaven? The answer is, *he uses the saints to do it for him.* Anytime you see one brother accusing another, Satan is at work. Satan knows the authority God has given to any two that will agree. (See Matthew 18:19.)

* * *

So walk in love today and become a direct threat to his domain.

LAYING IT ALL ASIDE TO SERVE

* * *

He riseth from supper, and laid aside his garments; and took a towel, . . . and began to wash the disciples' feet.

John 13:4-5

They would *never* forget this night. He alone had the right to be called *Master*, but He laid it aside to serve. Paul said, "Let this mind be in you, which was also in Christ Jesus: . . . Who . . . took upon him the form of a servant" (Philippians 2:5-7).

The secret of great ministry is seen in the things we lay aside to respond to His call. Laying aside the comforts of home to go where His name hasn't been heard. Laying aside the things that *most* enjoy to experience the things that *few* will ever know.

There are evangelists, pastors, and workers who never sold a tape or wrote a book, never drew a crowd or gained national fame, but they paid the price. Like Noah, whose membership never exceeded eight souls, they ministered faithfully. They wanted to do more, they thought they would go further, but they *laid it all aside to serve the few.* They said, "If I'm not called to help *everybody*, then, please God, let me help *somebody*." Child of God, ask yourself today, "Am I willing to lay it all aside to follow Him?"

* * *

It's the most important question you'll ever answer.

CAN YOU RECEIVE FROM OTHERS?

* * *

Whoever accepts anyone I send accepts me.

John 13:20 (NIV)

You'd be surprised how many people live beyond help, because they have an image to uphold. It's a dangerous place to be. When trials come, not only must you be open to the Lord, but also to whomever He sends. Listen: "And he was there in the wilderness forty days, tempted of Satan; . . . and the angels ministered unto him" (Mark 1:13). *Even Jesus needed ministry.*

He created the angels, yet He permitted them to minister to Him. The greater was willing to receive help from the lesser. *What a lesson for you!* When your pain levels get high enough, you won't care who God uses. If you were in a burning house you wouldn't care who the firemen were. Their education, denomination, or ethnic background would mean nothing to you because of the urgency of your need.

Perhaps your problem is you need *someone*, but you don't trust *anyone. Start trusting God!* Who do you think brought you this far? Listen: " 'Though the mountains be shaken and the hills be removed, yet my unfailing love for you will not be shaken nor my covenant of peace be removed,' says the LORD, who has compassion on you" (Isaiah 54:10, NIV). When God extends His love and compassion to you, don't be too *proud* to accept it.

* * *

When you accept it, you're accepting *Him*.

POSITION YOURSELF TO RECEIVE

* * *

If you hold anything against anyone, forgive him.

Mark 11:25 (NIV)

Sometimes forgiving *is the hardest thing you'll ever do.* Jesus said, in effect, "Don't just dismiss it—throw the case out of court!" Make a decision never to discuss it again. When you consider how often God has forgiven you, how could you think of doing less? Don't wait for them to ask and don't criticize them if they never do, that's between God and them. Forgiveness is for *your* benefit! You're removing the roadblocks that stand between you and His blessing.

In Mark 11:23, Jesus told His disciples, to tell the mountain to move and it will move. Perhaps you're thinking, "I spoke to my mountain and it *grew.*" But notice that Jesus also said, "Whatever you ask for in prayer, *believe* that you have received it, and it will be yours" (Mark 11:24, NIV). Perhaps you're saying, "I prayed, I claimed, I believed, and *nothing* has happened."

Then you need to focus on this verse, "If you hold anything against anyone, forgive him, so that your Father in heaven may forgive you your sins" (Mark 11:25, NIV). Go ahead, child of God, open your heart, close the door on the past, stand in His presence and say, "Lord, I've done what you asked. I've forgiven *any* and *all* as you've forgiven me, and I'm ready now for everything you have for me today."

* * *

This word could be the key to your deliverance and the door to your future.

THE "NOBODIES" OF THE BIBLE

* * *

The Lord GOD hath opened mine ear.

Isaiah 50:5

God can speak to you today through anybody! The question is, can you hear Him? Naaman was the Commander-in-Chief of the Syrian army, but he was dying of leprosy. Did he want to be healed? Yes! *But he wanted it his way.* First, he wanted Elisha to come personally and speak to him, since he was a man of rank and prestige. But instead, Elisha sent his servant out to say, "Go, wash yourself seven times in the Jordan" (2 Kings 5:10). But he didn't like the Jordan, because it was dirty, "Are there not cleaner rivers?" (2 Kings 5:12). God wouldn't accommodate his pride—and He won't accomodate ours either.

Naaman received his healing. Only when he humbled himself and became *willing to listen,* first to a slave in his kitchen, and then to some regular soldiers in his army who said, "If the prophet had told you to do some great thing, wouldn't you have done it?" (2 Kings 5:13). *Our problem is, if God doesn't speak to us in a certain familiar way, we won't receive it.* Child of God, He can use anybody to speak to you—a kitchen maid or waitress, a nameless soldier, or even somebody you know.

* * *

Today be sensitive, be humble, and be willing to hear.

ACTING OR REACTING

* * *

He that is soon angry dealeth foolishly.

Proverbs 14:17

The little girl was in a bad mood so she took her frustration out on her younger brother. At first, she just teased him, then punched him, pulled his hair, and finally, kicked him in the shins. He could take it all until the kicking began. That hurt! So he went crying to his mother and she said to the little girl, "Mary, the devil made you pull your brother's hair and kick his shins."

The little girl thought it over for a moment and then answered, "Maybe the devil did make me punch him and pull his hair, *but kicking him was my own idea.*"

All the evil in the world doesn't come from direct satanic involvement. A lot of it comes from the heart. Jesus said, "Out of the heart proceed evil thoughts, murders, adulteries, fornications, thefts, false witness, blasphemies" (Matthew 15:19). What we do with our anger and frustrations is subject to our *will.* We can *choose* how we will respond to stress, or to the behavior of others. We either act or we *react.* When we react, we give control to other people or other things. But when *you act according to the Word*, you can change that person or circumstance, and you *always* finish up feeling better about yourself.

* * *

Today, you're going to get another chance to do it God's way.

FIND YOUR PLACE

* * *

And they stood every man in his place round about the camp: and all the host ran, and cried, and fled.

Judges 7:21

It's one of the greatest military victories in the Bible. Three-hundred men were willing to *stand in their place* and, as a result, the enemy was routed. All Gideon needed was a consecrated few who would stand in their place and God did the rest. *Have you found your place yet?* Are you totally identified with the cause of Christ? Is your light shining?

Perhaps things are not going well in your local church and you wonder what to do. The answer is a small group of believing Christians who will join with you to fast, pray, go out and bring in the lost, and refuse to yield an inch to the devil. The New Testament church started with 120, and before it was over they were accused of turning "the world upside down" (Acts 17:6). *Revival can begin with two or three people seeking the face of God and refusing to settle for anything less.* If you haven't found your place yet, get into God's presence and ask Him about it. He'll reveal it to you, and when He does, you will find greater joy there than anywhere else you've ever been.

* * *

Until you find that place, your successes will be hollow and you'll feel like a misfit at anything else you try.

VICTORY

* * *

Use every piece of God's armor to resist the enemy whenever he attacks, and when it is all over, you will still be standing up.

Ephesians 6:13 (TLB)

During World War II, Winston Churchill's words inspired the British people to believe in victory. Listen: "You ask what is our policy? It is to wage war by sea, land, and air, with all our might and all the strength that God can give us . . . You ask, what is our aim? I can answer in one word: Victory! . . at all costs, Victory! . . in spite of all terror, Victory! . . however long and hard the road may be; for without victory there is no survival.

"We shall go on to the end, we shall fight in France, we shall fight on the seas and oceans, we shall fight with growing confidence and growing strength in the air, we shall defend our island, whatever the cost may be; we shall fight on the beaches, we shall fight on the landing grounds; we shall fight in the fields and in the streets, we shall fight in the hills; but we shall never, never, never surrender."

Child of God, don't give up. You're on the winning side. No matter how bad things may look today, His word to you is, "The LORD himself goes before you and will be with you; he will never leave you nor forsake you. Do not be afraid; do not be discouraged" (Deuteronomy 31:8, NIV).

* * *

The word to you today is, "Victory!"

THE PRAYERS OF MANY

* * *

Then many will give thanks on our behalf for the gracious favor granted us in answer to the prayers of many.

2 Corinthians 1:11 (NIV)

It was the worst thing Paul had ever been through. Listen: "We were under great pressure, far beyond our ability to endure, so that we despaired even of life. Indeed, in our hearts we felt the sentence of death" (2 Corinthians 1:8, NIV). Paul is overwhelmed. and on the verge of giving up. Have you been there? If not, you will be, so listen carefully. Paul learned two important lessons.

First, *dependence on God:* "But this happened that we might not rely on ourselves but on God" (verse 1:9). It's humbling to have to admit, "I don't have what it takes. I can't handle it without God." But when He's all you've got, you'll find He's all you need.

Second, *dependence on others.* Listen: "In answer to the prayers of many." Don't carry that burden alone. Reach out to others for help and you'll be amazed at what happens. Jesus said, "If two of you on earth agree about anything you ask for, it will be done for you" (Matthew 18:19, NIV). Recently, a dear friend of ours was completely healed of terminal cancer because a group of churches and believers prayed and refused to give up until God answered. You can't beat "the prayers of many."

* * *

It's God's way, and you can't improve on it.

DO IT NOW

* * *

Redeeming the time, because the days are evil.

Ephesians 5:16

How many times have you said, "I'll do it tomorrow?" Sometimes you put things off because you don't think you *know enough* or can do it *well enough*. The fact is, there is no magic age at which excellence emerges or quality surfaces.

Thomas Jefferson was 33 when he drafted the Declaration of Independence. Charles Dickens was 24 when he began his *Pickwick Papers* and 25 when he wrote *Oliver Twist*. Newton was 24 when he formulated the law of gravity.

A second danger is to think that creativity and invention belong to the young. Not so! Emmanuel Kant wrote his finest philosophical works at age 74. Verdi at 80 produced *Falstaff*. Goethe was 80 when he completed *Faust*. Tennyson was 80 when he wrote *Crossing the Bar*, and Michelangelo completed his greatest work at 87. Moses was 80 when he led God's people out of Egypt, and 120 when he got to Caanan.

Seize the day! Redeem the *now* moments of your life for the time and age you're waiting for may never arrive.

* * *

The moment, once passed, will never return. So do it now.

TRUE GREATNESS

* * *

Whatsoever ye would that men should do to you, do ye even so to them.

Matthew 7:12

One afternoon in 1953, reporters and city officials gathered at a Chicago railroad station to welcome the Nobel Peace Prize winner. A giant of a man with bushy hair and a large mustache stepped from the train. Cameras flashed. City officials approached him with hands outstretched and began telling him how honored they were to meet him.

The man politely thanked them and then, looking over their heads, asked if he could be excused for a moment. He quickly walked through the crowd until he reached the side of an elderly woman who was struggling with two suitcases. He picked up the bags and, with a smile, escorted the woman to a bus. After helping her aboard, he wished her a safe journey. Returning to the greeting party, he apologized, "Sorry to have kept you waiting."

The man was Dr. Albert Schweitzer, the famous missionary doctor who spent his life helping the poor in Africa. In response to Schweitzer's action, one member of the reception committee said to the reporter next to him, "*That's the first time I ever saw a sermon walking.*" Today look for an opportunity to be kind—to *go out of your way* and bless someone even if it costs you to do it.

* * *

And remember the words, "Whatsoever good thing any man doeth, the same shall he receive of the Lord" (Ephesians 6:8).

WHEN YOU'RE FOLLOWING HIM, YOU CAN FACE ANYTHING

* * *

He goes on ahead of them, and his sheep follow him because they know his voice.

John 10:4 (NIV)

When you have to face someone bigger and stronger than you, keep in mind that they're not bigger than *your God*! He shut the mouths of the lions for Daniel, and he quenched the fire for the three Hebrew children. He opened the prison door for Peter who was about to be executed the next day. Why? Because Peter's job wasn't done yet. His assignment wasn't yet completed *and nothing could happen to him until it was.*

Don't be afraid today. David said, "Commit thy way unto the LORD; trust also in him; and he shall bring it to pass" (Psalm 37:5). You can either commit it or sweat it.

You can look at the mountain, or look at the Mountain Mover. If you've tried running away or manipulating the situation or giving in to doubt and despair, stop and give it *to Him.* Peter said, "Casting all your care upon Him; for He careth for you" (1 Peter 5:7). He may not do it in your time frame and He may not do it the way you think it should be done, but He'll do it right. Give it to Him! *Surrender is simply turning it over one more time than you take it back.*

* * *

Do it and you'll discover that when you're following Him, you can face anything.

PRAISE GOD BEFORE IT EVEN HAPPENS

* * *

He staggered not at the promise of God through unbelief; but was strong in faith, giving glory to God.
Romans 4:20

It's tough to have faith when you're sick in body or your purse is empty and you can't make ends meet. Yet those are the very times when you need faith the most. Abraham did something to strengthen his faith, and so must you. Jude says "Building up yourselves on your most holy faith, praying in the Holy Ghost" (Jude 1:20). When we pray in the Spirit, we are built up and strengthened. A car kept in a garage will never get you where you want to go. You've got to use it, and it's the same with praying in the Holy Spirit.

Have you been in the Word lately? If I were your doctor and you wouldn't take my prescription, I'd tell you how sick you really were, and before I was through you'd gulp that stuff down. Solomon said, "Those who discover these words live, really live; body and soul, they are bursting with health" (Proverbs 4:12, TM).

Finally, you'll note that Abraham praised God for the blessing before it even happened. This is where *praise will give birth to faith, strengthen faith, sustain faith, and keep you focused on the source of all your blessings*.

* * *

Now that you know this, take some time today and begin to praise the Lord for what you believe He's going to do in your life.

CONTENTMENT ISN'T GETTING WHAT WE WANT BUT ENJOYING WHAT WE'VE GOT

* * *

I have learned . . . to be content.
Philippians 4:11

A farmer lived on the same farm all his life. It was a good farm with fertile soil, but with the passing of years the farmer began to think, *maybe there's something better for me*. He went out to find a better plot of land to farm.

Every day he found a new reason for criticizing something about his old farm. Finally, he decided to sell. He listed the farm with a real estate broker who promptly prepared an advertisement emphasizing all the advantages: ideal location, modern equipment, healthy stock, acres of fertile ground, high yields on crops, well-kept barns and pens, nice two-story house on a hill above the pasture.

When the real estate agent called to read the ad to the farmer for his approval prior to placing it in the local paper, the farmer heard him out. When he had finished, he said "Hold everything! I've changed my mind. I'm not going to sell. *I've been looking for a place just like that all my life."*

When you start seeing what's good in your situation, you're likely to find it far outweighs the bad. Paul says, "Dwell on the fine, good things in others. *Think about all you can praise God for and be glad about*" (Philippians 4:8, TLB).

* * *

Today, practice living this way.

SATAN'S SCHEMES

* * *

In order that Satan might not outwit us.

For we are not unaware of his schemes.

2 Corinthians 2:11 (NIV)

God has a plan for your life, and when you walk in it, you'll have peace, joy, and real fulfillment. Satan also has a plan for your life and he counts heavily on one thing: *your ignorance.* If he can keep you in the dark, then he can play havoc with your life.

His scheme is to keep you *spiritually dull* so that you can't discern the need in other people's lives. He wants to keep you *spiritually weak* so that you can't respond. He wants to keep you living in *condemnation* so that you feel unfit and unworthy to speak into their lives or minister to them—and so those who could hear through you will be lost. In other words, Satan's goal is not just *you,* but those he can *get at through you.*

Once you know this, you've destroyed his advantage, and taken your first step toward victory. Take the weapon out of his hand today. Jesus said, "I give you power . . . over all the power of the enemy" (Luke 10:19). Today that power is found in His Word, in the place of prayer, and in fellowship with His people.

* * *

As you walk in obedience, you'll discover you have the power to defeat Satan on every front and do the job God has called you to do.

YOUR RAPIDLY INCREASING MONEY SUPPLY

* * *

The word of the LORD came unto Abram in a vision, saying, Fear not, Abram: I am thy shield, and thy exceeding great reward.

Genesis 15:1

The first man in the Bible to pay tithes was Abraham. Later, when he was going through a rough time, God spoke to him and said, "Fear not, Abram: I am thy *shield*"—meaning, "I am your protection—against inflation, theft, unemployment, sickness, and anything else that would try to devour your blessings." Then God continued "And [I am] thy *exceeding great reward*." Bob Yandian, one of the finest Bible teachers I know, says these three words have special significance in the Hebrew. The word "exceeding" means *rapidly*; the word "great" means *increasing,* and the word "reward" means *money supply*. Think of it! In his hour of need, God appeared to Abraham and said, in essence, "I am your protection, and your *rapidly increasing money supply.*" Hallelujah!

Since you and I are the seed of Abraham and the heirs to his promises, we can claim this same blessing. But remember what Abraham did—he tithed. If you haven't been tithing, I encourage you to pray about it and begin to obey God today in this matter.

* * *

When you do, you'll be living under His protection and you'll be able to say with Abraham, "He is my rapidly increasing money supply." What a promise!

RISE ABOVE YOUR FEAR

* * *

With Him on my side I'm fearless, afraid of no one and nothing.

Psalm 27:1 (TM)

Ray Blankenship looked out his window one morning to see a girl being swept along in the rain-flooded drainage ditch beside his home. He knew that farther downstream the ditch disappeared underneath the road and then emptied into the main culvert. Nobody could survive that!

He raced along the ditch, trying to get ahead of the little girl. Finally, he hurled himself into the water. When he surfaced, he was able to grab the child's arm. The two tumbled end over end and then, within three feet of the culvert, Ray's free hand felt something protruding from the bank. He clung to it desperately, with the force of the water trying to tear him and the child away.

Amazingly, by the time fire department arrived, Ray had pulled the child to safety. Both were treated for shock. In that heroic moment, Ray Blankenship was truly a hero—you see, *he couldn't swim!*

Today, let your courage respond to needs that you see, not the fear you feel. God is just waiting for you to do what you *can*, then He'll do what you *can't.*

* * *

When you make the effort, God will do the rest—but nothing happens until you make that first move.

TO BE LIKE JESUS

* * *

And we . . . are being transformed into his likeness.

2 Corinthians 3:18 (NIV)

Teaching is very important, but people are not changed just by knowing doctrines. Some of the most critical people, the most self-righteous people, the most self-serving people I've ever met, held positions in the church. Some were Bible school graduates and some even taught the Word. But try to do business with them and you'll come out on the short end of the stick. Don't cross them, for they have a temper like a tornado. When some of them are more than 100 miles away from home, it's amazing where you'll find them. Are you getting the idea? Don't get me wrong, sound teaching is critically important, we must have it, *but a few minutes in the manifest presence of the Lord, can accomplish more than weeks or even years of theology.* Remember Saul on the Damascus Road? (See Acts 9.)

Teaching that comes from the presence of the Lord, that is anointed by His Spirit, will lead those who hear into His presence, where the knowledge is transformed *from your head to your heart. The Living Bible* says, "As the Spirit of the Lord works within us, we become more and more like Him" (2 Corinthians 3:18).

* * *

Make the goal of your life today *to be like Jesus.*

AMBASSADORS

* * *

We are ambassadors for Christ.

2 Corinthians 5:20

Being an ambassador is a position of great honor and responsibility. Someone who gives his own opinions would never qualify. You have to know the mind of your king and represent *his* interests only.

Often the kings would recall their ambassador after only two or three years because they were afraid that if he stayed in the other country too long he would become more concerned with that country's interests than the interests of the king.

We, *too, must* guard our hearts from becoming more sympathetic to the interests of this present age than to the interests of Christ. Paul writes, "Demas hath forsaken me, having loved this present world" (2 Timothy 4:10). It can happen so easily. Demas was seduced by *things* and lured away by the appeal of the world.

The Lord does not change His ambassadors every few years, we have a lifetime commission. Therefore you must be careful to keep your mind and heart set on God's interests alone. Paul said, "If I were still trying to please men, I would not be a servant of Christ" (Galatians 1:10, NIV). As long as you fear men, or seek their praises, you can never properly represent your King and His kingdom.

* * *

Today, ask God to truly make you His ambassador. What a calling!

ARE YOU A SECRET DISCIPLE?

* * *

Joseph of Arimathaea, being a disciple of Jesus, but secretly for fear of the Jews.

John 19:38

Years ago a famous atheist gave a talk to 2,000 students in a North American university. For an hour she ridiculed religion, defied God, and attacked the Bible. When she finished, a Christian girl at the back of the auditorium stood up and began to sing, *"Stand up, Stand up for Jesus, ye soldiers of the Cross, lift high His royal banner, it must not suffer loss."*

Everyone was stunned for a moment. Then in a different section of the auditorium, a young man stood to his feet and joined in singing, *"From victory unto victory, His army shall He lead."* Others suddenly jumped to their feet and joined in until all over the auditorium hundreds of students were singing, *"From victory unto victory, His army shall He lead, 'til every foe is vanquished and Christ is Lord indeed."*

Enraged, the atheist stormed from behind the podium, swearing she would never be back. What she had tried to build for the devil in an hour-long speech was torn down in a few moments by the commitment and the courage of a young Christian who refused to be a secret disciple. Are you a "closet Christian" like Joseph of Arimithea?

* * *

Today, God is going to give *you* an opportunity to speak up for Jesus. Don't miss it!

DON'T STOP PRAYING

* * *

God forbid that I should sin against the LORD in ceasing to pray for you.

1 Samuel 12:23

Prayer is one of the highest expressions of your love. It's "standing in the gap" (see Ezekiel 22:30) on behalf of another. It's both a privilege and a great responsibility. James says, "Pray one for another, that ye may be healed" (James 5:16). When times are discouraging and things seem to be getting worse, *keep praying*. Paul says, "I make mention of you always in my prayers" (Romans 1:9).

My late Sunday school superintendent, "Pop" Magee, who died in his 90's, could remember the names of scores of people that others seemed to have difficulty remembering. When he was asked how he could do this, he said, "*Because I pray for them by name every day.*" You can't forget somebody you're praying for.

God works through your prayers. Listen: "Call unto me, and I will answer thee, and show thee great and mighty things, which thou knowest not" (Jeremiah 33:3). Your prayer becomes the bridge over which the answers pass, and the wire through which God's power flows into the situation. *When you stop praying, a door closes.* God comes by *invitation*. Even though Israel was in rebellion, Samuel knew that it would be a sin to stop praying for them. God says, "You who call on the LORD, give yourselves no rest, and give him no rest" (Isaiah 62:6-7, NIV).

* * *

Keep praying, child of God, for prayer changes things.

THE TONGUE

* * *

He who guards his lips guards his life.

Proverbs 13:3 (NIV)

"The boneless tongue so small and weak, can crush and kill," declares the Greek.

"The tongue destroys a greater hoard", the Turk asserts, "Than does the sword."

A Persian proverb wisely saith, "A lengthy tongue—an early death."

Or sometimes takes this form instead, "Don't let your tongue cut off your head."

"The tongue can speak a word whose speed," the Chinese say, "outstrips the steed."

While Arab sages this impart, "The tongue's great storehouse is the heart."

From Hebrew wit this maxim sprung, "Though feet should slip, ne'er let the tongue."

The sacred writer says the whole, *"Who keeps his tongue doth keep his soul."*

James says, "If anyone can control his tongue, it proves that he has perfect control over himself in every other way" (James 3:2, TLB). If *this* is the standard by which we are measured, how well are *you* doing? *It's so hard to keep quiet,* especially when you have strong opinions, or when you're being constantly provoked.

Listen: "They called Him [Jesus] everything in the book, and He said nothing back. He suffered in silence, content to let God set things right" (1 Peter 2:23, TM). As I read these words, my heart cries "Lord help me! I fall so far short of this standard."

* * *

Maybe that's a prayer you also should pray today.

SEEKING SPIRITUAL "HIGHS!"

* * *

My people have been lost sheep; their shepherds have led them astray and caused them to roam on the mountains. They wandered over mountain and hill and forgot their own resting place.

Jeremiah 50:6 (NIV)

The competition between some shepherds today is alarming. Recently, in a popular Christian magazine, I read these advertisements for different ministries: "The man with the mantle," "The happening place," "Catch the new wave." A friend of mine recently attended a service in which the pastor told his congregation that "the Word" was no longer what God was emphasizing. It was now "laughter and joy," referring to a new emphasis in his church.

Now, I thank God for every genuine experience the Holy Spirit has given us these days, but I'm concerned. God said, in essence, "My people have been led astray by shepherds who try to keep them turning aside, from mountain to hill"—*from spiritual high to spiritual high*! By keeping the people continually moving and occupied, we're depriving them of the very purpose of their calling: *to develop an intimate, personal relationship with the Shepherd.*

The challenge is not how much are you doing, but *how much of Christ can be seen in you.*

* * *

Until the world can see Christ in His people, they will never be attracted to His Church. Think about it.

KEEP YOUR PROMISES

* * *

Serve God with a feast of kept promises; call for help when you're in trouble and I'll help you.

Psalm 50:14-15 (TM)

When God makes a promise to you, He keeps it. It's His nature. James said that with God there is "no variableness, neither shadow of turning" (James 1:17). If you're His child, He expects you to have that same nature. Listen to what He says: "Pay thy vows unto the most High: And call upon me in the day of trouble: I will deliver thee" (Psalm 50:14-15). All of us experience days of trouble. They come in many forms and they come through many doors, but those who keep their promises to God have *confidence* before God, because they know they have fulfilled their vows and kept their word to Him. Nothing robs you of faith and confidence before God like broken promises. Listen: "If our heart condemn us not, then have we confidence toward God. And whatsoever we ask, we receive of him" (1 John 3:21-22).

What have you promised God? Praying? Witnessing? Tithing? Giving up that relationship or that habit? Your deliverance depends on how you deal with this, so go to God *today* and ask for His forgiveness and start making things right. If you can make amends for the past, do it. If you can't, then repent, put it under the Blood and do it differently in the future.

* * *

Today, ask God to make you a person who keeps their promise.

THE WAY UP IS DOWN

* * *

Humble yourselves in the sight of the Lord,
and He shall lift you up.
James 4:10

Wilson Boone says, *"If God hasn't raised you up high enough, it's because you haven't gotten down low enough.* To be a bridge for God you must be walked on." Someone said to me, "I feel used!" I thought about that and I realized *that's what we've been called to—we're servants.*

In a great house, servants wait on others. They clean up after them, they get up long before them to prepare breakfast, and they stay up when others have gone to bed so they can get everything ready for the next day. They always make sure the master's needs are met and that he is well pleased with all they do. *Servant* is only a word until you have to start *serving.* It's all about going the extra mile—turning the other cheek—giving yourself away. *The Message* says, "Get down on your knees before the Master, for it's the only way you'll get on your feet." You can only do it with joy when you do it on your knees and do it "as unto the Lord." Listen:

* * *

The songwriter says:

All the treasures I have, I have laid at thy feet;
Thine approval shall be my reward.
Oh thy ancient of days, thou art worthy of praise;
My wonderful, wonderful Lord.

GET UP AND FIGHT

* * *

Fight the good fight of faith . . . whereunto thou art also called.

1 Timothy 6:12

Some of us are strong in faith but weak in fight. Without fight, Caleb would never have gotten his inheritance. Listen: "Now therefore give me this mountain . . . if so be the LORD will be with me, then I shall be able to drive them out" (Joshua 14:12).

To subdue Goliath, David had to fight. What a scene! "Then David said to the Philistine . . . And all this assembly shall know that the LORD saveth not with sword and spear: for the battle is the Lord's (1 Samuel 17:47). Did you hear that? "All shall know that the battle is the Lord's!" *The world wants to know if the God we talk about is bigger than the Goliath they're looking at. Their weapons don't work and they're wondering if ours do.*

Jesus challenged religious systems that enslaved people to rules that nobody could live up to, including those who made a living preaching them. He had something to say and He had the courage to say it. How about you? *It's a lot easier to admire Jesus than it is to follow Him.* The moment you really decide to follow Jesus, you're in for the fight of your life—in the workplace, the community, the home, and anywhere else you happen to be.

* * *

But remember, child of God, it's the big battles that produce the big victories, and that's what God has in store for you today.

MAKE PRAYER A LIFESTYLE

* * *

Aaron shall burn . . . sweet incense every morning . . . And . . . at twilight . . . a perpetual incense before the LORD.

Exodus 30:7-8 (NKJV)

Aaron was to burn incense first thing each morning and the last thing each night. There would be "*perpetual incense before the Lord.*" If you begin your days with prayer and end them in prayer, you'll be able to stay in a perpetual attitude of prayer. The Lord does not want you to talk to Him once in awhile, He wants you to *abide* in Him. (See John 15:7.)

How much of your lifestyle would change if the Lord appeared in the flesh and went everywhere with you today? Are there places you wouldn't go, things you wouldn't say or do? Would your attitudes undergo a radical change? *The truth is,* if the eyes of our hearts were opened *we would see Him in all we do*, and the reality of His presence would be greater than what we see with our physical eyes. Ask the Holy Spirit to make Jesus real to you, so that you can *see* Him and *sense* Him in everything you do.

When Paul said, "Pray without ceasing" (1 Thessalonians 5:17), he was talking about being conscious of God *at all times* and in constant communication with Him.

* * *

Make prayer your lifestyle.

MAKE A CLEAN BREAK

* * *

Make a clean break with all cutting, backbiting, profane talk.

Ephesians 4:31-32 (TM)

Criticism is one of the ultimate manifestations of pride because it assumes superiority! God's reaction to it should be the only warning we need: "God resisteth the proud, but giveth grace unto the humble" (James 4:6).

The Bible says God is at work in each of us. (See Philippians 2:13.) So when you criticize your brother, you're actually saying that "God's workmanship" does not meet with your approval and that He could have done it better. What arrogance! The truth is, we all struggle and fall far short, so on what basis do *you* point out the faults of another? When you criticize somebody's children, who gets upset? *The parents.* It's the same with God. When we judge His people we're really judging Him. When we judge His leaders, we're saying that God doesn't know what He is doing by permitting such leadership. Look out! That puts you on very dangerous ground.

Grumbling and complaining kept the first generation of Israelites out of the Promised Land. They spent their entire lives wandering in *dry* places. Could this be why you've been going through such a *dry spell* lately? They went round the same mountain *(problem)* over and over again. Think about it! Paul says, "Make a clean break with all cutting, backbiting, profane talk."

* * *

Don't you think it's time we took it seriously?

THE DOOR OF OPPORTUNITY IS MARKED "PUSH"

* * *

Lazy people want much but get little, while the diligent are prospering.

Proverbs 13:4 (TLB)

Walter drove his friend, Arthur, out into the country to a huge piece of land with just a couple of old shacks. He stopped the car and began to describe vividly the things he was going to build on the land. He wanted Arthur to buy some of the land surrounding his project. Walter explained, "I want you to have the first chance at this surrounding acreage, because in the next five years it will increase in value several hundred times."

Arthur thought to himself, *"Who in the world is going to drive twenty-five miles for this crazy project? He's lost his common sense."* He mumbled something about a tight money situation and promised to look into the deal later. "Later on will be too late," Walter cautioned, "you had better move on it right now." *Arthur failed to act, however.*

And so it was that Art Linkletter turned down the opportunity to buy the land that surrounded what became Disneyland—the land his friend, Walt Disney, had tried to talk him into. *Every day opportunities are coming to you, or going right past you.* First you need to perceive them, then you have to step out in faith and act on them.

* * *

Today, ask God for the *wisdom* to see and the *courage* to act.

ACT ON WHAT YOU HEAR

* * *

Don't fool yourself into thinking that you are a listener when you are anything but, letting the word go in one ear and out the other. Act on what you hear.

James 1:23 (TM)

Charles Spurgeon said that for every ten men who would *die* for the Bible, he could find only one who would *read* it. I doubt if much has changed! You'll find ten men and women who will fight for prayer in public schools for every one who prays with his or her own children at home. You'll have ten men and women who complain about sex and violence on television for every one who refuses to watch it. *This must change!* Our power to be salt and light in the world doesn't depend on what we *applaud,* it depends on what we *apply!*

You can go to church, *enjoy* great preaching, and yet leave and do nothing about it. On the road to Emmaus, the disciples eyes were opened when they recognized that it was *the Lord* who was breaking the bread. It's the same with us. When we see Jesus as the one breaking the bread, regardless of the earthly vessel, then our eyes will begin to open. God help us to get our doctrine off the drawing board and into daily practice, that men and women may be drawn to Jesus.

* * *

It's time to start acting on what we hear.

WHO ARE YOU LIVING FOR?

* * *

Those who live should live no longer for themselves but for Him who died for them and was raised again.

2 Corinthians 5:15 (NIV)

The fire on the altar of incense was lit from the fire on the altar of sacrifice. It takes sacrifice to pray. We must give up our self-life. The Lord is not after a few minutes of our day—He wants our *every thought* taken captive and brought into obedience to Him.

The apostle Paul is one of the great examples—he died *daily.* He did all things for the sake of the gospel. He sacrificed his own *will, safety,* and *comfort* to serve the Lord and His people. Paul's great effectiveness in ministry can be directly tied to the degree to which he laid down his life for the purposes of God. Are you willing to do that today?

There is power in sacrifice. The Cross was the ultimate sacrifice and it is the ultimate power. The degree to which you will take up your cross daily, will be the degree to which you experience the power of God in your daily life. The priesthood is about intercession, and *intercession is not prayer for yourself, but for others.*

Listen:

Others Lord, yes others,
Let this my motto be;
Help me to live for others,
That I may live for thee.

* * *

Who are you living for?

LEARNING TO PRAY

* * *

After this manner therefore pray ye: Our Father . . .

Matthew 6:9

When you say "Our Father," you're acknowledging you belong to His family, and that includes all the rights and privileges that go with it. Have you learned what they are yet? One of the first words most babies say is "daddy." Knowing your father helps you understand your own identity as a son or daughter. I need to know *who my Father is, and how He feels about me.* If you had an abusive father, or one who wasn't there when you needed him, it will take you some time to believe and act on the fact that He's *your* loving heavenly Father, that you can come to Him any time day or night, and He'll be there for you.

Prayer is just talking with the one you call "Father." So why don't we spend more time talking to Him? *One reason is, that while His love draws me—His holiness intimidates me.* When Isaiah saw the Lord, he cried, "Woe is me for I am undone"(Isaiah 6:5). Have you ever felt that way? I have. Thank God, David saw His compassion and said, "Like as a father pitieth his children, so the LORD pitieth them that fear him"(Psalm 103:13). All of us long to be understood. It's exhausting to be around people who audit every move, and demand that you qualify every statement. But "our Father" isn't like that. We don't have to labor to create what's already there. He knows what your *speech* and your *silence* suggest, and sometimes you can say it all in just two words—*"Heavenly Father."*

* * *

Why don't you take a few moments today and do it—you'll be glad you did.

GOD GIVES STRENGTH ONLY FOR TODAY

* * *

So don't worry at all about having enough food and clothing. . . . your Heavenly Father already knows perfectly well that you need them, and He will give them to you if you give Him first place in your life and live as He wants you to. So don't be anxious about tomorrow!

Matthew 6:31-34 (TLB)

Some time ago, I read this little poem:

Said the robin to the sparrow, "Friend, I simply do not know,
Why these anxious human beings rush around and worry so."
Said the sparrow to the robin, "Friend, I think that it must be,
That they have no heavenly Father such as you and me."

Don't pull the roof of tomorrow in over your head today. God has lessons for you to learn *today*—steps of growth He wants you to take *today*—blessings He wants you to enjoy *today*. But you can't experience them if you're focused on tomorrow and anxious over the future. Ask God to teach you to enjoy the opportunities and experiences that are in your life now. Don't miss your kids growing up. Don't miss a chance to reach out with love to someone who is hurting. And whatever you do, don't miss a chance to stop, thank the Lord, listen to His Word, and fellowship with Him.

* * *

Don't just work for Him—spend time with Him. Today, put first things first.

HIS TOUCH AND HIS WORD

* * *

He touched me and gave me strength . . .

When he spoke to me, I was strengthened.

Daniel 10:18-19 (Paraphrase)

What you need today is a *touch* and a *word* from Him, especially if you're battling sin, sickness, or satanic attack.

Daniel sought God with all his heart for an answer, but for three weeks he got nowhere. Is that where you are today? Don't give up. *Things are happening that you don't fully understand yet.* There's a battle going on, and when it's over, you're going to come out a winner.

Listen to what the angel of the Lord told Daniel: "From the first day you set your heart before God, your words were heard. But for twenty-one days an evil spirit blocked my way. Then Michael, one of the top officers of the heavenly army, came to help me so that I was able to break through" (Daniel 10:12-13, Paraphrase). *When God assigns, Satan attacks. Expect it!* It may come through a source you least expect, even a family member. Remember Joseph and his brothers? But God has an answer for you today—His *touch* and His *Word*, and they can both be had *in His presence,* so take some time today to get together with Him.

* * *

Today, ask Him to touch you and speak to your heart.

THE REJECTION TEST

* * *

He came unto his own, and his own received him not.

John 1:11

How many of us would spend our last night with someone if we knew they were going to betray us the next day? Jesus did. He was faithful even when they were not. There is no greater opportunity for you to grow in Christian love than when you are rejected and abused. Jesus asked the Father to forgive those who crucified Him. Amazing!

How you handle rejection reveals whether you have truly died to self and to the world. It's impossible for a dead man to feel rejection. On the other hand, *being rejected without being offended is one of the greatest demonstrations of spiritual maturity—it's being Christ-like.*

In the Old Testament, a priest was not allowed to minister if he had *scabs*. (See Leviticus 21:20.) A scab is *an unhealed wound.* And when you have unhealed spiritual wounds, you're *touchy* and you can't function the way God wants you to, and it will show up in the things you *say.* You need to be healed, for it's only when you pass the rejection test that you can reach out in love and make others whole.

* * *

Ask God to help you live this way.

WHEN THE WORD IS BORN IN YOUR HEART

* * *

For whatsoever is born of God overcometh the world: and this is the victory that overcometh the world, even our faith.

1 John 5:4

If you try it any other way, you will be fighting the flesh in the power of the flesh, and so be fighting yourself. Jesus said, "The words that I speak unto you, they are spirit, and they are life" (John 6:63). It's what *He* says directly to *you* that becomes spirit and life. His Word is an energizing, creative power. When the Word is *born* and begins to *grow up* in you, your whole attitude becomes one of total expectation, real faith, and absolute confidence. You begin to rise up in your spirit and declare the Word over all your circumstances.

As more of the Word is born in you each day, you will begin to take back more and more ground that the devil has stolen from you. The devil can do nothing with the man or woman who knows the Word, walks in the Word, and is committed to respond to every attack, every obstacle, and every problem by using the Word. That's the key to your victory today!

* * *

Don't just *read* the Word, *seed* the Word into your heart daily and you'll begin to experience God's blessings in a way you've never known before.

NOTHING BUT THE BEST

* * *

I am the Lord your God who teaches you to profit, Who leads you by the way that you should go.

Isaiah 48:17 (AMP)

Can you imagine your heavenly Father wanting less for His children than you and I want for ours? I have two children. The oldest is Kathleen. She's working on her doctorate in counseling and she's bright and beautiful. My son, Neil, has his Master's Degree in business at Georgia State University. He's a high energy, lovable kid with a great future.

If you think I'm proud of them—you're right! *I delight in their success.* Whatever touches them, touches me. Whatever I can do to help them succeed, I will gladly do.

Are you getting the message? Your heavenly Father wants you to know that *He cares about your career, education, business, home, marriage, family, health, and everything that concerns you.* Furthermore, He has promised to *teach* you how to *profit* in everything you put your hand to. The question is, *are you listening and following His instructions?* The best teacher in the world can do nothing for you unless you acknowledge that you still have much to learn, so open your heart and mind to receive it.

* * *

As you walk in the Word, you'll discover that God wants nothing but the best for you.

TAKING POSSESSION!

* * *

How long will you wait before you begin to take possession.

Joshua 18:3 (NIV)

God promised them the land, and Joshua led them right to it, yet seven of the tribes of Israel had done *nothing* to possess it. Is that where you're at today? *Just because you know your destiny, and understand what God's promised you, doesn't mean you'll ever fulfill it*!

The Old Testament Saul could have been one of Israel's greatest kings, but instead, David took his place. Saul died tragically on Mount Gilboa with the words captioning his life,"I have played the fool and have erred exceedingly" (1 Samuel 26:21). But what a difference we find in the New Testament Saul,"I have fought a good fight, I have finished my course" (2 Timothy 4:7). *Your destiny is determined by your decisions; so seek God and consult His Word before you make them.*

Perhaps you're saying, "But I'm too busy." Doing what? God doesn't reward your *efforts,* He rewards your *obedience!* Build your life on what 's *important,* not what's *urgent.* Prayer may not seem important at the moment, but in the final analysis, nothing is more important. Getting into God's Word may not seem urgent, but in the light of your destiny, can you think of anything more important? Set your priorities according to your destiny, and you'll suddenly begin to see what really matters in your life today.

* * *

How long will you wait before you begin to take possession of the land the Lord has given you?

DRESS FOR SUCCESS

* * *

Put ye on the Lord Jesus Christ, and make not provision for the flesh, to fulfil the lusts thereof.

Romans 13:14

One of the best selling books on the market recently was *Dress for Success*. Your appearance makes a statement, it sends a message. A general's attire commands authority and inspires respect. It says, "I'm in charge here."

Now Satan may not think much of you, but when you "put . . . on the Lord Jesus Christ," he backs up immediately. Every encounter he had with Christ left him devastated and running for cover. Listen to what Paul said: "Throw off your old evil nature . . . that was . . . rotten through and through . . . Clothe yourself with this new nature" (Ephesians 4:22,24, TLB).

Note, it says, "*clothe yourself.*" This is something you have to do for yourself, and you have to do it *daily*. If some of us spent *a fraction* of the time on our inner man that we do on our outer man, we'd walk in constant victory and blessing.

* * *

It's only as you spend time in the Word and in prayer, that you can dress for success.

DO YOUR THOUGHTS MEET WITH HIS APPROVAL?

* * *

May my spoken words and unspoken thoughts be pleasing even to you, O Lord.

Psalm 19:14 (TLB)

When I was a boy I used to watch the big trawlers sail into the Belfast Lough (bay) for servicing and repair. It amazed me that something so huge could be controlled by one man in a tiny wheelhouse. All the steersman had to do was turn the wheel in the right direction and that ship would move safely into the dock. It goes without saying that had he turned it in the wrong direction it would have meant disaster for everyone on board.

I never really saw him turn that wheel, but I knew he did it because *I saw the results*. Little wonder that David cried, "Let my unspoken thoughts be pleasing to you." The greatest defeat in David's life didn't take place on a battlefield, it happened when he saw Bathsheba and thoughts of lust came in. Before those thoughts were through, the disastrous results would fill two entire chapters of the Bible. That's why David cried to God, "Let the words of my mouth, and the meditation of my heart, be acceptable in thy sight, O LORD" (Psalm 19:14). Today, before you let a thought in, stop it at the door, check it out, and line it up with the Word of God.

* * *

Remember, thoughts spawn attitudes and actions that will either bless or blight your life.

WHAT HAVE YOU LEARNED LATELY?

* * *

Trust in the LORD with all thine heart; and lean not unto thine own understanding.

Proverbs 3:5

Have you discovered how different your values are from God's? We'll work our fingers to the bone for money, but we won't crack a book, listen to a cassette, or set aside thirty minutes for wisdom. We work hard for *comfort*, yet God is more interested in our *character*. Education is not wisdom. You can memorize facts, pass tests, and earn degrees, yet not have wisdom. So what is the secret? The Word says, "Trust in the LORD with all thine heart; and lean not unto thine own understanding" (Proverbs 3:5). He didn't say, "Don't use it," He said, "Don't *lean* on it."

After you've read, researched, consulted others, and done all you know, you come back to one unchanging fact: Jesus Christ is your source, your strength, your guide, your deliverer—He's your all in all. Listen: "*In all thy ways acknowledge Him, and He shall direct thy paths*" (Proverbs 3:6). Have you talked it over with Him? Do you remember the song:

Oh what peace we often forfeit,
Oh what needless pain we bear;
All because we do not carry,
***Everything* to God in prayer.**

* * *

Turn to Him now with all your heart—He'll help you!

THINKING OF HOME

* * *

I will come again, and receive you unto myself; that where I am, there ye may be also.

John 14:3

In spite of the family I love, the blessings I enjoy, and the assignment I have been given, some days I feel like a misfit. At best, it's all temporary! When you lose that perspective, it's time to remind yourself again that the things which are seen are temporal, but the things which are not seen are eternal. (2 Corinthians 4:18.) *You're a pilgrim—stop thinking like a resident*! Paul never lost his feeling of being homesick for heaven. Listen, *"I am torn between the two: I desire to depart and be with Christ, which is better by far"*(Philippians 1:23, NIV) Did you hear that? *It's better by far*!

Many of us never thought we'd see the year 2000; but now we're not so sure! What is Jesus waiting for anyway? He's waiting for the whole world to hear the gospel,(see Matthew 24:14) and He's waiting for the Body of Christ to get ready:"His bride has made herself ready"(Revelation 19:7, NIV). *I can tell you for sure, whether He comes or you go first, you'll never be truly at home until you're in His presence.*

* * *

For though from out are borne of time and place, the flood may bear me far,

I hope to see my pilot face to face, when I have crossed the bar.

Alfred Lord Tennyson

HOW TO LEAVE

* * *

For ye shall go out with joy, and be led forth with peace.

Isaiah 55:12

It's always easier to leave a difficult situation, than to stay and grow in grace.

When it's time to leave, how should you do it? You can leave *offended,* and try to negatively influence as many others as possible. When you see yourself as a victim, you'll blame those you think hurt you, and you'll try to justify resentment. When you do, *you* lose!

Listen to these words: "For you shall go out with joy, and *be led forth with peace."* That's how you should leave—*because God led you to and do it peacefully.* Churches aren't like cafeterias, you can't pick and choose what you like! Paul says, "But now God has set the members . . . in the body *just as He pleased"* (1 Corinthians 12:18, NKJV). You are not the one who chooses where you go to church—God does! Satan will always try to offend you, to get you out of the place where God wants to bless you and make you spiritually fruitful. David says, "Those that be planted in the house of the LORD shall flourish in the courts of our God" (Psalm 92:13).

* * *

If God plants you, He's the only one who should uproot you!

WHO GAVE YOU THE RIGHT TO SIT THIS ONE OUT?

* * *

Moses said to the Gadites and Reubenites, "Shall your countrymen go to war while you sit here?"

Numbers 32:6 (NIV)

The world respects an ex-president. The world salutes an ex-captain or general. The world despises an ex-Christian! There is no retirement in the service of the King of Kings! At 70, Paul said he was ready to go to Rome. To Paul, Rome meant death, but death for him held no terrors. Listen "Since future victory is sure, be strong and steady, always abounding in the Lord's work, for you know that nothing you do for the Lord is ever wasted" (1 Corinthians 15:58, TLB).

Did you hear that? This is the only *"sure thing"* you can invest your life in. Everything else, regardless of how highly you may value it, is scheduled for demolition. Child of God, *live*—to the very day and hour you die!

If your "get-up-and-go" has "got-up-and-went"—*get up and go after it!* Get involved in something that will outlive you—something that will make a difference. The God who asked His people of old, "Shall your countrymen go to war while you sit here?" is asking *you* the same question today.

* * *

What are you going to do about it?

DON'T TAKE THE BAIT

* * *

It is impossible that no offenses should come.

Luke 17:1 (NKJV)

Jesus said that it is impossible to live in this world and not be offended. So why then are we so shocked when it happens to *us?* The Greek word for "offense" literally means *a trap with bait in it.* What a picture! When we *take offense*, we have taken the devil's *bait,* and we finish up in a trap. We become *self-absorbed* and *resentful.* We lose our joy and can't function properly.

So what can you do? Jesus told the end-age believers to, "Anoint your eyes with eye salve, that you may see" (Revelation 3:18). See what? See your own attitude in all of this! *You'll only repent when you see your own condition of heart, and stop blaming other people.*

The wonderful thing is, when the Spirit of God shows you your sin, He'll show it to you in such a way that it will seem *separate* from you. Hence you will feel *conviction*, not *condemnation.* When He does, don't carry that offense another step.

* * *

Forgive "the offending party" as God has forgiven you—and move on.

WHAT TIME IS IT?

* * *

All of us must quickly carry out the task assigned us . . . for there is little time left before the night falls and all work comes to an end.

John 9:4 (TLB)

When you're a child, time is endless. As you grow older, it begins to fly. In later years, it's a gift to be used wisely.

When He was thirty-three, the Master said, "I have finished the work which Thou gavest Me to do" (John 17:4). At 70, Paul said, "I have fought a good fight, I have finished my course" (2 Timothy 4:7). Let me ask you a question: *Have you found the will of God for your life yet?* There is *not* a more important question. If you want to know what His will is, ask Him. As you wait in His presence, I promise, He'll reveal it to you. (James 1:5)

The next question is: *Are you doing the will of God?* When your life ends, will you be able to say, "I have finished the work which Thou gavest me to do?" Is your life making a difference? Will there be souls in heaven because you witnessed, prayed, and gave so that they could hear the gospel? Please think about this, for it's *eternally important.*

* * *

One of America's first missionary martyrs in the Amazon said, "He is not a fool who gives what he cannot keep, to gain what he cannot lose." Think about it!

ROBBING GOD

* * *

"Will a man rob God? Surely not! And yet you have robbed me." 'What do you mean? When did we ever rob you?' "You have robbed me of the tithes and offerings due to me."

Malachi 3:8-9 (TLB)

"If He already owns everything, how could I be robbing Him?"

First, *you're robbing Him of the joy of blessing you.* God says He wants to open the windows of heaven and "pour out a blessing so great you won't have room enough to take it in" (Malachi 3:10, TLB). As a father, I am thrilled when my children are blessed—don't rob Him of that joy!

Next, *you're robbing Him of the honor of having first place in your life.* Often the reason we don't tithe is that we have nothing left over. How dishonoring to God! He doesn't want your *leftovers*, He wants your *first fruit.* Listen: "Honor the Lord by giving Him the *first part* of *all* your income" (Proverbs 3:9, TLB).

Finally, *you're robbing Him of having resources (food) in His house.* (See Malachi 3:10.) *God* doesn't need our resources—*people* do. In the Old Testament, believers gave over twenty-five percent of their income to the work of God, and widows, orphans, and those in need were cared for.

* * *

Should we do less under grace than they did under law?

NO RESERVE, NO RETREAT, NO REGRETS

* * *

Well done thou good and faithful servant.

Matthew 25:21

Bill Borden, of the famous Borden Milk family in America, turned his back on fame and fortune and went to China as a missionary. His friends in America thought he'd taken leave of his senses, walking away from a life of comfort and riches. He'd been missing for days when they found his body in a tent. Under his thumb was a note that read, "*No reserve! No retreat! No regrets!*"

Think of it, child of God, "No reserve"—holding nothing back. "No retreat"—never looking back or turning back from what God called you to do. "No regrets"—"a workman that needeth not to be ashamed" (2 Timothy 2:15). Today the spotlight is on *commitment*. When you look at yourself, what you see may not be a very nice picture, but be honest with yourself—painfully honest. Ask God to help you rebuild your altar, and then *place your life on it.*

* * *

Remember, there's only one way to do it: *No reserve, No retreat, No regrets!*

AN OPEN MIND

* * *

But the wisdom that comes from heaven is . . . peace-loving and courteous. It allows discussion and is willing to yield to others.
James 3:17 (TLB)

The wisdom God gives is not contentious or argumentative. *It will make you humble enough to listen to the counsel of others.* God will share His wisdom through them as well. The real test of knowing whether the wisdom we receive is from God or man, is that *God's wisdom brings peace.*

After years of counseling, I've found that people who are determined to have their own way, and are *not open* to correction or change often say, "The Lord told me. . . " When I hear that, I know then the door is closed and all they really want is my approval. When I can give it, I do; when I can't, I offer them my prayers and my love and urge them to keep an open mind.

Read this verse over again, and then ask God for the gift of an open mind. When you need an answer, *He will place it within your spirit.*

* * *

When He does, you'll know it's His wisdom working through you.

HE FRAMES YOUR LIFE IN PICTURES ONE DAY AT A TIME

* * *

This is the day the Lord has made. We will rejoice and be glad in it.

Psalm 118:24-25

So often, if we don't like our present scene, we try to escape into the next picture. But each picture the Lord paints, makes us a little *more* like Him, and a little *less* like we used to be. This is not a Polaroid shot, or "one day" service—it's lesson after lesson learned on the canvas of life. Day by day the picture changes and we move from weakness to strength, and from spiritual babyhood into full stature. In the picture there are mountains and valleys, storms and sunsets. It's all part of growing up. God wants you to see that the real joy of life is not in arriving, *it's in the journey itself.*

Be where you are today! *Live in the present, for that's where God is.* That's where victory is. That's where growth is. That's where joy is. Check the words that are coming out of your mouth. If the window you are looking through is framed in doubt and negativity, then this word is for you. You have the power to change what you focus on, and what you say. *Rejoice and be glad.* In what? In this day that the Lord has made and given to you.

* * *

It's the only one you've got—so make it count.

EITHER IT WORKS OR IT DOESN'T!

* * *

It is possible to give away and become richer! It is also possible to hold on too tightly and lose everything. Yes, the liberal man shall be rich! By watering others, he waters himself.

Proverbs 11:24-25 (TLB)

It's not the seed that you keep that multiplies, it's the seed you sow. *That seed will never leave your life; it moves from your present into your future. It goes ahead of you to rearrange tomorrow in your favor.*

The world doesn't understand this principle and some of God's children don't either. Because they don't, they're living on the wrong side of God's blessings.

Giving is proof that you have conquered *greed.* It's also proof that you have conquered *fear*. When you give, your gift tells God that He is first in your life. It says you're totally confident that He is going to meet your needs and bless you. If you're not sowing, *you're robbing yourself of the harvest.* Read it again: "It is possible to give away and become richer! It is also possible to hold on too tightly and lose everything." *Make giving your style of living.* Be alert today, for God will give you opportunities to water others—and as you do, watch it begin to pour back into your own life. Either it works or it doesn't.

* * *

Don't you think it's time you found out for yourself.

TODAY—HE'S WITH YOU

* * *

Blessed be the Lord, Who bears our burdens and carries us day by day.

Psalm 68:19 (AMP)

When the pressure is on, one of our greatest temptations is to TRY AND escape into tomorrow. We dream about the day when we will be "out of this mess." The problem is, today is the tomorrow you were dreaming about yesterday. And each time you do it, you lose another day, and another opportunity to grow. You lose a chance to learn a lesson—even if it's painful—that could enrich your life and prepare you to make tomorrow better. Listen to the promise again: "Blessed be the Lord, Who bears our burdens and carries us *day by day.*"

Remember: *Yard by yard, life is hard—but inch by inch, life's a cinch.* Use today to "inch" closer to Jesus than you were yesterday, to add another layer to your strength, and to make a new discovery of who you really are in Christ. Worry is *faith in the wrong thing.* Are you worried about your health? Your finances? Your kids? Your future? Are you projecting into the future? Don't do it! God won't give you tomorrow's answers *today.* He won't give you tomorrow's supply *today.* He wants you to enjoy *this day.*

* * *

And when you get to tomorrow, He'll be there, too.

ONE DAY AT A TIME

* * *

How precious it is, Lord, to realize that you are thinking about me constantly! I can't even count how many times a day your thoughts turn toward me. And when I waken in the morning, you are still thinking of me!

Psalm 139:16-18 (TLB)

Right now God is thinking about you! He did it yesterday and He'll do it tomorrow. Amazing! A God *powerful* enough to speak worlds into being, yet *personal* enough to know all about you. He saw you in your mother's womb; He has preserved you to this moment (which is truly amazing when you think of what you've been through and the things you have done to yourself). So today, slow down— take a little time— begin to meditate on Him.

Listen and He'll speak; and He'll plant His thoughts into your mind. If you'll read His Word, there will be something special that will leap from the sacred page to ignite your spirit, and you'll know that it's just for you. Instead of rushing around trying to organize every minute and *make things happen*, why don't you just *let go and let God* and see what happens.

* * *

What assurance: He's thinking about you today.

ARE YOU LED OR ARE YOU DRIVEN?

* * *

We are assured and know that [God being a partner in their labor], all things work together and are [fitting into a plan] for good to those who love God and are called according to [His] design and purpose.

Romans 8:28 (AMP)

We call it life in the fast lane. We've never had so many comforts or conveniences designed to lift the burden, ease the pressure, and lighten the load. Yet, we've never had so much stress and anxiety! That's because we've never learned that God has a personal plan for our lives. He usually gives it to us *day to day, hour by hour,* and sometimes *moment by moment.* He didn't ask us to *design* the plan, He only asks us to seek Him and *discover* it. Peace doesn't come from winning the World Series or becoming president of the company. Usually what it costs to get there and stay there is our health, our families, and our sanity.

Child of God, real peace comes from knowing that *everything* in your life is in God's hands, and is fitting into *His* plan because He loves you and has committed Himself to this eternal principle:

* * *

Everything will work out for your good and His glory.

MY STEPS AND MY STOPS

* * *

The steps of a good man are ordered by the Lord.

Psalm 37:23

Clinton Utterbach, who wrote "Blessed be the Name of the Lord" and several other great songs, recently said to me, "My *steps* and my *stops* are ordered of the Lord!" He explained it this way: "In music, a rest is as much an action as a note, it's an important part of the whole score." Think about it today! David said, "He maketh me to lie down" (Psalm 23:2). Why? To restore my soul, to strengthen and refresh me by green pastures and still waters. In other words, to keep me from burning out and falling apart. When He orders you to *stop*, it's because He knows what lies ahead and He wants you to be prepared for the journey. Don't be anxious, a *delay* is not a *denial.* Isaiah said, "they that wait upon the Lord shall renew their strength" (Isaiah 40:31).

If the door is closed, don't try to force it open. If He's giving you a red light, don't keep driving, for when you move beyond obedience, you move beyond protection. He knows what's on the other side of that closed door, no matter how appealing it may seem to you. David said, "He guides the humble in what is right, and teaches them His way" (Psalm 25:9 NIV). And if you need more, listen: "For this God is our God for ever and ever; He will be our guide even to the end" (Psalm 48:14, NIV). Jesus said that the Holy Spirit would guide us (John 16:13). The bottom line is—it's "a trust issue!"

* * *

Will you trust Him today to lead you?—and that includes your steps *and* your stops. Think about it!

WHAT DO YOU REALLY STAND FOR?

* * *

If you do not stand firm in your faith, you will not stand at all.

Isaiah 7:9 (NIV)

A man went to Sodom one day hoping to save it from God's judgment. He talked to one individual after another, but nobody would talk to him. Next, he tried carrying a picket sign that had "REPENT" written in large letters, but nobody paid attention. Finally, he went from street to street, shouting, "Men and women, repent! What you are doing is wrong. It will destroy you!"

The people laughed at him, but still he went about shouting. One day a someone stopped him and said, "Stranger, can't you see that your shouting is useless?" The man replied, "Yes, I see that." They asked, "Then why do you continue?" The man said, "When I arrived in this city, I was convinced that I could change *them.* Now I know I cannot. But I continue shouting *because I don't want them to change me!"*

Speak out for those things you believe in. If you remain silent, others may interpret your silence as agreement. After all, evil can only prevail if good men do nothing about it. Jesus said, "Let your light so shine before men, that they may see your good works, and glorify your Father which is in heaven" (Matthew 5:16).

* * *

Today, lovingly take your stand.

IT'S UP TO YOU!

* * *

Obey the laws of God and . . . you will prosper in everything you do.

1 Kings 2:3 (TLB)

An American moved to my hometown in Ireland. He worked hard, developed real expertise in understanding our laws and economy, and, within ten years, he owned land everywhere and was a multimillionaire. On the other hand, a friend I grew up with graduated from one of our finest colleges as one of the most "promising" students in school. Tragically, he broke the law and ended up in prison. *The same laws that prospered one man, punished the other.*

It's the same in God's Kingdom. You can live in God's blessing and prosper because you *know* the laws of the Kingdom and *walk* according to them. By contrast, some of God's children are in trouble and in want because they haven't read those laws, or they're not bringing their lives into alignment with them. Listen again: *"If you will keep His commands you will prosper in everything you do, wherever you turn."*

* * *

The truth is, it's up to you!

DO YOU HAVE TROUBLE WITH YOUR TEMPER?

* * *

He that hath no rule over his own spirit is like

a city . . . without walls.

Proverbs 25:28

When a person loses his temper we say he "flew off the handle." (This refers to the head of a hammer coming loose from its handle as the carpenter attempts to use it.)When this happens, 3 things always follow:

First, the hammer becomes useless. When you lose your temper, you lose your effectiveness. You lose respect, you lose control, and anything you say is usually unproductive.

Second, the hammer head will hurt anything in it's path. Our children can carry the scars of our anger with them until the day they die. We may not realize we inflicted scars, and may never have intended to, but angry words cause wounds, and become the pattern of abuse that our child-ren pick up and use with *their* children. Anger has a long reach.

Third, repairing the damage can take time. The person who loses their temper may recover quickly, but the one who is the victim of their anger rarely does.Solomon says, "He that is slow to anger is better than the mighty; and he that ruleth his spirit than he that taketh a city" (Proverbs 16:32).

* * *

Ask God to help you keep your temper today.

WHEN GOD BLESSES YOU

* * *

Command those who are rich . . . not to be haughty, nor to trust in uncertain riches but in the living God, who gives us richly all things to enjoy. Let them do good, that they be rich in good works.

1 Timothy 6:17-18 (NKJV)

Everything you have, God gave you, so don't "ego-trip" over it! Enjoy all God gives you, but don't trust in anything but *Him*. It could all be gone in a day. Elijah discovered that when the brook dried up, God was still his source (1 Kings 17). The most important thing you've got is your relationship with God.

Anything you put before that—you're going to lose! So what's this all about? Simply this: If your possessions are just a status symbol or a security blanket, then you've missed it. Jesus said, "Freely ye have received, freely give" (Matthew 10:8). My greatest joy has not been what I've *acquired*, but what I've been able to *give*, and the problems I've been able to solve for hurting people. My wife tells folks, "I want God to bless me so much, that every time I open my checkbook the devil will tremble and run for cover." If she proves herself faithful with little, God will trust her with much.

* * *

Child of God, that includes you, too.

HE'S THE LIGHTHOUSE

* * *

I am the LORD, I change not.

Malachi 3:6

One night, the captain of a battleship spotted a strange light rapidly closing in on him. He ordered his signalman to flash a message to the unidentified vessel, "Alter your course ten degrees to the south." Back came the reply, "Alter your course ten degrees to the north." More determined, he snapped a second order. "Alter *your* course ten degrees—I am the CAPTAIN!" The response came back, "Alter your course ten degrees, I am Seaman Third Class Smith!" By this time the light was growing brighter and larger. Infuriated, the captain personally signaled, *"Alter your course. I am a battleship!"* The reply came back quickly, *"Alter your course, I am a lighthouse!"*

Over six-hundred times in the Bible, Jesus is called "Lord"—that means He's the boss. In the New Testament, the believers greeted one another by saying, "Jesus is Lord!" It meant His word is final. He can call for any change He wants or demand any price He chooses. His Word demands it, and His love deserves it!

* * *

Even if you think you're a battleship, remember, *He's the lighthouse!*

TODAY GOD IS ON YOUR SIDE

* * *

This I know . . . God is for me.

Psalm 56:9

When you know that God is for you, you can face anything. That doesn't mean life will be a bed of roses. Paul said to "endure hardness, as a good soldier" (2 Timothy 2:3). The new birth brings new battlefields and a new enemy to conquer. The war against you is on three fronts, and, by yourself, you're not equal to the enemy you're facing.

First, *the world,* whose pressures and influences seek to mold you every day. Next, *the flesh*, which will try to get you to live by what feels good and not by the Word. Finally, *the devil*, whose strategy is to get you off track and make you so weak you're no threat to his kingdom and no benefit to God.

But the good news is you're not alone. The God who opened the Red Sea and shut the lions' mouths is *your* God. Sure, the Israelites had to face the Red Sea, there was no other way. And Daniel probably wouldn't have chosen to spend the night in a lion's den if they'd given him a another option. But God brought them through victoriously and since He says, "I am the LORD, I change not" (Malachi 3:6). He's going to do it for you, too.

* * *

Now begin to say it: "This I know, God is for *me*."

WHEN YOU DON'T KNOW—JUST CALL

* * *

Call unto me, and I will answer thee, and show thee great and mighty things, which thou knowest not.

Jeremiah 33:3

Today, you may be facing a problem or a situation that's just too big for you. Perhaps you've even thrown up your hands and said, "It's going to take somebody bigger than me to figure this one out." Child of God, *I know just the person!* He knows what you don't know, and He can do what you can't do. He's called a "counselor" (Isaiah 9:6). He's just waiting to be brought into the picture.

He'll never force His way into your life; He comes by invitation. In the Book of Revelation, He says, "Behold, I stand at the door and knock. If anyone hears My voice and opens the door, I will come in" (Revelation 3:20, NKJV). Isn't it too bad that we usually wait until everything and everyone else has failed us before we turn to Him. Even then, He is faithful. Listen to His promise again: "I will answer thee, and show thee great and mighty things, which thou knowest not."

* * *

Today, take some time and get into His presence, for all the answers you need are waiting there.

YOUR YEAR OF JUBILEE

* * *

Cause the trumpet of the Jubilee to sound

. . . throughout all your land.

Leviticus 25:9

In the Year of Jubilee every prisoner was set free, every debt was canceled, and everything that had been taken from you was restored. (See Leviticus 25:10.) Praise God! *How would you like God to do that for you?* God can restore your health, or your relationships—but He can do *more* than that. He said, "I will restore to you the years that the locust hath eaten" (Joel 2:25). God can take the losses of a lifetime, and make it all up to you. *Yes, He can!* He's asking you today, "Is there any thing too hard for me?" (Jeremiah 32:27). The answer is *No*! "With God all things are possible" (Matthew 19:26). Today, get into God's presence and pray:

> Lord, I declare this to be my Year of Jubilee. I repent of any attitudes or actions that have caused me to sin against You. Wash me in Your blood and lead me by Your Spirit. I turn my life and my will over to You. I declare that this year, You are going to restore back to me everything that has been taken away. This is Your promise, and I believe it. Thank you, Lord! Amen.

* * *

Remember, this is your Year of Jubilee!

INSULATION OR ISOLATION?

* * *

Love not the world.

1 John 2:15

Ye are the light of the world.

Matthew 5:14

By trying to insulate ourselves against the evils of this world, we have isolated ourselves from its problems. We're out of touch! One out of every seventeen Americans is an alcoholic. One in two households is a single parent family. Children are now sexually active at twelve years of age. People are frightened because this is the most violent generation in history. The question is, *what are we going to do about it?*

In the story of the Good Samaritan (see Luke 10:30), Jesus described this generation perfectly: *stripped*, *wounded*, and *left to die*. He said that religion "passed by on the other side" (Luke 10:31). This is how the world still sees us—we're on one side and they're on the other. We are answering questions they're not even asking. They aren't looking for another religion, they're looking for a relationship that satisfies. *All they need is to meet Jesus, and I promise it will be love at first sight.* He's still the answer! Child of God, Stop isolating, and take the message to the marketplace, and tell them about Jesus.

* * *

***Today* would be a good time to start.**

HAVE YOU EVER BEEN IN LOVE?

* * *

We will rejoice in you and be glad; We will extol your love more than wine.

Song of Solomon 1:4 (NASB)

There is no feeling like it! You can't wait to be together. Even if you don't have much materially, it doesn't matter. Being together is enough. That's why we call our daily prayer time, *our devotions*—it's a love affair with Jesus. Prayer is my heart to His ear. Bible reading is His heart back to my ear. Sometimes I've much to talk to Him about, other times I just sit quietly in His presence singing, or weeping with joy because of that overwhelming sense of His nearness. Do you know what I mean?

His Word is like a mirror revealing those defects of character in me that He wants to remove. The more time I spend with Him, the more I long to be like Him. King David had a love affair with God—he was devoted to Him. Listen: "As the deer pants for the water brooks, So pants my soul for You, O God (Psalm 42:1, NKJV). Be like David—get into His presence, open your heart and sing:

> I love Thee in Life, I will love Thee in
> death,
> And praise Thee as long as Thou
> lendest me breath,
> And sing should the death dew lie cold
> on my brow,
> If ever I loved Thee, My Jesus, 'tis now.

* * *

If you're too busy to spend time with *Him*, you're just too busy!

RESTORATION

* * *

I will heal their waywardness, and love them freely, for My anger has turned away from them.

Hosea 14:4 (NIV)

Have you ever gone astray? Have you ended up being wounded, because you took the wrong turn on the road? In the parable of the Good Samaritan, Jesus said, "A certain man went down from Jesusalem to Jericho and fell among thieves" (Luke 10:30). Jerusalem was the place of God's blessing and Jericho was the place of judgment. when you leave one for the other, you're "*going down*" and you can count on one thing, it will always end the same way. "They stripped him, they wounded him and they left him to die." No matter what your friends or your instincts tell you, the last chapter is always the same. But there's hope! God says, "I will heal your waywardness and love you freely."

Some of us don't find God until we hit bottom, and hit it hard. Others hit "false bottoms" only to discover that the elevator can go even lower. When the prodigal finally "came to himself," he was wasted. But the story doesn't end there. Those wounded feet were bathed in the tears of a father's love and fitted with shoes that only a child of the king can wear. His scars of sin were covered with a robe of righteousness and those hands that had been used for evil were washed and given the ring of sonship. Listen: "Kill the fatted calf" (Luke 15:23). How long does it take to fatten a calf? Think about it! The father had been preparing for a long time for this moment and the *God who never stopped loving you, is waiting for you to come home today.*

* * *

He'll welcome you with open arms—all you have to do is come!

TAKE THAT PAIN AND MAKE IT A PEARL

* * *

Until Christ be formed in you.

Galatians 4:19

Pearls are made in a fascinating way. The oyster literally takes the grain of sand that causes it irritation and pain and wraps it in layer after layer of "mother of pearl." Instead of trying to escape the pain, it works with it until a pearl is produced. That worthless piece of sand is now a precious stone that has great value.

So what has been irritating you lately? What about that problem you've asked God to take away, but it's still there? God has given you an opportunity to take that thing and cover it with a layer of grace, a layer of patience, a layer of faith, and a layer of compassion. *It takes years for a grain of sand to become a pearl, and the work God is doing in you will not be accomplished overnight.*

Paul promised the Christians in Galatia that he would pray until "Christ be formed in you." There it is! God's goal for us is to have the world look at us and see the character of Jesus—the Pearl of Great Price. What a high calling!

* * *

Now read it again, and begin to seek His face "until Christ be formed in you."

ARE YOU HURTING ?

* * *

He healeth the broken in heart, and bindeth up their wounds.

Psalm 147:3

If you're not hurting, before this day is over, you'll meet someone who is. Behind that smile, you'll find a broken heart or a wounded spirit. But you have the answer: "He healeth the broken in heart." Often it's because they took the wrong direction, or never consulted God in the first place. After Peter denied his Lord, he went out and wept bitterly. He remembered how wonderful it had been to walk with Jesus. He remembered the Master's words, "You will deny Me three times" (Matthew 26:75, NASB). He was so sure that it could never happen to him, but it did. Sound familiar?

Maybe you find yourself today in circumstances you never dreamed you would be in. Divorced? Unemployed? Sick and depressed? Without the will to live? *Never discuss your problem with someone who is incapable of solving it—take it to Jesus.* He's a heart specialist. He has walked every path and felt every pain. Everything you need is available through Him today, but you've got to reach for Him, "Cast thy burden upon the LORD, and he shall sustain thee" (Psalm 55:22). That doesn't mean He'll take you *out*, but it does mean He'll bring you *through*.

* * *

Why don't you go to Him today. He's the healer of broken hearts.

SETTLE IT ONCE AND FOR ALL

* * *

He has settled in his mind that Jehovah will take care of him. That is why he is not afraid but can calmly face his foes.

Psalm 112:7-8 (TLB)

Never rewrite your theology to accommodate a tragedy. The thing you can count on in life is change. People change. Circumstances change. But the one who died for you, rose for you, and rules in every area of your life "is the same yesterday, today, and forever" (Hebrews 13:8, NKJV). I remember as a boy singing these words from an old hymn:

Change and decay, in all around I see,
Oh thou that changest not, abide with me.

When sickness tries to write a chapter into the book of your life, don't start wondering whether the day of miracles is passed. It hasn't. He's "the LORD that healeth thee" (Exodus 15:26). When the bottom drops out and you find yourself in need, don't start speaking doubt and wondering if maybe it's the will of God for you not to be able to pay your rent. Paul said, "My God shall supply *all* your need according to his riches in glory by Christ Jesus" (Philippians 4:19). Stop wavering and start trusting in the Lord!

* * *

Declare with David, "My heart is fixed."

RELIGIOUS PEOPLE RIDICULE, SPIRITUAL PEOPLE RESTORE

* * *

If someone is caught in a sin, you who are spiritual should restore him gently.

Galatians 6:1 (NIV)

How do you act when a child of God fails? There have been times when I have fallen flat on my face, even though I have been in ministry for years. *Everyone fails! The winners are just the ones that get back up again!* But they don't get up by themselves. They do it because God has some wonderful children who reach out with hands of love to "help him back onto the right path" (Galatians 6:1, TLB).

When a child of God has been wounded, do you walk away and leave him for the wolves to devour? Do you take the sword of judgment and finish him off? Or do you move quickly to his side and begin to pour in oil and wine and restore him (Luke 10:30). Recently, God has been convicting me of judging others. Since God alone knows their struggles and why they do things, my only job is to pray and restore. Here is my prayer—perhaps, you can make it yours also:

> *Father, if I can't find something good to say, let me say nothing at all.*
>
> *If I can't lift them up, then help me not to pull them down.*
>
> *If I can't speak to them about You, then at least, let me speak to You about them.*

* * *

Remember, spiritual people restore!

STOP STRIVING

* * *

Just keep traveling steadily along His pathway and in due season He will honor you.

Psalm 37:34 (TLB)

David's brothers were lining up to be the next king of Israel. They were competing for fame and glory. Not much has changed. But Samuel passed them all up and went out into the fields looking for David. When he found him, David was doing what he had been doing for a long time—tending his sheep. Now child, here's the word for today: *Stay where He puts you, and when you're ready, He'll come and get you.!*

It took one slain lion, one dead bear, and years of getting to know God, but David was now ready. God has always been ready—He lives that way. The problem is us! Restless, competitive, and discontented, we strive for success. We reach, and over-reach, and finish up empty-handed. God sees what men don't—our hearts. The difference between David and his brothers was they were *striving*—he was *yielding*. See the difference?

Let others strive for thrones and crowns. The right place for you to be today is in His presence, doing faithfully what He has called you to do.

* * *

Just live that way and when you're ready, He'll come and get you.

THE POWER OF HABIT

* * *

He kneeled upon his knees three times a day, and prayed.

Daniel 6:10

Mike Murdock says, *"Men don't decide their future. Men decide their habits, and their habits decide their future."* I think he's right. Recently, I decided to rise earlier and spend the first hours of my day in prayer and the Word. To do it, I had to give up late night television. Experience has taught me that if I don't get into God's presence and stay there, nothing else goes right. It was a decision of my spirit—my flesh has been opposed to it from day one. Some days are easier than others, *but the rewards are worth it!*

The men who have made a difference "were creatures of habit." Even in the face of death, Daniel "kneeled upon his knees three times a day, and prayed." Paul said, "I . . . cease not to give thanks for you, making mention of you in my prayers" (Ephesians 1:15-16). *In the life of every great man or woman of God, you will discover a foundation of holy habits from which the power and the presence of God flows.*

* * *

You might need to take some time today and think about your habits—especially the ones you need to establish.

GETTING BACK UP

* * *

As the disciples stood round about him, he rose up, and came into the city.

Acts 14:20

They stoned Paul and left him for dead, and the other disciples stood around, waiting to see if he would get back up. Child of God, *if you're waiting for others to come and lift you, it probably won't happen.* The first move is up to you—when you make it, God will send others to help.

Paul said, "We were troubled on every side; without were fightings, within were fears. Nevertheless God, that comforteth those that are cast down, comforted us by the coming of Titus" (2 Corinthians 7:5-6). We need more believers like Titus with the ministry of encouragement. We give in so quickly. We blame circumstances or we blame others. Adam started it all: "The woman whom thou gavest to be with me, *she* gave me of the tree, and I did eat" (Genesis 3:12). When God asked Eve about it, *she blamed the devil!*

Until you can accept responsibility for yourself, you can't get anywhere with God. Until you can accept correction without resentment, your life will remain on hold. Get up! Your problems aren't unique—you're not the first person to fail. You would be amazed at how many of us are fighting the same battle and showing some of the same scars. Your problem isn't *that you fell, it's that* you haven't gotten back up!

* * *

Be like the man who said, "I'm never down, I'm always getting back up!"

THE GRATEFUL HEART

* * *

Giving thanks always for all things unto God.

Ephesians 5:20

A monk in a monastery took a vow of silence. Every seven years he was permitted to speak. When asked if he had anything to say after his first seven years, he replied, "Yes. The bed is too hard." Another seven years went by and he was asked again if he'd like to say something. He said, "Yes. The food is terrible." Finally another seven years went by and he was asked once again if he had anything to say. He replied, "Yes. I quit." Whereupon the head of the monastery said to him, *"I'm glad, because you've done nothing but complain since you got here."* That brings up our point: What will *you* be remembered for—the *good* you always found, or the *bad* you never failed to point out?

Jesus once healed ten lepers, but only one came back to thank Him: "And Jesus answering said, 'Were there not ten cleansed? but where are the nine?' " (Luke 17:17). Can you hear the disappointment in His voice? He noticed their lack of gratitude, and He still does. Then He turned to the one who came back and said, "Thy faith hath made thee whole" (Luke 17:19). What a statement! The others were *healed,* but the one who had a grateful heart was made *whole.*

* * *

Today, child of God, practice being grateful!

TESTED BY SUCCESS

* * *

Promotion and power come . . . from God.

Psalm 75:6-7 (TLB)

When you're successful, it exposes you to four things:

1. *Jealousy in those around you.* The elder brother was angry, because the attention he once had was now focused on somebody else and he couldn't stand it. When God blesses you, resistance and resentment will surface in those who feel left out.

2. *Insecurity in those around you who are fearful.* When you move to a new level of blessing, it usually involves change, and that's threatening to those who only know how to do things a certain way

3. *The attacks of the devil.* He doesn't mess with *low impact* Christians. He *always* targets those who are of special value to God. So you better put on your armor and get ready for battle today.

4. *Success will test every relationship in your life.* Those who feel dwarfed or displaced by your success will often say, "He's just not the same anymore." Some will seek to control you out of the fear of losing you. You'll be tested—so get ready.

* * *

Remember, walk in love toward *everyone*, for the one who promoted you can demote you just as easily.

KEEP LOOKING THROUGH THE STORM UNTIL YOU SEE HIM

* * *

Be of good cheer; it is I; be not afraid.

Matthew 14:27

Jesus sent His disciples into the storm, knowing that they would be different when they came out. They had seen Him heal the leper, and even raise the dead, but they didn't know He had authority over the wind and the waves. There are things you can only learn by getting into the boat and going through the storm. *He revealed Himself to them in the worst experience of their lives.* He defied impossible conditions to reach them. He proved there is no circumstance you're facing today in which He will not be with you.

Peter said, "Lord, if it be thou, bid me come unto thee on the water" (Matthew 14:28). When Jesus said, "Come," Peter did not step out on the *water*, he stepped out on the *Word*. He believed that if Jesus told him to do the impossible, *the power to obey would be inherent in His Word!* So why did Jesus rebuke him? *Because he stopped short of what might have been. He accepted less than what he could have had.* Sound familiar?

* * *

His Word to you today is "Be of good cheer; it is I; be not afraid."

HOW EAGLES DIE

* * *

The course I was set I have finished.

2 Timothy 4:6 (Philips)

I'm told that eagles die with their feet on the rock and their face toward the sun. What a way to go!

My mother went to be with the Lord on her 74th birthday. A few month's before her death she had a complete physical, and the doctor said she was fine. Nevertheless, she went to the undertaker, picked out her casket, and put in writing what she wanted read at her memorial service, including the Scriptures. She then packed her best dresses in a box and sent them to her sister in Ireland with a letter saying, *"Dear Phyllis, These were my favorite dresses, but I won't be needing them anymore. I'm going home! I love you, Martha."*

Somehow, she knew that her course was finished. A few weeks later, she went into the hospital with chest pains. The next day, while sitting up in bed, without pain or fear, she was gone in less than two minutes. We buried her in Ireland beside my dad. Her headstone nearby reads, "The parting is for a moment, but the meeting will be for eternity." *Death loses its power when you know your feet are on the Rock, and your face is toward the Son.*

* * *

Remember, if you live ready, you'll die right.

ARE YOU KEEPING YOUR COVENANT

* * *

With thee will I establish my covenant.

Genesis 6:18

A covenant is the strongest promise two people can make. C*ovenant* means *"to bind together."* Sometimes they would exchange swords, signifying that they would always defend each other. Other times they would pass a sandal between them, pledging to go to any lengths for each other. Again, they would take an annual sacrifice, split it down the middle and walk between the halves, signifying *they were one, and* without the other, they were incomplete.

God has entered into a covenant to bless you. Listen: "There, in the presence of the LORD your God, you and your families shall eat and shall rejoice in everything you have put your hand to, because the LORD your God has blessed you" (Deuteronomy 12:7, NIV). Read the promises of your covenant: health, safety, prosperity, guidance, victory—*if you obey the rules.* God put those rules into the Ark of the Covenant, and when Israel went to war, the Ark went before them and nobody could stand up to them. *The covenant was their power source; God Himself was their ally in battle. And He is your ally too.*

The covenant *sword* is God's promise to fight for you. The covenant *sandal* says no matter how far gone you may feel, just call and He'll come. The covenant *sacrifice* means you're an heir to all that He has promised.

* * *

Are you keeping your covenant with Him today?

THE POWER OF THE BLOOD

* * *

When I see the blood, I will pass over you.

Exodus 12:13

God told His people to put blood *over* their door, which meant He would see them *through the blood.* He said to put blood on the *side posts*, meaning the blood would *separate* them from the world. Finally, He told them to *stay* in the house and when He saw the blood, He would pass over them. *And the blood is still the sign that marks us as His.*

When I was growing up, some of the major denominations removed all mention of the blood from their preaching and their hymnals. One prominent leader called it "a slaughter house religion," and said it was out of step with the space age. The results were disastrous. Multitudes left the church.

If you take the blood out of your Bible, it becomes dead history. If you take the blood out of your church, the body becomes a corpse. If you take the blood out of your preaching, men and women will die in sin. They may call us fundamental or *completely mental*—but as long as we have breath, we must preach that "the blood of Jesus Christ his Son cleanseth us from all sin" (1 John 1:7). When you pray, "plead the power of the blood of Jesus" and watch God move and Satan flee.

* * *

Remember, we overcome the devil *"by the blood of the Lamb"* (Revelation 12:11). That's why he's so scared of it!

IS IT WELL WITH THEE?

* * *

Is it well with thee? is it well with thy husband? is it well with the child? And she answered, It is well.

2 Kings 4:26

In the hour of need, Elisha asked this woman a question we must all face. Listen: *Mother, is it well with thee?* Are you serving the Lord? Are you teaching your children the Word? I owe so much to my mother. She didn't *send* us to church, she *took* us. She didn't *preach* it, she *lived* it.

Father, is it well with thee? Are your footsteps leading your children to heaven or to hell? Time will fly, and you won't have another chance to teach and mold them for God. Lot sacrificed his kids for his career, but Abraham saved his because he put God first. How about you, sir?

Son or daughter, is it well with thee? Listen: "Sin, when it is finished, bringeth forth death" (James 1:15). Before you decide to take the trip, *please* check the destination. Drugs may be fun today, but what happens when you can't quit? You can have sex in 20 minutes, but raising the child will take you 20 years. Young person, God has a destiny for you, and the most important thing in your life today is finding it and filling it.

* * *

Is it well with thee?

DON'T COME DOWN

* * *

I am doing a great work, so that I cannot come down.

Nehemiah 6:3

Four times Nehemiah's enemies tried to bring him down, and each time he said "No, I'm doing a great work and I cannot come down." There are times in your life when you are vulnerable and the enemy will try to bring you down. First, when you're *exhausted*. My wife tells me I have no limits where work is concerned, and I've paid a high price for it. Jesus said, "*My yoke* is easy, and *my burden* is light" (Matthew 11:30). When we wear yokes He never designed for us and burdens He never gave us, we get into trouble.

Another vulnerable point is when you're *successful* and everyone around you is telling you so. Be careful—pride will bring you down faster than anything, for it makes you play God in your own life. Another point of vulnerability is when you're *alone*. Peter was alone when he denied his Lord. David was alone in his palace when he saw Bathsheba. You need fellowship. David said, "God setteth the solitary in families" (Psalm 68:6). The Living Bible says, "He gives families to the lonely."

* * *

Make sure you're in a spiritual family that will feed you and fellowship you, and then tell the devil, "I'm doing a great work, and I can't come down."

TWO KINDS OF HONOR

* * *

How can ye believe, which receive honour one of another, and seek not the honour that cometh from God only?

John 5:44

Honor comes from two sources—Christ and the crowd. If you see the crowd as your source, then pleasing them becomes everything. John the Baptist publicly rebuked the sins of a king and it cost him his life. The three Hebrew children refused to bow to another god—they wouldn't even *nod* in his direction. Paul rebuked Peter for his racial prejudice, and God put it in the Bible for all of us to learn from.

These men didn't know crowd psychology or marketing strategies, *they knew God,* and that's why they prevailed. Daniel said, "The people that do know their God shall be strong, and do exploits" (Daniel 11:32). What we need is not more talent, or more pulpit finesse, *we need men and women who hear from God* and aren't afraid to declare what He says. They may not be popular with the crowd, but God will honor them. And when it's all said and done, can you think of anything more important?

* * *

Honoring Him! Make it the goal of your life.

KEEP YOUR EYES ON JESUS

* * *

No doubt about it, God is good . . . But I nearly missed it . . . I was looking the other way

Psalm 73:1 (TM)

David almost "went over the edge" looking at people. The ones who really bothered him were those who broke all the rules, yet seemed to prosper. It's one of the oldest weapons in the devil's arsenal—getting you to look at people. The trouble begins when *you* try to figure it out. God will settle the score. The first time Jesus came to *save,* the next time He comes to *reign*—and settle all accounts.

When you're tempted to ask, "What's going on here?" Just remember, the last chapter hasn't been written. John said, "And I saw the dead, small and *great,* stand *before* God; and the books were opened" (Revelation 20:12). *There will be an audit.*

But if you're not careful, you can develop a *negative* attitude and ruin your own future. You don't have to understand everything, and thank God you don't have to explain it. David said, "When I *thought* to know this, it was too painful for me; Until I went into the sanctuary of God; then understood I their end" (Psalm 73:16-17). Just ask God to give you *patience* under provocation, and *love* in the face of injustice. Above all, *never* let your attitudes and actions be determined by other people.

* * *

Just keep your eyes on Jesus—He's your source, He's your security, and He's your peace.

A PRAYER FOR EVERY DAY

* * *

Order my steps in thy word.

Psalm 119:133

David knew from painful experience where his flesh would take him, and he didn't want to go there anymore. So he cries, "Order my steps in thy word: and let not any iniquity have dominion over me." Iniquity means *to bend in the direction of*, or *incline toward*. He's asking God to deliver him from a nature that is bent toward sin and always inclined to go the wrong way. Sure sounds familiar to me. How about you?

In the Christian life the only way to win is to *surrender*. *You* can't live it, but *He* can. Listen to Paul: "I live; yet not I, but Christ liveth in me" (Galatians 2:20). Slide out from behind the wheel today and let Him take over. You know what happens when *you* drive!

Maybe you're saying, "But what's my part in all of this?" First, to *live in the place of constant surrender to Him;* and second, to *fill your heart with His Word.* Listen: "Thy word have I hid in mine heart, that I might not sin against thee" (Psalm 119:11). Also, remember to stay filled with the Spirit, for the Christian life is not the product of fleshly effort, it's the fruit of the Spirit. (See Galatians 5:22.)

* * *

Today, and every day from now on, pray, "Order my steps in thy word."

BEFORE AND AFTER

* * *

But ye shall receive power, after that the Holy Ghost is come upon you.

Acts 1:8

The best argument for the Spirit-filled life is those who live it. No illustration is more powerful than the life of Peter. *Before* Pentecost, he denied Jesus in weakness. *After* Pentecost, he faced the crowd with boldness and proclaimed that Jesus is Lord. That day, 3,000 were born into God's family. That's the power of the Holy Spirit!

Before Pentecost, Jesus gave Peter one of the harshest rebukes in the Word of God, "Get thee behind me, Satan: . . . for thou savourest not the things that be of God, but those that be of men" (Matthew 16:23). Peter was opinionated, critical, and he often spoke without thinking.

But what a difference we find in Peter *after* Pentecost. Now He is *filled, broken,* and *channeled.* Listen to him: "You should be like one big happy family, loving one another with tender hearts and humble minds. Don't repay evil for evil. Don't snap back at those who say unkind things about you. Instead, pray for God's help for them, for we are to be kind to others, and God will bless us for it" (1 Peter 3:8-10, TLB). Is this the same guy? No! He's the new Spirit-filled model, and he's the example of what God wants you and me to be today.

* * *

So, child of God, get into God's presence today and ask Him to fill you again with His Spirit.

MOTHER, STAND BY THE CROSS!

* * *

Now there stood by the cross of Jesus his mother.

John 19:25

Where were His disciples? Listen: "Then all the disciples forsook him, and fled" (Matthew 26:56). Couldn't you have understood if His mother had turned her back and walked away too? Or collapsed under the pain watching them crucify Him? But no—the record reads for all time, "And there stood by the cross of Jesus his mother." I'm convinced that *few things can get the attention of God faster than the prayers of a godly mother.* More than once, in some of the worst moments of my life, I was so aware that it was my mother's prayers that sustained me and kept me alive. I'm convinced that many of the blessings I've enjoyed have simply been *transferred credits* from her life and walk with God.

Many times in the Bible, it was a woman's voice that settled the issues and changed history. Remember Deborah, and Huldah, and Ruth? Solomon says, "Charm is deceptive, and beauty is fleeting; but a woman who fears the LORD is to be praised" (Proverbs 31:30, NIV). If, as we are told, men are what their mothers make them, then what we need today is an *army of committed Christian mothers* who will *stand by the Cross* and refuse to allow one more generation to go to hell.

* * *

Mother, are you living for Jesus today?

GET TO KNOW HIM!

* * *

The LORD is good, a strong hold in the day of trouble; and he knoweth them that trust in him.

Nahum 1:7

What you believe about God will determine everything else in your life. If you believe He is *good*, then you'll have the confidence to go to Him in the day of trouble. If you're not *convinced* of this, you'll turn to everybody and everything else—and only when you've exhausted all other possibilities, will you turn to Him. Listen: "When trouble comes, He is the place to go! And He knows *everyone* who trusts Him!" (Nahum 1:7, TLB). He also knows those who *don't!*

Now there are two parts to this thing. First, *what you know* and believe about God; and second, *what God knows* and believes about you. Many of us wait until the day of trouble comes, only to discover the faith we *thought* we had isn't there. You can't even approach God without faith, and you certainly can't please Him without it. (See Hebrews 11:6.)

Child of God, are you so wrapped up in business and in other things that you've neglected your spiritual life? If you are, then start doing something about it today. Get into God's word. Get acquainted with just how good He is, and how great His promises are.

* * *

Get to know Him now so that when trouble comes, He'll know you!

GOD LOVES EVERYBODY—DO YOU?

* * *

"How can I [understand]," he said, "unless someone explains it to me?"

Acts 8:31

This man was of a different race and had a morally questionable background—but he was searching for God! To get to him, Philip had to overcome prejudice and tradition. But when the man found Christ, he went back to Ethiopia and introduced the queen to Him. Before it was all over, multitudes turned to God. What if Philip had been like some of us?

We put up barriers and think God put them up. He didn't! God loves the world, and that includes the worldly. Remember the woman at the well? How about adulterous David—could he join your church? God deliver us from petty preconceived notions of who deserves God's love and who doesn't. "Grungers" with spiked hair and nose rings, hard-drinking brawlers, lonely single gays, up and outers who walk the halls of government or business by day and search for pleasure in questionable places by night. They *all* need Jesus! Listen to what this man said: "How can I understand, unless someone explains it?" Before we can explain anything to them, we have to love *them.*

* * *

God does—do you?

DEALING WITH FAILURE

* * *

When thou art converted strengthen thy brethren.

Luke 22:32

Peter denied his Lord three times and went out into the night and wept bitterly. Jesus told him it would happen, but he couldn't believe it. That's why it was so shattering. Child of God, have you experienced failure in your life lately? Do you feel like you're not worthy of His love and forgiveness? Remember, Peter's failure was no surprise to Jesus. *He knew what Peter was when He picked him, and He knew what you were too. Nothing about you is a surprise to Him.*

Since He didn't pick you because of your virtue, He's not going to throw you away because of your shortcomings. Moses told the Israelites, "The LORD thy God turned the curse into a blessing" (Deuteronomy 23:5). The same one who told Peter that he would fail, also told him he would be fully restored and would be able to minister to people he could never have touched before.

Some denominations would have put Peter out of the ministry and disqualified him forever. But God not only restored him, He made him spokesman on the day of Pentecost. That day, God used him to win 3,000 souls to Christ.

* * *

Let God turn your mistakes into miracles today. Let Him use the lessons and the low points of your life to strengthen and bless others.

HOW TO MAKE THINGS TURN OUT RIGHT

* * *

Whether we like it or not, we will obey the Lord our God. . . . For if we obey him, everything will turn out well for us.

Jeremiah 42:6 (TLB)

A lot of us are cafeteria Christians. We walk down the line and decide what we like and don't like. We pick some things and leave the rest. But it doesn't work. Listen: "Whether we like it or not, we will obey the Lord our God."

If you're a parent, you know that your job is not to make your children *happy*, but to make them *obedient*—for obedience brings happiness, while disobedience brings trouble. For example, if you let your children play with matches, you may make them happy for a while, but only until they burn the house down. Breaking the speed limit may bring happiness to an immature teenager, but when it lands him in court or he has a wreck, he'll change his mind in a hurry.

It was *after* David had been chastened that he wrote, "Your laws are my guide. I used to wander off until you punished me; *now I closely follow all you say.*" (Psalm 119:66-68, TLB).

* * *

Child of God, the promise to you today is that *if you will walk in obedience, everything will turn out well for you.*

HIGH PLACES

* * *

And unto Him shall the gathering of the people be.

Genesis 49:10

When Hezekiah came to the throne, the first thing he did was to remove *the high places*. (See 2 Kings 18:4.) High places—what are they? *Other* objects of worship. *Other* sources of trust. There's a lesson here for us to learn in the hour when movements are built on a personality, or a place God once used. In the 1950's, William Branham had a truly great miracle ministry. But his followers *idolized* him, and started calling him the prophet Elijah returned. (See Malachi 4:5.) One day he confided to some friends, "If the people don't stop doing this, God will have to remove me." Two months later he was killed by a drunk driver in a car wreck. How sobering!

God won't tolerate *high places*! Thank God for the *people* God has used. But James reminds us, "Elijah was a man subject to like passions as we are" (James 5:17). Thank God for *places* where God once moved—but don't make them shrines. Listen again: "Unto *Him* shall the gathering of the people be."

* * *

Today, fall in love with *Him!* Lift *Him* up! Keep your eyes on *Him*!

DITCHED!

* * *

Remember ye not the former things, neither consider the things of old. Behold, I will do a new thing.

Isaiah 43:18-19

After helping a lady whose car was in a ditch, I asked her what happened. She said, "I was looking in the rearview mirror instead of looking at the road ahead." What a thought! *There is no way to go forward if you're focused on what's behind.* You'll end in a ditch! Disconnect from the past, focus on the future, and move on with God. *Give up all hope for a better yesterday.* You can't change the past. You can only obsess over it, run from it, or accept it and be wiser.

There are over 500 Scriptures that tell us God is merciful and forgiving. But none of them are worth anything unless you accept God's forgiveness—*and then forgive yourself.* Listen: "I, even I, am he that blotteth out thy transgressions for mine own sake, and will not remember thy sins" (Isaiah 43:25). God says *He* has forgiven and forgotten your sins, therefore *you* must—otherwise you make yourself better than God. That's spiritual pride in its worst form. *The devil can hurt you every day of your life if you don't forgive yourself and let the past be the past.* Child of God, take that weapon out of his hands today.

* * *

God wants to do a new thing in your life—let Him.

YOU'LL FIND HIM WHERE YOU LEFT HIM

* * *

But they, supposing him to have been in the company, went a day's journey; and they sought him among their kinsfolk and acquaintance. And when they found him not, they turned back again to Jerusalem, seeking him.

Luke 2:44-45

It happens so easily. We get so busy with our battles, our projects, our ministries and 101 other things, that we fail to notice that Jesus is not with us. Jesus' parents returned to where they had last seen Him, *and so also must we.* To renew us, God brings us back to our most recent encounter with Him. Back to basics. Yesterday's anointing will not sustain us in today's battles. David cried, "I shall be anointed with fresh oil" (Psalm 92:10). God sent manna to His children in the wilderness *each day.* Jesus taught His disciples to pray, "Give us this day our *daily bread*" (Matthew 6:11). Have you gathered your manna today? Have you eaten your *daily bread*?

In the world of banking we are told that if you *give out* more than you *take in,* you'll end in *bankruptcy.* Are you on the verge of burnout and bankruptcy? If so, you need to move from being a Martha to being a Mary and sitting at His feet.

* * *

Child of God, make sure *He's* with you.

SUBMIT AND RESIST

* * *

Submit yourselves therefore to God. Resist the devil, and he will flee from you.

James 4:7

Unless you're *submitted* to God and walking in obedience to His Word, you'll have no power to *resist* the devil. Don't even try it. Your power comes out of your relationship with the Lord, and if that's been neglected lately, you can be sure Satan knows about it and he'll give you a bad time. Jesus said, "The prince of this world cometh, and hath nothing in me" (John 14:30). Satan couldn't find one unsurrendered area in the life of Jesus—not one square inch where he could establish a beachhead from which to either control Him or attack Him. Why? Because He had been with His Father, and He carried that divine presence with Him wherever He went.

How about you today? Without prayer you have no power. You can be busy and be barren, and be no match for the enemy. Child of God, take some time out and get alone with your Father. The truth is, if you don't get into His presence and stay there, you're always going to fail. You know I'm telling you the truth. Submit your will, your ways, your words, and your all unto Him.

* * *

Then go out and really show the devil who's in charge.

SETTING BOUNDARIES

* * *

I will establish your borders

Exodus 23:31 (NIV)

You won't know what your inheritance is, if you don't learn to set boundaries. How far? How wide? Where's the fence line? You'll never enjoy or protect your inheritance without clearly defined boundaries, for people (even well-meaning ones) will violate them and walk "roughshod" through your life. In the Old Testament, Shammah fought for a tiny lentil patch, and the bible, the most important book in the world, recorded it. Why? Because that lentil patch was an *inheritance* from his father—it put food on his family's table and it guaranteed *his children's future*. Listen: "Shammah took his stand in the middle of the field . . . and the Lord brought about a great victory" (2 Samuel 23:12, NIV).

Your boundaries are your values. What's important to you defines who you really are. Recently, a friend of mine told some people she worked with, "*When you violate my boundaries, you force me to make a decision and you may not like that decision. I know where I got my boundaries from, and you wouldn't like me without them. That old me was not a nice person. My Father is pleased with me the way I am and you are the beneficiary of that. So please, respect my boundaries, and we'll get along just fine.*" Like Shammah, she took her stand and laid down boundaries.

There are areas of your life that belong to God alone and no one else should be allowed to come there. Are you getting the message?

* * *

Child of God, the word for you today is "Establish your boundaries."

WOUNDED HEALERS

* * *

And with his stripes we are healed.

Isaiah 53:5

Because Jesus was wounded, He received authority to bring healing to you and me. Out of His brokenness, others were made whole. Child of God, *there's purpose to the pain.* "Only the broken become masters at mending." Paul said that God "comforteth us in all our tribulation, that we may be able to comfort them which are in any trouble, by the comfort wherewith we ourselves are comforted of God" (2 Corinthians 1:4).

Find God's purposes in the reversals of your life, and you'll turn them into stepping stones to blessing. God doesn't waste experience. All of us have gone through things that we never imagined could have happened to us—but they did. The problem is, the same sunshine that melts the butter, hardens the clay. Experience can make us hard and cold, or *drive* us into the arms of Jesus—where we find answers and compassion.

Today, you're going to meet people who are hurting. They'll relate to your experience, not your theories. Most won't even listen unless you've "been there."

* * *

Child of God, let God take your wounds and your pain and make you an instrument of healing wherever you go.

GOD'S STRANGE CHOICES

* * *

God hath chosen the foolish things . . . weak things. . . base things . . . and things which are not . . . That no flesh should glory in his presence.

1 Corinthians 1:27-29

God wants you to see things like *He* sees them. He wants you to look beyond the *obvious* and see the *actual.* Five loaves and two fish were just enough to feed one small boy for a day, but when he put it into the hands of Jesus, it fed 5,000 with plenty left over. When Mary and Joseph brought the baby Jesus into the temple, Simeon saw in that small child God's salvation for the whole world. (See Luke 2:28-30.) *May God help you today to see in what you've got, the potential to make a difference in this world around you.* Listen: "Though thy beginning was small, yet thy latter end should greatly increase" (Job 8:7).

God's not looking for ability—He's looking for use-ability. If you've grown up believing that you're "less than" or that you never "measure up," then it's time you start renewing your mind on the Word. God can take a tiny acorn and produce a mighty oak. He can take a tiny seed and produce a great harvest. He can take one surrendered, dedicated life and affect a whole family and all its generations.

* * *

Child of God, ask the Lord to use you today and go out expecting Him to do it.

STRUGGLING TO BELIEVE

* * *

Lord, I believe; help thou mine unbelief.

Mark 9:24

The man in our story asked Jesus to heal his demon possessed son. Jesus told him to believe. His answer is worth noting, "Lord I believe, help thou mine unbelief." We've all been there. We've reached inside ourselves to find a faith that wasn't there. If you find yourself in this position today, then there are some things you need to do. First, *get into the Word of God immediately.* "So then faith cometh by hearing, and hearing by the word of God" (Romans 10:17). The Bible is *faith food,* and as you read it, faith will begin to grow inside of you.

Next, *bring some people with faith into your life.* Multiply your faith by the faith of others, and make your prayer *a faith offering* to God. Jesus said, "If two of you shall agree on earth as touching any thing that they shall ask, it shall be done for them of my Father which is in heaven" (Matthew 18:19).

Finally, remember that you're not coming to an auditor who's examining your books, *you're coming to a loving heavenly Father who knows your struggles.*

* * *

When you have reached up as far as you can, He'll reach down the rest of the way.

THE *ROPE HOLDERS*

* * *

They risked their lives for me.

Romans 16:3-4 (NIV)

When Paul was saved, word spread like wildfire. The religious leaders hired assassins to kill him. Some Christians took him by night to the top of the city wall and, using ropes, lowered him over the side in a basket. He escaped, and went on to write Epistles, build churches and change history. The Bible doesn't tell us who these Christians were, but we know that, had they been caught, it would have cost them their lives.

In Romans 16, Paul writes a doxology to the rope holders who risked their lives for him. They waved no banners, blew no trumpets, demanded no applause, but without them the work of God would *never* have been accomplished.

Child of God, you may never be a preacher, or a singer, or a missionary; but by your praying, your words of encouragement, and your financial support, you can *hold the rope* for those who do. The Day of Judgment will be a day of *surprises*. Many who have enjoyed the limelight will get little reward—for God saw their hearts and their selfish motives. And many who seemed so unimportant will be called to the frontline of service to hear the words, "Well done, thou good and faithful servant" (Matthew 25:21).

* * *

If God has made you a *rope holder*, He has given you a place of honor in His kingdom.

GOD HEARS AND ANSWERS PRAYER

* * *

I cried unto the LORD with my voice, and he heard me.

Psalm 3:4

Mike Murdock once told me of a lady who came for prayer at the end of one of his services. When he invited her to pray with him, she said, "No, it wouldn't do any good. I just don't think God hears me." He looked at her and said, "Would you mind saying a few curse words?" Greatly offended, she said, "No!" He said, "But why not?" She said, "Because God would hear me!" Mike said to her, "So what you're telling me is, God hears you if you *curse*, but He doesn't hear you if you *pray*?" She got the point.

Have you been feeling like that lately? Maybe you've even given up praying altogether because you feel like it just doesn't work for you. Nothing could be further from the truth. Listen to His promise: "Call unto me, and I will answer thee, and show thee great and mighty things, which thou knowest not" (Jeremiah 33:3). One of the keys to answered prayer is to *center your life around Christ*. David said, "Delight thyself also in the LORD; and he shall give thee the desires of thine heart" (Psalm 37:4). Don't go to Jesus for a miracle—go to Jesus for a *relationship*. Once you have a relationship with Him, then you can have a miracle every day of your life.

* * *

Child of God, take some time today to work on your relationship with Him.

DAILY

* * *

Exhort one another daily.

Hebrews 3:13

Often when we can't handle the pressure of today, we escape into remembering *the good old days*—or we dream of tomorrow when *things will be better.* But until you learn to live *now,* you miss what God has for you. The Christian life is lived one day at a time. Listen: "Exhort one another *daily.*" Someone you know is going through a rough time, and the Word you have is just what they need. It was a kitchen maid who led Naaman, captain of Syria's army, to the Lord, and to his healing.

In Acts 2:46, it's written, "And they, continuing *daily* . . . breaking bread from house to house." Get out and fellowship with someone! Beware of isolation. When you're by yourself, you may be in the worst possible company. God wants to use *others* to bless you, strengthen you, and be a support system in your life.

Finally, Jesus said, "Take up [your] cross *daily*, and follow me" (Luke 9:23). Cross bearing and self-denial have almost become dirty words. Not many Christians seem to use them anymore. Yet the heart of the Christian life is *daily* saying, "No." No to self and "yes" to Jesus.

* * *

Child of God, when these things are working in your life on a *daily* basis, you will have joy and fulfillment such as you've never known before.

A WARNING AND A PROMISE

* * *

And some who are most gifted in the things of God will stumble in those days and fall, but this will only refine and cleanse them and make them pure.

Daniel 11:35 (TLB)

In the Bible, the Holy Spirit reveals the mistakes of some of God's most gifted leaders in both the Old and the New Testament. There are reasons why. One is to let you know that there are *none* of us so strong as to be incapable of falling. President Kennedy once said, "If we don't learn from the past, we are doomed to repeat it." Paul said, "All these things happened to them as examples—as object lessons to us—to warn us against doing the same things" (1 Corinthians 10:11, TLB).

If you are suffering today because of mistakes you made yesterday, then God says, "This will only refine you, cleanse you, and make you pure." David wrote his greatest Psalms *after* his encounter with Bathsheba. The Bible says, "And the word of the LORD came unto Jonah *the second time*" (Jonah 3:1). He's the God of the second chance. Today, He will pick you up where you have fallen, and restore you by His grace.

* * *

Please remember, child of God, when God restores something it's not *secondhand*—it's *brand new*.

LOVE

* * *

Love is the fulfilling of the law.

Romans 13:10

In his famous little book, *The Practice of the Presence of God*, Brother Lawrence points out, "When you truly love God and your neighbor, you will go through life, keeping the Ten Commandments." After all, if you really love the Lord, you won't take His name in vain, and you won't put anything or anyone before Him. On the other hand, when you truly love your neighbor, you would never dream of stealing from him, committing adultery with his wife, or envying anything he had, and certainly you would never want to kill him. So when you truly love, you will fulfill all the demands of the law, and *it will become a lifestyle instead of a set of rules.*

You may ask, "How is such a love possible?" I only know one answer. Paul said, "The love of God is shed abroad in our hearts by the Holy Ghost" (Romans 5:5). If you're having trouble loving your husband, your wife, or your children, or those you live and work with, get into the presence of God and ask Him to melt you afresh. Then ask Him to fill you with His Spirit, and you will discover that the Holy Spirit will do *through* you and *for* you what you could never do by yourself.

* * *

From that point on, child of God, you will find it easier to "walk in love."

LESSONS FROM THE STORM

* * *

And straightway he constrained his disciples to get into the ship, and to go to the other side.

Mark 6:45

He'll never send you on a trip that you can't make. That doesn't mean it will be *easy*, or that you won't be *frightened* by the waves. Remember Psalm 23, "Yea, though I walk through the valley of the shadow of death, I will fear no evil: for thou art with me" (Psalm 23:4.) He doesn't *send* you—He *leads* you and sustains you. How reasurring!

Something else; *when you can't see Him, He's still watching over you*. Jesus was on a mountain praying to the Father, but the Bible says "He saw them toiling in rowing" (Mark 6:48). He sees your toil and your tears today. As Ethel Waters once sang, "His eye is on the sparrow, and I know He watches me."

And don't forget, *He is the master of the wind and the waves.* There's no situation He can't handle. Listen: "And the LORD, he it is that doth go before thee; he will be with thee, he will not fail thee, neither forsake thee" (Deuteronomy 31:8).

Finally, *before the storm's over, God will be glorified in it, and your faith will grow stronger.* Remember, your Father is a lot more interested in your *character* than He is in your *comfort*.

* * *

So rejoice today, He's going to bring you through.

BE GENEROUS

* * *

If God has given you money, be generous in helping others with it.

Romans 12:8 (TLB)

God didn't say you had to be *rich* to give, He just said you had to be *generous*. It's interesting what Jesus noticed. He noticed a widow who put two copper coins into the alms box and said that she had given more than the others because she had given her *all*.

Sometimes we excuse our hardheartedness by saying, "If they want money, let them go out and work for it like I did." I agree, we must never reward laziness, but all around us are people who did nothing other than be born in the wrong place at the wrong time. Many of them don't want *a hand out,* they want *a hand up*.

Recently, I came back from Romania where I visited the orphanages. When children who have never felt the love of a mother's arms reach up to me and say, "Papa," I fight back tears and rage at the system that enslaved them. I can't walk away. And neither can you. James says that pure religion is, "To visit the fatherless and widows in their affliction" (James 1:27).

* * *

Today, be sensitive to His voice when He speaks to you about ministering to others, for *what you make happen for others, God will make happen for you.*

WHO ARE YOU KIDDING?

* * *

Even while they were in their kingdom . . .

they did not serve you.

Nehemiah 9:35 (NIV)

So you think that if your life were easier, you'd be a better Christian? If you had *more* money you would tithe. Think again! 90 million Americans go to church regularly, yet only 3-5% of them tithe. We live in the most affluent society in history. In our quest to make sure our kids have the things we didn't have, we forget to give them the things that matter most. Things like "values" they can live by when they face temptation. Things like knowing the difference between "getting ahead", or "going on with God."

"They enjoyed God's great blessings but they did not serve Him or turn from their evil ways. Think about it! *The very things that are supposed to bless us, burden us to the point that we can't give God His rightful place—first place in our lives.*

If you can't give God $1 when you have $10, you wouldn't give Him $100 if you had $1,000. The mortgage on a bigger home, the payments on an extra car, and the need to "put more by for retirement," would push Him to the end of the line. Don't get me wrong, your Father longs to bless you, but if He's already crowded out by the things you have, can you imagine what would happen if He gave you more?

* * *

Perhaps you need to get back into His presence and discuss all of this with Him. What do you think?

ANOTHER LOOK AT REJECTION

* * *

The stone which the builders rejected, the same is become the head of the corner: this is the Lord's doing, *and it is marvellous in our eyes.*

Matthew 21: 42

Jesus concluded that the rejections of men were actually "the Lord's doing." After Joseph had been rejected by his brothers, he said, "Ye thought evil against me, but God meant it for good" (Genesis 50:20.)

How many times have things happened, and later you realized they were necessary? If you hadn't sustained that loss, or walked through a difficult time, you wouldn't be ready for the blessing you're now enjoying, or the assignment you're now carrying out. It's when you begin to see the hand of God in it, that it becomes "marvellous" in your eyes!

To be "more than conqueror" means you stand up and say, "Here's how *I see it. It took all I've been through to make me who I am today, and to teach me what I know. I chose to be better—not bitter! I trust the faithfulness of God more today than ever before. If faith doesn't remove the mountain today, it will give me strength to endure until tomorrow. If it's not gone by tomorrow, I'll still believe He is able, and I'll trust Him until until the mountain is gone."* Your steps are being *arranged* by God, and they're being *observed* by Him!

* * *

Rejection brings new direction—and it can actually become marvellous in your eyes" when you see it from God's perspective.

LONG SERMONS

* * *

Then Peter preached a long sermon . . .

Acts 2:40-41 (TLB)

It's interesting how some Christians can sit at home and watch a commercial-packed, two hour, television movie and never complain—and never look at their watch. But if the pastor preaches over thirty minutes, they want to reassign him to a mission post in outer Mongolia. I'm not promoting long sermons, I'm concerned about our lack of hunger for the Word. *Amos spoke of a day when there would be "a famine . . . of hearing the words of the LORD" (Amos 8:11). We're living in that day.*

Paul once preached until midnight. The service took place on the third floor, and a chap by the name of Eutychus "sunk down with sleep, and fell down from the third loft, and was taken up dead." Then Paul stopped preaching, went and laid hands on him, brought him back to life, took him back upstairs, put him back in the window, and made him listen to the rest of that sermon—which lasted until dawn.

Maybe you're smiling, but these believers thought the Word was more important than *sleep, work,* or *socializing with friends.* You see, *if you get the Word in you, you'll live—if you don't, you'll die.*

* * *

Child of God, you need to develop a Bible-study life so that you'll know the Book from cover to cover.

ACCORDING TO WHAT?

* * *

But my God shall supply all your need according to his riches in glory by Christ Jesus.

Philippians 4:19

"His riches." Think about it; who else would tell a prophet in the middle of a famine to go sit by a stream in the mountains and birds will show up every evening with fresh meat? Who would tell exhausted fishermen who had "fished all night and caught nothing" to cast their net on the right side? How about filling pots with water, and then pouring it into the wineglasses of the guests, and believing that what went *in* as water, would come *out* as wine? How about manna from heaven? Or blessings that pursue you until they *overtake* you? These things can only be found in God's storehouse. When God says He'll meet *all* your needs, *according to His riches,* He's saying your job is not your source, and your bank account is not your security.

Do you really believe the Bible, or are you just reading stories? Isn't it time that you made up your mind that the God who did all these things for His people in Bible days is willing, waiting, and wanting to do them for you, too? Go ahead, *place your needs beside His riches, and you'll see just how well off you really are.*

* * *

Then say with David, "The Lord [the one who's in charge of everything] is *my* shepherd, I shall not want [for anything]." What a way to face the day!

GOD'S WATCHDOGS

* * *

Surely goodness and mercy shall follow me all the days of my life.

Psalm 23:6

When I was growing up in Belfast, there was this guy in our neighborhood named Burt who owned two big watchdogs. Everywhere he went they were at his heels. We lived in a pretty rough neighborhood and you had to know how to take care of yourself. But Burt never had any trouble. Folks just took one look at those dogs and treated him respectfully. Are you getting the message? God has two big watchdogs called *Goodness* and *Mercy,* and He's told them to follow you and look after you wherever you go.

If you haven't seen them, it's because you probably weren't looking. *Mercy* will pick you up when you fall, and protect you from anything that would hurt you. *Goodness* will provide you with all the blessings God has promised. Recently, I've been reading a lot in Deuteronomy and I keep coming back to this one great verse: "And all these blessings shall come on thee, and overtake thee, if thou shalt hearken unto the voice of the LORD thy God" (Deuteronomy 28:2). Imagine, instead of you running after God's blessings, they're running after you. *What a thought! Overtaken by the blessings of God.* That's what goodness and mercy are all about.

* * *

They're with you today, and they'll be with you all the days of your life.

PROTECTION AND CORRECTION

* * *

Thy rod and thy staff they comfort me.

Psalm 23:4

The tall staff with the crook was what the shepherd used to slip around the neck of a sheep that had wandered off and fallen into a ditch. He'd gently reach down, lift it up, hold it in his arms and comfort it.

The rod was used for a different purpose. It was a weapon that could be used to drive off the wolves lurking in the shadows. Even though the sheep couldn't see the danger, the shepherd could. At times, he'd use the rod to prod a *wayward* sheep back on to the path, or a *reluctant* one to go forward.

If the pattern of your Christian life these days seems to be a blessing and a beating, it's because your Shepherd knows that some days you need *the rod of correction*, and other days you need *the staff of protection*. Either way, isn't it comforting to know that He will take care of you and lead you safely home? Has He been prodding you lately? Has He lifted you out of any ditches?

* * *

Child of God, as long as you're following your Shepherd, nothing can get at you without first coming through Him. Praise God!

HE'S NOT SENDING YOU, HE'S LEADING YOU

* * *

He leadeth me.

Psalm 23:2

Aren't you glad He didn't redeem you and leave you on your own? If He had saved you and said, "Here's a road map, see you in heaven some day," you would never make it. Listen to this promise: "He leadeth me beside the still waters." Why? To *restore* you when life is too much. Sometimes we get so busy that we don't take time to read His Word, or talk to Him in prayer, or wait quietly in His presence for the strength we need. As a result, we finish up "running on empty." At times like this that *He'll make you lie down* while He does a work of restoration in you. Remember, He's much more interested in what you *are to Him*, than what you *do for Him.*

Listen again: "He leadeth me in the paths of righteousness"—right direction for my life. As I look back at the problems and painful situations I've been in, I confess that it was my best thinking that got me there. So I need His guiding, protecting hand in my life every day. How about you? Child of God, your Shepherd knows where the wolves are lurking, where the poison pasture is waiting, or how close you are to the ditch. You don't.

* * *

So trust Him, follow Him, commit everything to Him, and He will take care of you.

THE DAYS OF TIME AND CHANCE

* * *

Time and chance happeneth to them all.

Ecclesiastes 9:11

Live every day like there was no tomorrow. Speak that kind word, send those flowers, make that phone call, spend time with your children or grandchildren, volunteer to teach that class, visit that shut-in. Stop merely *thinking* about it, and start *doing* it.

I once ministered to a man in his mid-forties. I had just preached his father's funeral. Twenty years before they had a bitter argument, and apart from exchanging pleasantries at family gatherings, not a word had been spoken between them since. They were both stubborn, and neither of them would give in. Now at the graveside, this successful young executive collapsed into my arms weeping, and said, "*I loved him so much, but somehow I could never tell him . . . and now I'll never have a chance to.*"

You get better perspective at a funeral than you do at a party. In my autumn years, I find myself thinking a lot about the seasons of my life and about what is really important. Was I so busy paying the mortgage that I didn't get to enjoy the house? Did I put my career ahead of my loved ones and now there's so little time left to enjoy them? When you reach the end, what will you wish you had done in the days of "time and chance"?

* * *

Child of God, you need to give this some thought today.

THE HARVEST LAW

* * *

But remember this—if you give little, you will get little.

2 Corinthians 9:6 (TLB)

God operates according to set laws. One of them is *sowing and reaping*. Listen: "A farmer who plants just a few seeds will get only a small crop, but if he plants much, he will reap much" (2 Corinthians 9:6, TLB).

The most sensitive nerve a man has is the one connected to his pocketbook. Money represents our *time*, *security*, and *hard work*; so when God talks to us about sowing some of it, there are several things we usually do. First, we *bargain*, because we're used to giving at a certain level. But if God talks to you about a *bigger seed*, it's because He has a *bigger harvest* in mind. If God's telling you to *sow* at a higher level today, it's because He wants you to *reap* at a higher level, and you'll never break out of your present circumstances until you take that step of faith.

Maybe you're saying, "Someday, when things get better, I'll try it." However, since your seed is the door to your harvest, that day may never come. God said in Malachi, "Prove me" (Malachi 3:10). He's saying the same thing to you today. If you want to know what God can do, give Him something to work with. And remember, *every* seed produces a harvest, but your *faith* is the *magnet* that pulls that harvest into your life.

* * *

Today, God wants to talk to you about *giving*—are you listening?

HAMMERED BY THE WORD

* * *

Is not my word like as a fire? saith the LORD; and like a hammer that breaketh the rock in pieces?

Jeremiah 23:29

What you hear often enough you will eventually believe, and what you believe will determine your direction, your decisions, and your destiny. Paul told the Philippians, "I never get tired of telling you this, and it is good for you to hear it *again and again*" (Philippians 3:1, TLB).

How often do you have to *listen* before you really *hear*? How often do you have to hear before you start putting it into practice? Someone suggested that when you put something into practice consistently for thirty days, it becomes part of you. Not every page in this devotional may be just what you need; but when you find one that is, read it over and over until it becomes part of you.

Jesus said, "The flesh profiteth nothing: the words that I speak unto you, they are spirit, and they are life" (John 6:63). First His Words enter your *spirit*, and then they become part of your *life*. Otherwise you're simply going through the motions. The point is, you need to be hammered continually by the Word until your carnal nature has been crushed and broken. Then you can start getting somewhere with the Lord.

* * *

Child of God, are you letting the Word work in your life today?

ME ALSO

* * *

He brought me up also out of an horrible pit, out of the miry clay, and set my feet upon a rock, and established my goings.

Psalm 40:2

Ray McCauley, who pastors a great church in South Africa, tells of a night in a hotel when he encountered an old drunk. The man was reeking of booze, staggering, and bumping into people. Ray said, "At first I was angry and wanted to straighten him out, but I just walked off in disgust. By the time I reached the elevator, however, God spoke to me clearly and said, 'Ray, the only difference between him and you is Me.' " That night in his room, Ray knelt in prayer and repented of his attitude.

We forget so quickly. We get so religious and critical. Could it be that you need to be reminded of where God found you, of what He saved you from, and all that He has done for you? Paul asks the Corinthians a question you would do well to ponder, *"What do you have that you did not receive?"* (1 Corinthians 4:7, NIV). *Child of God, you don't have a thing He didn't give to you—and that includes your salvation.*

* * *

With this in mind, ask God today to give you a new love and compassion for those who are still stuck in that horrible pit, for the only difference between *them* and *you* is *Him*.

WHAT IS SUCCESS?

* * *

Lord, what wilt thou have me to do?

Acts 9:6

If you asked six different people that question, you'd probably get six different answers. But God has only one answer: *obedience*. Doing what God tells you to do, when He tells you to do it. Mordecia Ham preached "one of the most unsuccessful crusades of his career" in North Carolina, early in the century. After weeks of preaching, only one ten-year-old boy gave his life to Christ. The evangelist was completely discouraged. What he didn't know, however, was that the boy, Billy Graham, would someday preach to more people and win more souls than any evangelist on record. If bringing Billy Graham to Christ was the only thing Ham ever accomplished, he was a great success.

It was an obscure Sunday School teacher who led D. L. Moody to Christ when he was a boy. Years later it was said of Moody, "He took two continents and shook them for God." When my father died, my mother raised three children alone. She took us to the house of God faithfully, and drilled the Scriptures into us. For her it was a lonely, difficult, and often discouraging path. But her two sons grew up to become ministers of the gospel who have taken the principles she taught them and reached multitudes with the love of Jesus.

* * *

So the only question that really matters today is, "Lord, what wilt *Thou* have me to do?" Think about it.

HEARTBURN

* * *

Did not our heart burn within us, while he talked with us by the way, and while he opened to us the scriptures?

Luke 24:32

On the Emmaus Road, a man and his wife walked in silence and despair. Jesus was dead. Their hopes has been destroyed. We've *all* been on the Emmaus Road—maybe that's where you are today. But suddenly *Jesus came!* (Don't you love those words?) They didn't know it was Him—they thought He was a stranger. On resurrection morning, Mary thought He was the gardener; and on the Sea of Galilee the disciples thought He was a ghost. The Bible says, "Some have entertained angels unawares" (Hebrews 13:2). Keep your eyes and your heart open and before the day is through you might be saying, "It's Him! It's His voice! He's here." In that moment, you can reach out and touch Him and be made whole.

You say, "How will I know it's Him?" *Heartburn!* Listen: "Did not our heart burn within us, while He talked with us by the way." You'll know it's Him all right. There's no voice like His. No touch like His. No peace like His. As you open the pages of your Bible, He'll open your understanding.

* * *

When He does, your heart will burn and you'll feel the warmth and glow of His presence. There's nothing like it!

AREN'T YOU GLAD?

* * *

This is the day which the LORD hath made; we will rejoice and be glad in it.
Psalm 118:24

I'm glad God doesn't greet us in the morning and remind us of how *badly* we did yesterday. No, "The LORD'S mercies . . . are new every morning" (Lamentations 3:22-23). Every day is a new beginning and *you can start your life over again any day you like.*

A friend told me the other day that he had smoked again. He said it was *pressure* and he just reached for the old crutch. If you've ever been a smoker, you'll understand. In despair he asked me, "Will I got to hell?" I said, "No, but you'll probably smell like you've just been there. And it's a poor testimony to the God who's supposed to be able to set you *free*. After all, we're His demonstrators, and if the demos keep breaking down, who's going to buy the product?" He was disgusted with himself and wanted to do better—*and that's all that is required for a new beginning.*

With the shape your books are in sometimes, aren't you glad God's not an auditor? To repeat David, "This is the day which the LORD hath made; we will rejoice and be glad in it." It begins with your decision to close the door on yesterday and move into today rejoicing.

* * *

Everybody needs a new beginning and *today He's offering one to you.*

ARE YOU WASHING YOUR NETS?

* * *

He noticed two empty boats standing at the waters edge, while fishermen washed their nets.

Luke 5:2 (TM)

How strange. Why would fishermen wash nets that hadn't been used? Nets that hadn't caught fish? The answer: they were *quitting—quitting* because of *an overnight problem.* Listen: "We have fished all night and caught nothing." *Don't you know how that feels?* They believed that the way things were, was the way they would always be. They were beaten. That's when Jesus loves to show up. He walked right into the middle of their problem with a solution.

First, He asked them for their boat (their business) and *used* it to preach to the crowd. Child of God, turn it all over to Him—all you have and all you'll ever be—and let Him use you for His highest purposes.

Next, He gave them a Word that only *faith* could receive, "Launch out into the deep, and let down your nets for a draught" (Luke 5:4). Can you see why He has to wait until you've done everything you know to do? *Only then are you ready to listen and to obey without question.*

You may be washing your nets today, but it's not over. Who told you God wasn't going to bless you again? Who told you He wasn't going to bring victory out of your ashes?

* * *

If He can fill empty nets for those discouraged disciples, then you don't have a problem He can't take care of.

THE CURE FOR DEPRESSION

* * *

O my God, my soul is cast down within me: therefore will I remember thee.

Psalm 42:6

The Message says, "When my soul is in the dumps, I rehearse everything I know of you." David talked to himself and you've got to learn to do that, too. Listen: "Bless the LORD, O my soul, and forget not all his benefits: Who forgiveth all thine iniquities" (Psalm 103:2-3). The charges against you have all been dropped. It doesn't matter how many court records there are, or how many fingers point in accusation. John wrote, "He is faithful and just to forgive us our sins, and to cleanse us from all unrighteousness" (1 John 1:9).

Read the rest of Psalm 103:3, "Who healeth all thy diseases." Has He ever healed you? Or better yet, has He *kept you healthy?* Isaiah says, "The Lord will guide you continually, and satisfy you with all good things, and keep you healthy too" (Isaiah 58:11, TLB) If you can *speak,* then praise Him. If you can *move*, then lift up your hands and begin to exalt Him. If you can *think,* then begin to rehearse His goodness to you.

We forget so easily, and before we know it we're complaining about things that don't amount to a hill of beans. Come on, child of God, it's time for a rehearsal. David said, "Let the redeemed of the LORD say so, whom he hath redeemed from the hand of the enemy" (Psalm 107:2).

* * *

Try it! It's the Bible cure for depression!

THE POWER OF PURPOSE

* * *

And we know that all things work together for good to them . . . who are the called according to his purpose.

Romans 8:28

Before you ask for *prosperity*, ask for *purpose.* Before you ask for *relationships*, ask for *direction.* When it comes to people, the right ones *add* to you and the wrong ones *subtract* from you. If God didn't send them, you don't need them.

The Bible says, "There was a man sent from God, whose name was John" (John 1:6). God can *send* people into your life. Ask the widow of Zarephath. When she was willing to put God first, she prospered in the middle of a famine. (See 1 Kings 17:9-24.) She could have held on to what little she had—but she knew that as long as it was in her hand, one meal was all it would ever be. In *God's hand*, however, it could start a harvest that would last seven years. When what you have is not enough, make it a seed for the harvest you need.

Success is not at the top of the ladder or pastoring the biggest church in town. It's not being married to a "10," or driving a Rolls Royce. No! Success is being in the middle, smack in the center, of God's will for your life.

* * *

When you're there, you *know* that all things are working together for your good. What a way to live!

A PLACE AND A PRICE TAG

* * *

The thing I seek most of all, is the privilege of . . . living in his presence every day.
Psalms 27:4 (TLB)

There's no place like God's presence. Things happen there that can't happen anywhere else. Moses found that place, and when he did, the bush burned and he talked face to face with God. Awesome! But look at the price tag. He had to leave the crowd, leave his family, climb a mountain, and spend forty days alone with God. Most of us can't spend forty minutes with Him. God won't take second place to your appetites or agenda or anything else in your life. His word to you today is, *don't tell Me—show Me!*

David said, "One thing have I desired of the LORD" (Psalm 27:4). He said that *after* he'd tried all the *other things* we spend our lives pursuing. Then he went further and said, "That *will I seek after.*" If you desire Him, you'll pursue Him and get rid of anything that comes between you and Him. Read on, "That I may dwell in the house of the LORD all the days of my life." This is for those who are tired of commuting in and out. It's for those who've decided that what really matters is not *seeking His hand for a handout, but seeking His face for a relationship.*

* * *

Is that how you feel today?

HE CAN MAKE IT UP TO YOU

* * *

I will . . . replace for you the years that the locust has eaten.

Joel 2:25 (AMP)

Fifty-two percent of all marriages in America end in divorce. One out of every four people have been molested. Tragically, they will grow up feeling like "damaged goods."

But there's good news! Jesus heals wounded emotions. I know, because He did it for me. The first step is always forgiving the person that hurt you. *If you don't, they not only take your past, but you give them your future.* Don't do it, child of God! Forgiving may be hard, but it's not nearly as costly as holding on to the hurt. God says He'll *restore* and *replace* the years that were taken from you.

Life is about seasons. (See Genesis 8:22.) You have a choice—you can keep lamenting the harvest you've lost, or you can start a new one. All you have to do is *sow.* Sow your love, sow your abilities, sow your resources—every seed begins a new harvest. Other people don't determine your harvest, *you* do! Decide what kind of harvest you want and then you'll know what kind of seed to plant. Don't speak words that reinforce your resentment and memorialize your past. Start announcing what God is going to do in your future. Come into agreement with Him.

* * *

If He says He's going to restore and replace those lost years, then it's time you started making plans.

WILLING TO LISTEN

* * *

Is not this the carpenter's son?

Matthew 13:55

Your decision to follow Jesus will upset some people and your *family* may be the first place you'll feel it. Not everybody was happy when the prodigal came home, just ask the elder brother. When you dance at a man's funeral, it's hard to celebrate his resurrection—especially when he wants his old bedroom back.

Listen to what his friends and acquaintances said about Jesus: "Is not this the carpenter's son? . . . And they were offended in Him" (Matthew 13:54, 57). When you step out and follow the Lord, some of those who have known you the longest will be *offended,* and they'll probably let you know it.

How is it that we can be so *open* to someone we don't know, and yet so *closed* and even *resentful* toward someone we do? Last week Debby said to me, "When *I* told you that, you acted like you never heard a word. But when *someone else* comes along and tells you the same things, you act like it's divine revelation." What an amazing concept—God can actually speak to us through our wives. Today, ask God to help you open the channel and fine tune your receiver, for He may want to bless you or speak to you through somebody you know.

* * *

Are you ready to receive?

WHEN THE GIVER DELIGHTS IN HIS GIVING

* * *

God loves it when the giver delights in his giving.

2 Corinthians 9:7 (TM)

I was sitting in church one day when a special offering was being taken for missions. I'd given a lot that month and, financially, I felt tapped out. I said to myself, "Let somebody else do the giving tonight." No sooner had I thought the words, than a familiar voice said to me, "*If somebody else does your sowing, somebody else will do your reaping—is that okay with you?*" I didn't have to think about it for long.

Paul said, "Let us not be weary in well doing: for in due season we shall reap, if we faint not" (Galatians 6:9). Did you hear that? There is a date scheduled for your harvest. The only thing that will keep you from reaping is if you get *cynical* or *discouraged* or *impatient.* When someone has a need, or a letter arrives asking for your help, ask yourself, "Could this be God giving me a chance to schedule another harvest?" Offering time is not how God gets money *from* you, it's how He gets it *to* you! As Paul said to the Corinthians, "Take plenty of time to think it over and make up your own mind what you will give. For God loves it when the giver delights in His giving" (2 Corinthians 9:7, TM).

* * *

Your giving is the bridge to your future.

TAKE NO THOUGHT

* * *

Take therefore no thought for the morrow.

Matthew 6:34

Somehow, we've picked up the idea that *we're in control* of our lives. Satan told Eve, "In the day you eat . . . you will be like God" (Genesis 3:5, NASB). What a deal—you'll be in *control.* So we try to *control* our lives, then we get ambitious and try to *control* the lives of others. When things don't go the way we think they should, we feel like we've let ourselves and everybody else down. Then we worry ourselves sick.

Then someone says to us, "Only believe." So we stack up on tapes and books and start naming and claiming things, but still nothing happens. Then someone else tells us we don't have enough faith, or we're not worthy. So we try going through some man of God, hoping *he* can get it for is.

Finally, in despair you turn to God and say, "I just can't *think* anymore—it's all Yours!" At this point, God smiles and says, "That's what I've been trying to tell you all along: *take no thought.*" When you take thought, you take *charge,* and you know where that gets you. When you take thought, you take *stock*, and you begin looking at what you've got, instead of what He's got. Instead of thinking, start trusting.

* * *

Put it all into His hands today and don't take it back.

STOP WORRYING

* * *

Therefore take no thought, saying, What shall we eat? or, What shall we drink? or, Wherewithal shall we be clothed?

Matthew 6:31

When Moses asked God what His name was (See Exodus 3:13), God replied, "I AM." He was literally saying, "I AM—the one who feeds you in the wilderness; I AM—the one who heals you when you're sick; Whatever you need—I AM. So don't be afraid of having needs, for your needs just reveal who I AM." Your problems are just disguised opportunities for God to show you how big He is and how much He really loves you. Don't run from them, welcome them.

Listen to *The Message*: "All this time and money wasted on fashion—do you think it makes that much difference? Instead of looking at the fashions, walk out into the fields and look at the wild flowers. They never primp or shop, but have you ever seen color or design quite like it? The ten best dressed men and women in the country look shabby alongside them. If God gives such attention to the appearance of wild flowers . . . don't you think He'll attend to you? *What I am trying to do here is to get you to relax, to not be so preoccupied with getting, so you can respond to God's giving*" (Matthew 6:28-32).

* * *

Today, His word to you is: *Relax, stop worrying, and put it all into My hands.*

A QUICK RESPONSE

* * *

When thou saidst, Seek ye my face; my heart said unto thee, Thy face, LORD, will I seek.

Psalms 27:8

It's sad to see two people who couldn't wait to be together, reach the place where they treat each other with indifference. There's no unfaithfulness, no fighting—and *no passion*. They park in the same garage and write checks on the same account—but they pass like ships in the night, without closeness, commitment, or communication. Jesus said, "The love of many shall wax cold" (Matthew 24:12). Child of God, if this is the way things are in your life today, do something about it.

When David heard the voice of God, he responded *immediately,* "Thy face, LORD, will I seek." How's your response time? Do you remember when the slightest tug or the smallest whisper was all you needed? Something has happened.

Look at the life of Noah. In Genesis 6:9 we read, "Noah walked with God." In Genesis 7:5 we read, "And Noah did according unto all that the LORD commanded him." Finally, we read that Noah got *blessed,* got *busy,* and got *drunk.* Listen, "And Noah began to be an husbandman, and he planted a vineyard: And he drank of the wine, and was drunken; and he was uncovered within his tent" (Genesis 9:20-21). What a progression! Child of God, *don't let this happen to you.*

* * *

You can say and do all the right things, but it means nothing until your heart says, "Thy face, LORD, will I seek."

BENT IN THE WRONG DIRECTION

* * *

The LORD hath laid on him the iniquity of us all.

Isaiah 53:6

Iniquity means *"to be bent or inclined toward."* The Bible says, "Lot . . . pitched his tent *toward* Sodom" (Genesis 13:12). It proved to be a fatal attraction. He lost everything he'd spent his life working for, including his family, because he *leaned* the wrong way. It works like this: you sow a thought and you reap a *deed*, you sow a deed and you reap a *habit,* you sow a habit and you reap a *character*, you sow a character and you reap *a destiny.*

When you give into certain inclinations, you're *hooked.* I've been there! You can get hooked on sex, food, alcohol, drugs, and a lot of other things. The good news is: Jesus came to get you *off the hook.*

Iniquity means to be *bent*, but Jesus came to straighten you out, and He's only waiting for your permission to do it. If you're tired of fighting those inner drives and inclinations, let Him have your life. He'll say to you what He said to Isaiah, "And thine iniquity is taken away, and thy sin purged" (Isaiah 6:7).

* * *

Don't wait—do it today.

TO THOSE IN CHRISTIAN SERVICE

* * *

They made me the keeper of the vineyards;
but mine own vineyard have I not kept.
Song of Solomon 1:6

Last year, I sat listening to Jim Bakker, former President of the PTL Ministry, tell 7,000 pastors at a conference, "*Don't make the mistake I made. I had to go to prison to give my son one whole day of my life.*" A pastor from Arkansas came to him in tears after the service and said, "I came for the conference, but I'm not staying, I'm leaving tomorrow to go back home. You see, I haven't spent a day with my son in four years."

A few years ago, a popular preacher told some friends of mine, "This is not the way it's supposed to be. I never see my wife, and my kids hardly know me." Last time I checked, not much had changed, the ministry *has* him. He has books to write, TV programs to prepare, a donor base to be developed, and speaking engagements to be fulfilled to reach his goals. The question is, who set those goals? The woman in the *Song of Solomon* said they made her the keeper of the vineyards of others, *but her own were neglected.* Relationships don't just happen, they must be worked on.

* * *

So I'm going to end this now and go spend a little time with my family. How about you?

A FRIEND WHO STICKS

* * *

There is a friend that sticketh closer than a brother.

Proverbs 18:24

A relationship is like riding a bus—you have to move over and make room for somebody else and all their baggage, too. Your willingness, not your words, is what sustains real friendship. Willing to forgive. Willing to adjust. Willing to believe the best.

The pastor of one of the largest churches I know, is one of the loneliest people I've ever met. He once told me, "I don't have *one* real friend. I trust nobody." He's a prisoner of his own image and other people's expectations. He can't show his humanity in case they reject him. What a terrible way to live.

So often we throw away a good person because he made a mistake. We forget all the good and dwell on only the thing they did to hurt us. Would you throw your car away because of a bad battery? Is there any possibility of repair? You say, "No." *Then how does God ever love you?* If He forgave you your debts in the same way that you forgive your debtors, could you stand? Are you getting the idea?

* * *

Today, ask God to make you a friend who *sticks.*

GOD IS BIGGER THAN AIDS

* * *

Is there any thing too hard for me?
Jeremiah 32:27

One day I sat in the *Cathedral of the Holy Spirit* in Atlanta, Georgia, looking up at the stained glass windows and struggling to keep back tears as I remembered the artist who created some of them. He arrived at the church a few years ago. He was a skeleton of a man, dying of AIDS. He had been to several other churches requesting help, but all of them had turned him away. One day at the cathedral ,the pastors were praying, and one pastor called him out and said, "Young man, God has just told me that you are being given a blood transfusion and you are being healed." When he went back to the doctor they could not find any trace of AIDS.

That was three years ago and he's still healthy and serving the Lord. The last time I saw him, he was making another beautiful stained glass window of Jesus touching the leper. As I spoke with him, his face shone with joy as he told me what God has done for him.

God is bigger than *AIDS!* He is also bigger than *cancer,* bigger than *drugs,* bigger than *habits* or *lifestyles* or *past hurts.* Don't give up on religion until you've tried Jesus. He's not a creed, He's a person and He wants to have a relationship with you.

* * *

Whatever you're facing today, remember that *there is nothing too hard for Him.*

MAKE SURE THE CAPTAIN IS ON BOARD

* * *

Take fast hold of instruction; let her not go: keep her; for she is thy life.
Proverbs 4:13

A young ensign was given an opportunity to display his ability at getting the ship out of port. He had the decks buzzing with men, and soon the ship was steaming out of the channel. He actually set a new record for getting the destroyer underway, and he was feeling good until he received a *radio message* from the captain that read, "My personal congratulations upon completing this exercise according to the book and with amazing speed. However, in your haste you have overlooked one of the unwritten rules—*make sure the captain is on board before getting underway.*"

Before you make that important decision about your family, your job, or your life's goals, first take time to read your Bible. Jesus said, "The words that I speak unto you, they are spirit, and they are life" (John 6:63).

* * *

Remember, before you launch out on the voyage, *make sure the Captain is on board.*

A WORD ABOUT VALUES

* * *

For the LORD is a God of knowledge, and
by him actions are weighed.

1 Samuel 2:3

Before you set your *goals,* determine your *values.* If you don't, your gift could carry you to heights at which your character can't sustain you. Before you tell *others* how to live, determine what you really believe yourself.

I learned to be a preacher a long time before I learned to be a real Christian. I spent a lot of time developing ministry skills, but not enough developing a relationship with the Lord. But your ministry is not where you draw strength in the hour of testing, that comes from your *relationship* with God.

The pulpit is a two-edged sword. First, it introduces us to men and women of God who bless our lives. But if you haven't heard clearly from God for yourself, it can pressure you into thinking, *"Wouldn't it be wonderful to be up there with them."* But if *God* didn't tell you to do it, you're setting yourself up for disappointment. Jesus said, "I have finished the work which *thou* gavest me to do" (John 17:4). What has God told you to do? If you don't get a vision for your own life, you'll probably spend your life helping somebody else fulfill theirs.

* * *

Today ask yourself: ***"Do I really know what I believe? Do I have a clear sense of His leading for my life?"***

OVERLOOKED

* * *

"Are these all the sons you have?" "There is still the youngest," Jesse answered, . . . Samuel said, "Send for him."

1 Samuel 16:11 (NIV)

When it came to looks, experience, and position, David couldn't compete with his brothers. Although Jesse had eight sons, he only brought seven of them out for Samuel. Where was David? In the fields feeding his sheep and fellowshipping with God. He had been overlooked—but not by God. God knew *who* he was, *where* he was, and *when* the time for him to be brought out of obscurity would be. He didn't have to do a thing to promote himself. He just walked with God and stayed in God's presence. When the time was right, God sent Samuel to get him.

God knows who you are. He sees where you are today, and in Jeremiah 29:11, He says, "I know the plans I have for you" (NASB). Your future is not in the hands of an organization or an individual, it's in the hands of the Lord, and when the time is right, He'll move on your behalf.

You haven't been overlooked, you've been *looked after*. In the midst of boils, bankruptcy, and bereavement, Job could say, "He knoweth the way that I take: when he hath tried me, I shall come forth as gold" (Job 23:10). Your time of waiting is not wasted.

* * *

Use it to draw closer to the Lord and build a relationship with Him that will prepare you for your future.

FOR MEN ONLY

* * *

Husbands, love your wives, just as Christ loved the church.

Ephesians 5:25 (NIV)

How did Jesus love the Church?

He always put it first. This calls for the death of self-serving, self-seeking, and self-centered living. That's hard!

He lived to develop it. Jesus spent most of His ministry grooming twelve men to be world-changers. Their success didn't threaten Him, it thrilled Him. Sadly, some men are happy to have a wife who is a good mother, a good cook, and a good entertainer. But if God calls her to ministry, they feel they have to blow her light out to let their light shine, but a secure man can rejoice in that calling.

He was patient and loving with them. One of His disciples denied Him, one of them doubted Him, and others wanted to call down fire upon some who disagreed with them. What a bunch! But He poured His life into them.

So there you have it, sir! That's how Christ loved the Church and that's how *you* and *I* are supposed to love our wives.

* * *

That's enough to get any man on his knees!

HAVE YOU LEFT THE PATH?

* * *

You don't love me as at first! Think about . . . your first love . . . and turn back to me again.

Revelation 2:4-5 (TLB)

Once we take the wrong road, it will never become the right road. The only way to get back to the right road is to go back to where we missed the turn. Jim Bakker wrote a book called, *I Was Wrong*. In it, he tells of being at the top of a mega-ministry with 3,000 employees, 180 million dollars a year budget, and 200 television stations. He says, "*I got so busy working sixteen hours a day that I had no time to read, no time to pray, no time for my family, and, when the attack came, I had nothing to fight back with.*" What a lesson!

Paul says, "The fire will test the quality of each man's work" (1 Corinthians 3:13, NIV). Why go on building something if we know it's going to be burned up? Frances Frangapane says, "The Lord inspects his house by walking through it and throwing matches." It's better to have it burn up now and start afresh, than to spend a lifetime working on it, only to have it go up in smoke. *The single most important action you can take today is to get closer to the Lord.* If you do that, everything else will work out. If you don't, everything else will continue to be burned up, regardless of how much you try to save it.

* * *

His word to you today is, "Turn back to Me again."

MENDING AND RESETTING

* * *

If someone falls into sin, forgivingly restore him, saving your critical comments for yourself. You might be needing forgiveness before the day's out.

Galatians 6:1 (TM)

Geoff Jackson, a Greek scholar, says the word *restore*, in the original Greek, gives us two pictures. First, *fishermen mending their nets;* and second, *a doctor resetting a dislocated bone*. What an insight! A broken net can't catch fish, so it must be taken out of service and repaired. And what about the doctor who resets a broken bone? Not long ago I broke two bones in the back of my hand. They operated on it, put me in a cast for several weeks, and told me not to use it.

Forgiveness and restoration are first cousins, but with a big difference: forgiveness can happen in an instant, restoration often requires time. The good news is that our God is in the business of resetting and restoring. Doctors that set broken bones tell us that once bones are truly healed, they're stronger than the original. Hallelujah! He can do that for you. Don't be afraid of *time out* and *time alone* with Him. Jeremiah was told to go down to the house of the potter and watch him take a broken vessel and skillfully work with it until it was beautiful once more.

* * *

Today, the Potter wants to put you back together again.

LOOKING AT A DIFFERENT PILE OF STONES

* * *

That all the people of the earth might know the hand of the LORD, that it is mighty.

Joshua 4:24

Jericho was too big, so God gave His people an interesting plan. He told them to walk around it's walls once a day, and then come back home each evening to Gilgal. From there, they could see the River Jordan and a monument of stones, erected to commemorate the day that God miraculously dried up its waters. (God's people were circumcised at *Gilgal*, so it also represents putting away the flesh.) The plan was this, don't look at Jericho through the eyes of the flesh, for that only frames it in fear. No! We've circumcised our hearts. We're walking in faith. We're looking at it through the eyes of our spirit and we're getting stronger each day. *We're looking at a different pile of stones.*

Jericho was what men could do. Jordan's monument was what God could do. Before you face tomorrow, check with yesterday. Surely! Surely! Surely! Keep saying it until you believe it. "*Surely* goodness and mercy shall follow me all the days of my life" (Psalm 23:6). Come on, child of God, He has promised to bring down those walls in your life. The thing that stood between Israel and the promised land was flattened when God's people stepped out in faith and obeyed His Word.

* * *

The word to you today is: *Start looking at what God can do!*

THE GREAT CARROT WAR

* * *

Train up a child in the way he should go:
and when he is old, he will not depart from it.
Proverbs 22:6

In Ancient Israel, when a child was born, the midwife would rub oil on its tongue to give the infant a desire to suck. Our verse could also read, "*Give your children a taste of the things of God when they are little, and when they grow up the world will never satisfy them.*"

When I was a child I hated carrots. My mother was determined that I would love them, however, so we had *the great carrot war!* Three times a week we would meet for battle. My mother would sound the opening volley, "Eat your carrots, dear, they're good for you." I responded with light rifle fire, "No thank you, I don't like them." She responded with a bazooka, "Boy, eat your carrots, they're good for your eyes; you've never seen a rabbit with glasses." I responded with a bomb, "I hate carrots, carrots are killing me, and what good are eyes if you're dead?" Finally, like a four-star general, she would draw the lineand say, "Not another word! Eat them!"

During a twelve-year period we fought 1,762 carrot battles and I lost every one of them. But a funny thing happened—today I love carrots. I drink carrot juice. I eat carrot cake, and for forty years I haven't needed glasses—she was right!

* * *

Today, give your children a taste of the good things of God and when they grow up, the world will never satisfy them!

"ISN'T THIS THE CARPENTER?"

* * *

The Spirit of the Lord is upon me, because he hath anointed me to preach the gospel to the poor; he hath sent me to heal the brokenhearted, to preach deliverance to the captives, and recovering of sight to the blind, to set at liberty them that are bruised.

Luke 4:18

Think of the opportunity they missed. The one who could calm the sea and open the eyes of the blind, was standing in their midst. But all they could say was, "*Isn't this the carpenter? And they took offense at him*" (Mark 6:3, NIV). It takes *humility* to say, "I don't have all the answers," or, "I need help." They were afraid of the changes that following Jesus would bring, so they failed to seize the moment. They placed themselves beyond His reach and His blessing.

Have you been doing that? Perhaps you have said, "I'm a Baptist, I'm a Catholic, I'm an Anglican, etc., so therefore I'm not open to anything new or different. Our theology is sealed, signed, and settled." *Don't do it, child of God! If you honor a man's anointing, you put yourself in a position to receive from his ministry.* Today, God is using men and women from every denomination, and every walk of life, to minister and to bless. Open your heart to the blessing and the changes God wants to bring to you today. Don't miss your day of visitation.

* * *

Ask yourself, "Am I truly open to God today?"

GOD DIDN'T CALL YOU TO FIGHT EVERY BATTLE

* * *

the battle is not yours, but God's.

2 Chronicles 20:15

Some battles are not yours—they're God's! Listen: "Ye shall not need to fight in this battle: set yourselves, stand ye still, and see the salvation of the LORD" (2 Chronicles 20:17). *What a relief!* Now, if the battle is the Lord's, guess who chooses the weapons, the battlefield, the strategy, and the timing? That doesn't mean we don't have anything to do. God's people were told to "stand ye still" and trust in His unfailing faithfulness. *Don't discuss your problems with people who are incapable of solving them.* Give them completely to the Lord, then begin to praise Him for victory.

God told them to put the choir in front of the army, and have them march out to meet the enemy. Can you imagine their reaction? But *praise moves God!* It brings Him into your circumstances. While the choir sang, God moved among the enemy, and they began to fight each other. Israel never fired a shot, they never took a casualty, and the victory they won was so great that it took three days to pick up the spoils of battle. Child of God, the word for you today is, "The battle is not yours, but the Lord's."

* * *

Begin to *trust* Him and *praise* Him for the victory that He is going to give you.

THINGS

* * *

But seek ye first the kingdom of God, and his righteousness; and all these things shall be added unto you.

Matthew 6:33

Have you become absorbed with the very things that Jesus told you not to? Things like having enough to eat, or having clothes to wear, or having a home to live in. Over the last ten years a rash of books and tapes about how to get your needs met have flooded the Christian market. Don't get me wrong. Your heavenly Father knows exactly what you need, and He has promised that if you will put His Kingdom first, all the things you need will be added unto you.

But listen to Hebrews 11:3: "Through *faith* we understand"; Hebrews 11:6, "Without *faith* it is impossible to please Him"; Hebrews 11:33, "Who through *faith*, subdued kingdoms." If language means anything, then these verses mean that God didn't give us faith just to get temporal things, but to first get *understanding,* then to *please Him*, then to *subdue kingdoms.* The wonderful thing is, when we place the needs of God's kingdom first, He makes sure we have everything we need.

* * *

Child of God, are you putting things before Him? Think about it prayerfully today.

WHERE THERE IS UNITY, GOD COMMANDS HIS BLESSING

* * *

Behold, how good and how pleasant it is for brethren to dwell together in unity . . . for there the LORD commanded the blessing

Psalm 133:1, 3

When God sees us working together in unity and love, He *commands* His blessing upon us. Since we know that, why don't we work harder for unity? One word that comes to mind is "striving." "An argument started among the disciples as to which of them would be the greatest" (Luke 9:46, NIV)—Jesus had to deal with the spirit of striving among His disciples. Someone has wisely said, "There is no limit to what can be accomplished if nobody cares who gets the credit."

Another reason for lack of unity is our *failure to walk in love.* We are unwilling to accept people as they are, to love them, and let the Holy Spirit change them. After all, *that's His job.*

Sadly, some of those who are most guilty of striving can be found in the pulpit. They are more interested in protecting their reputation, their influence, and their turf. Today, you need to pray that God will help you transcend the spirit of striving, pettiness, and selfishness, and begin to reach out to others in *love*. Only a united Church can bring healing to a divided world.

* * *

Child of God, *if it doesn't work for us, how will it ever work for them?*

IF YOU CAN'T HEAR FROM A MAN OF GOD YOU CAN'T HEAR FROM GOD

* * *

He that receiveth whomsoever I send receiveth me.

John 13:20

When God gets ready to bless you, He usually sends a person to do it. It may take the form of correction, stretching your faith, or deepening your devotion to the Lord. *If you want to take big steps, follow in the footsteps of big people.* Who inspires you? Who do you read? Timothy was an Apostle by the time he reached seventeen, because he had spent much of his life under the influence of Paul. Elisha was influenced by Elijah, and did twice as many miracles as his teacher had done before him.

The greatest man I ever knew was my pastor. I spent months in his home, and years in his company, listening to every word and opening my life to his counsel. *God never meant you to do it alone.* Solomon said, "Two are better than one; . . . For if they fall, the one will lift up his fellow: but woe to him that is alone when he falleth; for he hath not another to help him up" (Ecclesiastes 4:9-10). Jesus sent His disciples out in companies of *two*. Child of God, ask God to give you the humility and the hunger to open your life to those that God would send, and to give you a willingness to listen to them.

* * *

After all, your destiny depends on it.

ARE YOU REALLY SERIOUS?

* * *

Wilt thou be made whole?
John 5:6

A pastor friend once shared with me three questions he asks every person wanting counseling. By the time they've answered these questions honestly, *over seventy-five percent of them discover they don't need counseling after all.* They've gotten a handle on the situation themselves. They are asked to *write* down their answers, which is always the first big step toward solving any problem.

Here are the questions:

1. *What exactly is the problem?* We get so lost in our feelings, our circumstances, and our excuses, we lose sight of what the problem really is. Just writing it down for the first time can change our whole perspective.

2. *What have you already done to solve this problem*? What steps have you already taken? What does the Word say about it? What Scriptures are you standing on?"

3. *What do you think we can do for you that you cannot do for yourself?*

By answering these questions, you'll discover whether they're looking for *solutions* or *sympathy*, *answers* or *attention*. These questions, when honestly faced, bring to the surface such things as blaming others, making excuses, unwillingness to change, and dishonesty. Either way, you'll get to know what you're dealing with and have the option of either solving it and moving on, or remaining stuck. Now, take another look at the questions.

* * *

Child of God, which option are you taking?

GUARD YOUR *HEAD* AND YOUR *HEART* TODAY

* * *

Above all, taking the shield of faith, wherewith ye shall be able to quench all the fiery darts of the wicked. And take the helmet of salvation.

Ephesians 6:16-17

In ancient times, the Roman soldiers were trained to aim for the head or the heart, because that was the fastest way to kill a man. This is still the devil's strategy. Paul said, "Put on the whole armour of God" (Ephesians 6:11). *Child of God, the enemy is out today to get your head,* so *put on your helmet.* The real battleground is your thought life. Solomon said, "As he *thinketh* in his heart, so is he" (Proverbs 23:7).

The other day, I heard Beverly Crawford say, "I've *been* poor, but I've never *thought* poor." What an attitude! Today she pastors a great church of 2000 in Los Angeles and her life is touching a city for God. *If you don't learn to think for yourself, your mind will become a playing field for others.* They will do your thinking for you. Today, decide to take back your mind, and renew it with the Word of God. David said that the man or woman who would succeed must meditate day and night in the Word of God. (See Psalm 1.) Since you can *think* your way into victory or defeat, joy or sorrow, life or death, then you need to start renewing your mind daily with the Word.

* * *

The time to start is today.

YOU CAN START AGAIN

* * *

You will give me added years of life, as rich and full as those of many generations, all packed into one.

Psalm 61:6 (TLB)

I once saw a bird's nest lying on the ground. It had been destroyed by a storm. I thought sadly of the time and work it must have taken to build it, but suddenly my thoughts were interrupted by a bird singing. When I looked up into the tree, I saw a wonderful sight—*the little bird was busy building another nest.*

You can't go back. You can't rewrite the past. But you don't have to wallow in regret or remorse. Your experiences have made you the person you are today, and if you're still breathing, then you can start your life over again, beginning right now. David's mistakes were bigger than those of most people. But he decided not to be a prisoner of his past. Listen: "You will give me *added years* of life as rich and full as those of many generations, all packed into one." *Everything begins with a decision—decide to live again!* All of us have things we wish we had done differently, or hadn't done at all. What is past is past. Rearview mirrors were made to glance at, not stare at! Put it under the blood and move on.

* * *

Child of God, your best days are ahead—*if you can accept God's promise and act on it.*

LONGING FOR GOD

* * *

As the deer pants for streams of water, so

my soul pants for you, O God.

Psalm 42:1 (NIV)

Something deep within me understands David's heart cry for the presence of God. It's a "thirsting" and a "longing" that nothing else will satisfy. When I've been in God's presence, I'm *different!* I'm *confident* about the future, I'm *sensitive* to the needs of others around me, and I'm definitely more *loving* and *long suffering.* Isn't it that way in your life too?

Other animals can go for days or even weeks without water, but not the deer. *He must drink from the stream every day*. The New Testament believers were like that too. When the "business side" of the church became too demanding, they refused to let *anything* take the place of fellowship with God, and studying His Word. Listen: "*We will give ourselves continually to prayer, and to the ministry of the word"*(Acts 6:4). The original Greek word for "give" is *addict*. Did you hear that? They were addicted to the Word of God and prayer. What a way to live!

By the way, hind's feet belong in *high* places! Others may live in the valleys or on the plains, but *the deer was born to live in high places—and so were you, child of God!*

* * *

Get into God's presence today.

TELL THE DEVIL TODAY, "NOT AN INCH."

* * *

Living or dying we follow the Lord. Either way we are His.

Romans 14:8 (TLB)

If Satan can't have everything, he'll take whatever he can get. When Moses told Pharaoh, "Let us go that we may serve the Lord," Pharaoh made him three offers. First, "Go serve the Lord, but *leave your children here."* Next, "Serve the Lord but *leave your cattle and goods here."* Last, *"Go, but don't go far."* Moses said, "No!" and so should you!

Satan is making you the same offer today: "Serve the Lord but let me have your kids." Or, "Serve the Lord, but let me have your business." "Limit your Christianity to Sunday—act like me the rest of the week." His final offer is, "Serve the Lord, *but don't go far."* "Why read the Bible? It's more enjoyable watching TV. Why pray? It's hard work that's better left to others. Why tithe? Think of what you could do with that money. Be a Christian but don't go too far."

Child of God, do you recognize those words? Has the devil been talking to you lately? Have you been cold in heart and compromising in your attitudes? *Don't give the devil an inch.* Don't let him have your children. Don't let him have your business. Don't let him keep you on a short leash.

* * *

Tell him today that you are going to serve the Lord and you're taking everything with you!

WE'RE NOT ORNAMENTS, WE'RE VESSELS

* * *

I must be about my Father's business.

Luke 2:49

Somehow we've picked up the false notion that we could have Jesus as *Savior* without having Him as *Lord*. Sometimes when we try to get others to help in God's work we say, "If you have the time." Or, "Would you please consider." What nonsense! Jesus said, "I *must* be about my Father's business." Paul cried, "The love of Christ constraineth [me]" (2 Corinthians 5:14). One translation reads, "The love of God leaves me no choice."

Service is not an option, it's an obligation. You're not just a son or daughter, you're a servant. If God gave you a voice to sing, you should not have to be coaxed, you should volunteer. If God has blessed you with money, remember that you're not an owner, you're simply the administrator of God's estate in your life. Listen to these words: "Everything comes from you, and we have given you only what comes from your hand" (1 Chronicles 29:14, NIV).

Are you getting the message, child of God? Listen again to the words of Jesus in Matthew 21:28: "Son, go work today in my vineyard."

* * *

It's not a suggestion, it's an order—and it's your call to service today.

GOD'S WAY

* * *

Then was Jesus led up of the spirit into the wilderness to be tempted of the devil.

Matthew 4:1

Jesus was baptized in the Holy Spirit and immediately led into a place of temptation. This is God's way. He will confront us as soon as possible with our need to say "No" to the world, the flesh, and the devil. The will of God is never easy! There are mountains to be climbed. Remember, *spiritual blessings enjoyed on the mountaintop are to equip us for the valley that lies ahead.*

When Jesus faced the enemy, He used the Word of God. Three times He said, "It is written." He knew what God had said, therefore He was more than a match for the devil. Do you know the Word? If not, then you need to get into it right away.

It's not just one big fight, and after that smooth sailing. Every morning when you wake up, the enemy will be there to face you through a circumstance, a health condition, a financial problem, a critic, or even a close family member.

Even if you've failed and fallen in the battle in recent days, get back up, take the sword in your hand, and remember His promise, "I give unto you power . . . over all the power of the enemy: and nothing shall by any means hurt you" (Luke 10:19).

* * *

Child of God, He wants you to be an overcomer today.

POSTAGE STAMP CHRISTIANS

* * *

Let us throw off everything that hinders and the sin that so easily entangles, and let us run with perseverance the race marked out for us.

Hebrews 12:1 (NIV)

John Mason tells of a tree called the Chinese Bamboo. During the first four years, they water and fertilize the plant with seemingly little or no results. Then, in the fifth year, they again apply watcr and fertilizer and in *five weeks time,* the tree grows *ninety feet* tall. The question is: did the tree grow ninety feet in five weeks, or did it grow ninety feet in five years? The answer is: it grew ninety feet in five years. *Because, if at any time during those five years people had stopped watering and fertilizing the tree, it would have died.*

Perhaps your dreams and plans don't seem to be succeeding. Are you tempted to give up? Don't do it! Continue to water and fertilize your dreams.Charles Spurgeon said, "*By perseverance the snail reached the ark.*" We need to be like that snail. Perhaps you've failed and feel discouraged. Remember, failure is not fatal! Mistakes are not final. Paul said, "We get knocked down, but we get up again and keep going" (2 Corinthians 4:9, TLB). Get back up! Josh Billings said, "Consider the postage stamp! It's usefulness consists in the ability to *stick to something until it gets there.*"

* * *

Don't give up! By His grace, you'll make it!

HAVE YOU DISCOVERED YOUR "TRUE CALLING"?

* * *

For God's gifts . . . can never be withdrawn.

Romans 11:29 (TLB)

Some people live and die without discovering their gifts. Others seem to spend a lifetime trying to *change* theirs. Today, you need to get into God's presence and ask Him to show you clearly your gifts and strengths and begin to build on them. Even if you've never done anything with them, or if you've failed time and time again, God's gifts are still resident within you. His call can never be withdrawn.

Iif you choose not to use the talents He has given you, you will probably spend your life helping someone else reach their goals. Most people let others control their destiny. Don't do it! Don't allow anyone to take over the driver's seat in your life. Fulfill your own dreams and determine your own life's course.

Remember, there are people whose lives are waiting to be affected by what God has placed within you.

* * *

Take some time out today and get alone with your Father, and ask Him to reveal to you the *gifts* that He has placed within you.

TAKE CONTROL OF YOUR TIME, AND YOU'LL TAKE CONTROL OF YOUR LIFE

* * *

So teach us to number our days, that we may apply our hearts unto wisdom.

Psalm 90:12

We're all equal in one respect: *each person has been given twenty-four hours each day.* We need to choose to give our best time to our most challenging situation. It's not how much we *do* that matters, it's how much we *get done.*

One of the best timesavers is the ability to say, "No." Not saying no when you should, is one of the biggest wastes of time you will ever experience. Jesus said, "The thief cometh not, but for to steal, and to kill, and to destroy" (John 10:10). The first thing he wants to steal is *time*, for time is the stuff your life is made of.

The difference between people is determined by what they do with the amount of time at their disposal. Don't be like the airline pilot flying over the Pacific who reported to his passengers, "We're lost, but we're making great time." Remember that the future arrives one hour at a time. Child of God, make David's prayer your prayer today, "Teach me to number my days and recognize how few they are—and help me to spend them as I should" (Psalm 90:12, TLB).

* * *

Make up your mind to *be all that you can be today.*

THE HABIT OF LYING

* * *

Lie not one to another, seeing that ye have put off the old man with his deeds.

Colossians 3:9

T. L. Osborne once said, *"Always tell the truth, and you'll never have to remember what you said. No one has a good enough memory to be a successful liar."* A lie may seem to be the easiest way out. Even if it solves your present problem, it can begin future problems that will eventually blur your vision, cause you to lose your confidence with God in prayer, and eventually forfeit the respect of others. Worst of all, some lies can only be defended and propped up by more lies—and worse lies.

The ninth commandment could be summarized in these words, "Thou shalt not lie." I can tell you from personal experience that this is one of the most difficult commandments to keep. More than once I have failed to tell the truth in an effort to spare someone else's feelings, avoid confrontation, or look good. One writer says, "Hope built on a lie is always the beginning of loss. Never attempt to build anything on a foundation of lies and half truths, it will not stand." Child of God, if you are to walk with confidence toward God and men today, then ask God to give you the courage to walk in the truth and to tell the truth.

* * *

Anything less will distort God's plan for your life and lead you into places God never meant you to be.

FIRST WRITE IT, AND THEN RUN WITH IT

* * *

Write the vision, and make it plain upon tables, that he may run that readeth it.

Habakkuk 2:2

There is power in putting your dream down on paper. While it's merely in your mind, other things can crowd it out. When God wanted to change the world, He wrote a book. He put His heart in writing and it's been changing lives ever since. Here are a few questions from John Mason to get you going:

What would I do if I knew for sure I could not fail?

What one thing should I eliminate from my life because it's holding me back from reaching my full potential?

Am I on the path of something marvelous or something mediocre?

Am I running from something, or toward something?

Note the word "run." Child of God, get going! You've wasted too much time already. Get rid of your excuses for not taking decisive action. If you wait for perfect conditions, you will never get anything done. (See Ecclesiastes 11:4.) *The longer you take to act on God's direction, the more unclear it becomes.* Perhaps others have told you that your plans are impossible, or that it will never work. That's what they told Edison, Ford, Columbus, and Paul. Don't listen to them.

* * *

Involve yourself with something bigger than you are. You'll discover that's where God is.

THE PEACE TEST

* * *

And let the peace of God rule in your hearts.

Colossians 3:15

Have you noticed that when you're in doubt, you're easily swayed by the opinions of others, the circumstances around you, and the fears that the devil will bring to your mind. Indecision can be deadly. Someone has said, "The most dangerous place to be is in the middle of the road."

The challenge for you today is to be *decisive.* Harry Truman once said, "Some questions cannot be answered, they must be decided." Most of the time we don't have all the facts available about any given situation, but we usually have all the facts we need to make a decision. This is when we need to rely on God. Paul said, "Let the peace of God rule in your hearts." The Greek word for "rule" means "umpire." You need an umpire to *call the close ones.*

Listen to what God said to Joshua when He told him to take the Israelites into the Promised Land in just three days: "Have not I commanded thee? Be strong and of a good courage; be not afraid, neither be thou dismayed: for the LORD thy God is with thee whithersoever thou goest" (Joshua 1:9).

* * *

Child of God, He is speaking those same words to you today. So listen, and let His peace be your guide.

WHAT TO DO WHEN YOU ARE DISCOURAGED

* * *

And he arose, and did eat and drink, and went in the strength of that meat forty days and forty nights unto Horeb the mount of God.

1 Kings 19:8

Elijah had just experienced his greatest victory. In one day, both fire and rain fell from heaven. Yet nothing changed. In fact, things got worse because Jezebel vowed to kill him and he had to flee for his life. Sitting under a Juniper tree, discouraged and exhausted, he said, "It is enough; now, O LORD, take away my life" (1 Kings 19:4).

Have you reached that place? Are you frustrated by your inability to change things at home, on the job, or in the circumstances around you? Like Elijah, you want to quit.

There is an answer. Elijah laid down and slept, and as he did an angel touched him, and said, "Arise and eat; because the journey is too great for thee." The journey before each of us is "too great." *We need strength that can only come from the touch of God.* If we get so busy working *for* God that we have no time to spend *with* God, we will become fragmented, weak, and unfruitful. To restore our souls, the Lord brings us *back to basics.* Jesus rose early each morning to spend the first hours in prayer with the Father. There He got His instructions for the day *and His strength.*

* * *

Today, He's calling you back to the place of prayer—there you'll find guidance and strength.

HIS WILL WILL NEVER TAKE YOU WHERE HIS GRACE WON'T KEEP YOU

* * *

My grace is sufficient for thee.

2 Corinthians 12:9

We've all had days when we'd like to quit. I've had lots of them. But where are we going to go? Back to our old lifestyle of sin and shame? Back to depending upon our own ability? Remember all the trouble you used to get into? *It was your best thinking that got you there.* When I was a boy we used to sing, "Stand up, stand up for Jesus, stand in *His* strength alone; the arm of flesh will fail you, ye dare not trust your own."

Perhaps you feel like you're fighting for your life. People have let you down. Satan has attacked you, and you haven't done as well as you thought you would. Cheer up, child of God, His *enablement* will always exceed His *requirement*. He has a larger plan in mind. He's dealing with some areas in your life that have been holding you back. Things like *doubt; fear of people; fear of failure; spiritual pride; self-centeredness*. These things usually only float to the surface when we find ourselves in hot water. Be encouraged, God has a plan for your life, and today He is working that plan out. On days like this, heed the words of Paul: "Having done all . . . *stand*" (Ephesians 6:13).

* * *

And remember, tomorrow will be better, for His blessings are new every morning.

DESPERATION

* * *

Blessed are they which do hunger and thirst after righteousness: for they shall be filled.

Matthew 5:6

My friend, David Robinson, called me after he had spent the day fasting and praying. He said, "I told my Father that if I cannot walk in the power of the Spirit, and see the results He promised in His word, then I don't want to hang around. He can just take me home." Does that sound extreme? Paul cried, "I could wish that myself were accursed from Christ for my brethren, my kinsmen according to the flesh" (Romans 9:3). Jacob cried, "I will not let thee go, except thou bless me" (Genesis 32:26). Listen to the results: Paul changed history and Jacob became known as "Israel," a prince with God. *Something happens when we get desperate.* God hates apathy and indifference. Listen: "So then because thou art lukewarm, and neither cold nor hot, I will spue thee out of my mouth" (Revelation 3:16).

God responds to *passion.* He told Jeremiah, "Ye shall seek me, and find me, when ye shall search for me with all your heart" (Jeremiah 29:13). Maybe this sounds fanatical to some, but God can do more with a fool on fire, than He can with a scholar on ice. John Knox, the great Scottish reformer, prayed, "God give me Scotland, or I die." That cry was heard, and the fires of revival swept through the land.

* * *

God has not changed. He still responds to those who seek for Him with *all* their hearts.

QUICK, CHEAP, AND NOT DEEP ENOUGH

* * *

The stream beat vehemently upon that house, and could not shake it: for it was founded upon a rock.

Luke 6:48

Listen to Jesus: "But all those who come and listen and obey me are like a man who builds a house on a strong foundation laid upon the underlying rock. When the floodwaters rise and break against the house, it stands firm, for it is strongly built. But those who listen and don't obey are like a man who builds a house without a foundation. When the floods sweep down against that house, it crumbles into a heap of ruins" (Luke 6:47-49, TLB).

Both houses experienced the same storm, but only one was able to stand. The other fell because it was built *quick, cheap*, and *not deep enough*. Beware of the snare of instant things. Don't seek for an *experience*, seek for a *relationship*. One can be had in a *day*—the other is the product of a *lifetime* of walking with the Lord.

Both houses looked identical. The storm revealed the difference. You can count on the fact that *you will go through storms.* Paul said, "All that will live godly in Christ Jesus shall suffer persecution" (2 Timothy 3:12). He asked of the Galatians, "Ye did run well; who did hinder you?" (Galatians 5:7). The answer was, they built *quick, cheap*, and *not deep enough.*

* * *

Child of God, will the house you are building today stand the storm tomorrow?

THE DAY OF TEMPTATION

* * *

He that covereth his sins shall not prosper.

Proverbs 28:13

At the end of a service in Estonia where I was preaching, a young woman came forward for salvation. Approaching the pastor, who was my friend and translator, she asked, "Do you remember me?" He said, "No." She continued, "We met in Siberia." As one of the counselors prayed with her, my friend, who pastors this great church of over 1,000 people, turned to me and said, "Now I remember!" Five years ago he had flown to Siberia at the invitation of the President of Estonia and his cabinet, to conduct a memorial service for thousands of Estonians who had died there in exile.

That night, as they all stood around a fire celebrating the independence of Estonia, an attractive young woman came and linked arms with him. At first he thought nothing of it, but as she continued to hold his arm, he began to feel uneasy. He loved his wife and had never been unfaithful to her, *but in that moment, far from home, he found himself suddenly entertaining the idea.* Shocked, he he broke free and went back to his room. The next morning, one of the President's cabinet said he had spent the night with the same girl and a bottle of vodka!

Now 5 years later, she came walking down the isle of his church. Visibly shaken, he said, *"What if I'd given in?"* Child of God, the day of temptation will come for you, too.

* * *

And when it does, remember, *the battle is not just over your present—it's over your future!*

THOSE WHO CANNOT ADMIT THEY ARE WRONG ARE NOT WORTHY OF OUR TRUST

* * *

If we say that we have no sin, we deceive ourselves, and the truth is not in us.

1 John 1:8

We violate trust when we cannot admit we are wrong. After all, if we'll lie to ourselves, why would others trust us? None of us is perfect. We didn't come from a perfect family, and we don't have a perfect family. I often tell people, "There are no perfect churches. And if *you ever find a perfect church, don't join it, you'll ruin it.*" It brings a smile, but the fact is that neither the preacher in the pulpit nor the member in the pew is without fault. The church is not a society for the perfect, it's a hospital for those who are being made whole under Jesus, the Great Physician.

So when someone can't admit they're wrong but has to defend their position as always being right, they are not worthy of your trust. The Living Bible says, "[They] are only fooling [themselves] and refusing to accept the truth." Thank God there is a solution. Listen: "If we confess our sins, he is faithful and just to forgive us our sins, and to cleanse us from all unrighteousness" (1 John 1:9).

* * *

It takes honesty and humility to admit to ourselves and to others when we are wrong, but it's the gateway to blessing and honor.

"NO" DOESN'T MEAN "NEVER"

* * *

In due season he will honor you with every blessing.

Psalm 37:34 (TLB)

Why do we usually think that when God says *no* it means *never*? Because of past disappointments? Are you naturally pessimistic? Have you been taught more about suffering with Christ than about the blessings He has promised to His children? More often than not, "no" simply means "not now." You're not ready yet! *No* is temporary; it's transitional. In a transition you do what you *know*, what you have been *taught*, and you keep *standing on the truth* you have received until you get further revelation and instructions.

Waiting time is never wasted time— it's preparation time. Abraham waited, worshipped, and walked with God for *twenty-five years* before Isaac was born. Moses spent *forty years* in the wilderness learning to trust, and to recognize the voice of God, before he was finally ready to lead the children of Israel out of bondage. One commentator said Moses spent his first forty years learning to be *something*; he spent his next forty years learning to be *nothing*; and he spent his last forty years learning that God is *everything*. If God has you in the school of the Spirit today—and some days it feels more like the school of hard knocks—don't complain, don't get impatient, and don't try to run.

* * *

Rejoice, for you're on your way to graduation day.

REDEMPTIVE STUBBORNNESS

* * *

If ye endure chastening, God dealeth with you as with sons.

Hebrews 12:7

Dr. Kirby Clements first introduced me to the term "redemptive stubbornness." When I asked him what it meant, he said, "It's both a strength and a weakness. God needs stubborn people. They hang on. They don't run. They won't back up or retreat. But the other side of the coin is, when it's time for change, they usually resist it." Does this sound familiar?

This is why our *chastening is an ongoing process*. Listen to these words: "For whom the Lord loveth he chasteneth, and scourgeth every son whom he receiveth. If ye endure chastening, God dealeth with you as with sons; for what son is he whom the father chasteneth not? . . . Now no chastening for the present seemeth to be joyous, but grievous: nevertheless afterward it yieldeth the peaceable fruit of righteousness unto them which are exercised thereby" (Hebrews 12:6-7, 11).

The fruit of the Spirit and the character of Christ are *the products of His chastening hand.* The process usually goes like this: first, He will *break* you; next, He will *make* you; finally, He will *take* you—because now you are ready to carry out His will.

* * *

His chastening also means that He won't let you slip through His fingers, He loves you too much. Think about it.

HOW TO BECOME "GOOD SOIL"

* * *

Still other seed fell on good soil, where it produced a crop.

Matthew 13:8 (NIV)

When I first took up gardening, I think I set a new record for killing flowers. Part of the problem was the *soil*. We have hard, red, Georgia clay, and it's not easy to grow things in it. So I dug it out and put in loads of good planting soil. Now you should see the garden! The solution was in the soil.

Jesus said the seed fell on four kinds of ground. Only one was "good soil." The question is: *how do you become good soil?* First, you need to get *broken up*. Hosea said, "Break up your fallow ground: for it is time to seek the LORD, till he come and rain righteousness upon you" (Hosea 10:12). The *Living Bible* says, "Plow the hard ground of your hearts." The breaking process can be painful. Sometimes God will permit your critics to have a part in it. Other times He'll permit you to be stripped of everything until you have nothing left but *Him*.

Next, you need to be *fertilized* and *watered* constantly by the Word. Jesus said, "Now ye are clean through the word which I have spoken unto you" (John 15:3). When this process begins to work in your life, you'll discover that you are becoming "good soil."

* * *

Now you can receive the Word, bear fruit, and produce life.

LET GO AND LET GOD

* * *

Casting all your care upon him; for he careth for you.

1 Peter 5:7

My mother was a wonderful Christian and I loved her dearly. But among her defects of character was the need to *always be in control.* Guess what? "As the twig is bent, so goes the tree." I struggle with the same thing. It can be exhausting, for you can never take a day off. It can be frightening, for no human being on earth can give you that much assurance. It can alienate people because it makes you rigid and inflexible. Five minutes around a person like that could be four minutes too long.

Recently, God has been dealing with me about this. *He wants to set us free from the need to always be in control; to always have the right answer for everybody, and to know about tomorrow.*

It's not an easy transition. It's like a child letting go of the crib to take his first steps in learning to walk. There's a lot of falling and getting back up before it's finally accomplished. The point is, the longest road in the world is shorter when you take your first step.

* * *

Child of God, He wants to teach you to walk by faith and trust Him as your source.

THE END OF ALL ARGUMENTS

* * *

O taste and see that the LORD is good.

Psalm 34:8

Two professors were discussing the ingredients in a barrel of honey. A little boy standing by stuck his hand into the honey, tasted it, and said, "Suck it and see." That's the bottom line. *Your experience is not at the mercy of someone's argument.* Remember, it's *your* experience with God, not *theirs*. Saul of Tarsus had to be blinded and thrown to the ground in a life-changing confrontation with Jesus. Gideon was hiding in a cave when he met the Lord and heard these words, "Surely I will be with thee" (Judges 6:16). Isaiah had an entirely different experience, "In the year that king Uzziah died I saw also the Lord sitting upon a throne, high and lifted up, and his train filled the temple" (Isaiah 6:1).

Don't try to pour someone else into the mold of *your* experience. And don't cast doubt on their experience with the Lord because it's *different* from yours. No two of us are alike. *Remember, if any two of us are alike, one of us is unnecessary.* God knows what you need. When John saw the Lord on the isle of Patmos, he "fell at his feet as dead" (Revelation 1:17). Our experiences with the Lord will each be different. You don't have to understand somebody else's experience—so long as it produces the fruit of the Spirit and makes Jesus Lord in their lives.

* * *

That's the end of all arguments.

GETTING TO KNOW HIS VOICE

* * *

And the sheep follow him: for they know his voice.

John 10:4

Recently I heard of a tourist in the Middle East who paid a shepherd to exchange clothes with him, and see if this verse is really true. Imagine this—the shepherd is dressed like a tourist, and the tourist is dressed like a shepherd, and both men go out and begin to call the sheep. As you've already guessed, the sheep *ran to* the shepherd, and *away* from the tourist. Why? *Because they had spent enough time with the shepherd to know his voice.* What a lesson for you and me today. The burning desire of your heart, indeed the quest of your life should be, to *know* His voice—and that takes time spent in His presence. *Nothing else will do it!* Listen to what Jesus said: "He calleth His own sheep by name" (John 10:3). He knows your name. He has a plan for your life, and a destiny that was scheduled before you breathed your first breath.

Listen again to Jesus: "He leads them out" (John 10:3). That's not easy! Leaving the familiar for the unknown. Learning to stop seeing people as your supply. Trusting *Him alone* to meet your every need. Learning to stop using your *head*, and start using your *faith*. Don't implement your own plan and then ask Him to bless it. Don't kick doors open, or try to make it happen! Jesus said, "He goes on ahead of them, and His sheep follow Him, because they know His voice" (John 10:4, NIV). Did you hear that? *He's already gone before you!*

* * *

And when you get there, you'll discover that everything has been worked out.

DON'T LEAVE HIM STANDING OUTSIDE

* * *

Behold, I stand at the door, and knock.

Revelation 3:20

How long have you kept Him waiting? How often does He have to knock before you'll answer? The Prodigal Son had to hit bottom before he would say, "Father, I have sinned against heaven, and before thee" (Luke 15:18). Until then, he was too busy having a good time to listen.

The night I heard God's voice calling me I was in a little dance hall in East Belfast, packed with people. I was 12 years old. As the 19-year-old evangelist, James McConnell, preached, I felt like every word was for me. When the invitation was given, I went forward and gave my life to Christ. I had no idea where this path would lead me, or what changes it would produce in my life. But I can tell you this, *if I had a million lives to live, I'd live them all for Jesus.* How about you?

Hollman Hunt's famous picture shows Jesus standing with a lamp in front of a closed door. He's knocking, trying to get in. The interesting thing is there is no latch on the door. When the artist was asked why not, he said, "*The latch is on the inside, and only you can open it and let Him in.*" Letting Him in was the best decision I ever made—and if you have not made that decision, do it today.

* * *

You see, He may not be there tomorrow.

A HEART THAT'S FREE FROM DOUBT AND CARNALITY

* * *

Blessed are the pure in heart: for they shall see God.

Matthew 5:8

One Bible commentator defines a pure heart as "A heart that's trusting God; an attitude that is not mixed with doubt or carnality; a focus that is single." When I read those words I cried: "God give me a heart like that! A pure heart that can see You in very situation, regardless of the circumstances. A pure heart that can see the potential for a miracle, even when everything around it is falling apart."

Shadrach, Meshach, and Abednego refused to bow before the king's idols. When he threatened them with the fiery furnace, they answered from pure hearts, "Our God whom we serve is able to deliver us from the burning fiery furnace, and he will deliver us out of thine hand, O king. *But if not*, . . . we will not serve thy gods" (Daniel 3:17-18).

A pure heart can handle the "*but if not's*." If that job doesn't come through, if that loved one doesn't come back, if your health isn't restored, it still says, "I will serve the Lord." David said "No *good* thing will he withhold from them that walk uprightly [with pure hearts]" (Psalm 84:11).

* * *

Today, ask Him to give you a pure heart, an unmixed faith, and a single focus.

DESPISING THE SHAME

* * *

Who for the joy that was set before him endured the cross, despising the shame, and is set down at the right hand of the throne of God.

Hebrews 12:2

Some things in the Christian life were never meant to be enjoyed. Jesus didn't enjoy being rejected and misunderstood. He didn't enjoy being spat on, flogged, and crucified between two thieves. How was He able to do it? He looked *beyond* the Cross with it's shame, to the resurrection with its glory, and ultimately to the birth of a Church that was destined to change the world. *Champions are willing to do things they despise in order to create things they love.* Paul said, "I reckon that the sufferings of this present time are not worthy to be compared with the glory which shall be revealed in us" (Romans 8:18).

The other day, I heard Dr. Beverly Crawford say, "I'd go through it all again to get to where I am today; and to have what I have in Christ today." Moses had this perspective. Listen: "*By faith Moses, . . . refused to be known as the son of Pharaoh's daughter. He chose to be mistreated along with the people of God rather than to enjoy the pleasures of sin for a short time . . . because he was looking ahead to his reward"* (Hebrews 11:24-26, NIV).

* * *

Today, with God's help, you can go through anything when you realize the reward that's waiting for you up ahead.

HOW'S YOUR TESTIMONY?

* * *

Enoch . . . had this testimony, that he pleased God.

Hebrews 11:5

Enoch's testimony was that "he pleased God." How about you? Do you spend your life trying to *please yourself*? If you spend your life working for *things*, and protecting the *things* you have, the answer is obvious. Is your testimony that "you try to please *others*?" Many of us are caught in this trap. We're afraid to give out a gospel tract in case someone ridicules us. We pass up opportunities to witness for Christ out of fear of rejection. Jesus said, "But whosoever shall deny me before men, him will I also deny before my Father which is in heaven" (Matthew 10:33).

Child of God, there are forces at work today that seek to pull you down and compromise your testimony. When the angels were ready to destroy Sodom and Gomorrah, they gave Lot a chance to get his children. But when he warned them to get out, they laughed at him. The Bible says, "He seemed as one that mocked" (Genesis 19:14). What happened? Were they aware of his shady business dealings? The off-color stories? His pastimes? One thing is sure, when he needed his testimony most, he didn't have it. God is looking for people today who will live clean in a dirty world.

* * *

So you have a choice. You can have a testimony like *Lot*, or a testimony like *Enoch*—it's up to you.

REVELATIONS OF THE HEART

* * *

The LORD looketh on the heart.

1 Samuel 16:7

Sometimes we say, "Look what you made me do!" The truth is that the situation merely revealed what was in your heart. This may not be easy to accept, but until you're willing to, you'll never get anywhere with the Lord. Two women claimed to be the mother of the same child. Solomon took a sword and said, in effect, "Let's cut the child in half, and you can each have a part." The impostor stood silently by, but the real mother cried, "No! Give the child to her." *In that moment, Solomon revealed the secrets of their heart.*

Your heavenly Father will sometimes put you in places of difficulty that will surface in you things that need to be dealt with. When He does, don't fight—deal with it! For example, do you still carry resentment over wrongs done to you years ago? Do you find yourself responding with criticism when others irritate you?

You see, you can go to church seven days a week, and go through all the motions, and never deal with what's really in your heart. *Have you become hardhearted? There's nothing coming in, and nothing going out.* David said, "A broken and a contrite heart, O God, thou wilt not despise" (Psalm 51:17). By the way, you cannot work on everything at once, you'll overload your circuits.

* * *

So today, work on things as He brings them to your attention.

GUARDING THE EYE GATE

* * *

I will set no wicked thing before mine eyes.

Psalm 101:3

We need to take another look at the television viewing preferences of this generation. Most producers today admit that a movie is doomed unless it shows some violence, partial nudity, or profanity. I confess that I can now put up with some things I probably wouldn't have years ago, because the show is funny or exciting. How about you?

Does this mean we have matured, or does it mean we have been *desensitized*? At the risk of sounding old, *whatever happened to the noble art of conversation?* Malachi said, "Then they that feared the LORD spake often one to another" (Malachi 3:16). Now "they that fear the Lord" seem to spend time together watching TV.

What about Paul's advice to Timothy, "Give attendance to reading?" (1 Timothy 4:13). May I remind you again, *you do not determine your future, you determine your habits, and your habits determine your future.* Your TV can either be a curse or a blessing. It's how you use it. The same man who wrote, "I will set no wicked thing before mine eyes," also wrote, "Open thou mine eyes, that I may behold wondrous things out of thy law" (Psalm 119:18).

* * *

Don't you think that God at least deserves *equal time* with your television?

IS HE YOUR SAVIOR OR YOUR OBSESSION?

* * *

I want to know Christ and the power of his resurrection and the fellowship of sharing in his sufferings.

Philippians 3:10 (NIV)

You have an option: you can reach for His hand and make Him your source, or you can reach for His heart and make Him your obsession. The men and women God has used most, are those who have sought Him with a passion. Abraham's trip up Mount Moriah to offer up his son, Isaac, was all about one thing, and one thing only: was there anything he loved more than God? The Bible doesn't tell us a thing about Abraham's emotions—but how would *you* have done that day? Each step is taking you closer to plunging a knife into the heart of your child. Wouldn't you have bargained? Not Abraham—there was *nothing* he held nearer or dearer than the Lord. There was no possession that could ever take the place of God in his life. Try weighing yourself on those scales!

Paul said, "That I might *know* Him." The Bible tells us that Adam *knew* his wife, Eve, and she conceived. Nothing can be born unless it is first conceived, and nothing can be conceived unless there is first an act of intimacy between two people. Your destiny, your equipping, and your anointing, can only be conceived and sustained in the place of *intimacy.*

* * *

Today get alone with God and make it the cry of your heart: "That I might know you."

HOW TO DEAL WITH THE FLESH

* * *

Walk not after the flesh.

Romans 8:1

I smiled as a lady shared this testimony: "My carnal nature got up before me today. It waited for me at the breakfast table. It sat beside me in the car and whispered all sorts of things into my ear. Things like: *resentment* toward my husband for not being more loving; *anger* toward my boss for being insensitive; *fear*—the kind that says there won't be enough money this month to pay the bills? I thought, surely all this entitled me to a good dose of *self-pity*.

"Next I thought, If the day has barely started and it's this bad, what will it be like by supper time? Then I heard a familiar voice laughing in the background, and I knew exactly what was happening. *I was letting the devil do it to me again!* So I called 'time out!' The word says, 'Submit yourselves therefore to God. Resist the devil, and he will flee from you' (James 4:7). That was it! I hadn't taken time to submit to the Lord. I was operating in my flesh."

There is no sweeter sound than *footsteps*. The footsteps of Jesus when you invite Him in, and the footsteps of the enemy as he rushes to get out. You can't fight the flesh in the power of the flesh, you'll only end up fighting yourself. How do you neutralize it? Through the power of the Holy Spirit. And that power is yours today!

* * *

Try it, child of God—*it will work for you today.*

STALLED

* * *

The disciples went everywhere preaching, and the Lord was with them

Mark 16:20 (TLB)

The first car I owned was a 1957 Pontiac. One day, I pulled up to a traffic light in Houston. Next to me was a 1957 Chevy Convertible with 380 hp under the hood. I could tell he wanted to drag. When the light turned from red to yellow, he put his foot to the floor, revved the engine, and took off. He got about fifty feet when suddenly his car stalled and came to a humiliating halt in the middle of the intersection. I drove right past him, smiling.

A lot of churches are like that. It's my privilege to speak in different churches. Some of them have crowds, talent, and volume, but they're *stalled.* They're not winning souls. They're not changing the community. They have the power and the potential, but *they're not going anywhere.*

The New Testament believers had their power "geared down" to go somewhere. In Acts 2, *3,000* souls were won to Christ. By the end of the next chapter, *8,000* more had been saved. By the time you get to Acts 17, they're accused of turning "the world upside down." Are you getting the picture? The Holy Spirit wasn't given to make us *feel* the power. He was given to make Jesus Lord and to help us gather in the harvest before the Lord of the harvest returns.

* * *

So, ask Him to fill you with His Spirit today, and then *get going*.

CHEAP CROSS

* * *

This people draweth nigh unto me with their mouth, and honoureth me with their lips; but their heart is far from me.

Matthew 15:8

I stood in a small Mexican town where a religious festival was going on. On several street corners, vendors were selling crosses. Some were gold, others were silver, but most were cheap wooden crosses. At the top of his voice, one man cried, "Cheap cross! Cheap cross!" As I watched, nobody bought a gold cross, nobody bought a silver cross, everybody bought a "cheap wooden cross."

I remembered thinking, "Isn't that just like us." We give God one dollar out of ten, or one day out of seven, and occasionally we might even make a sacrifice. But generally speaking, we live by this formula: just enough salvation to make us feel safe, just enough religion to make us feel right, just enough to get by. It's called *lip service.*

Today, if your love has grown cold, and other things have taken *His place,* stop whatever you're doing and get back into His presence. Repent! Ask Him to cleanse you and restore to you your "first love." (See Revelation 2:4.)

* * *

I promise you, He will—He's only waiting to be asked.

THE PERIL OF NEGLECT

* * *

How shall we escape, if we neglect so great salvation.

Hebrews 2:3

On the dashboard of my car there's a series of gauges. They let me know about such things as the brakes, oil, transmission, and cooling system. I've never been mechanically-minded but I have learned, at considerable cost, to pay attention to those lights and gauges. Paul warns of the peril of *neglecting* our salvation. You don't have to neglect your garden for very long before the weeds will claim it. You don't have to neglect your car for very long before it breaks down. You don't have to neglect your marriage for very long before it becomes a statistic.

There are certain warning signs that let you know you've been neglecting your spiritual life. When you find yourself being *critical* towards others instead of *complimentary*; when you find it's easier to *tear people down* than to *build them up*; when you're too tired to go to church but not to tired to sit home and watch TV for hours; when you're not reading the Word, or praying, or sharing Jesus with others—these are *clear signals* that you're heading for a breakdown.

* * *

If you see them at work in your life today, then don't wait another day longer—do something about it now!

HOW GOD FEELS ABOUT INDIFFERENCE

* * *

"Curse Meroz," said the angel of the LORD. . . . because they did not come to help the LORD,

Judges 5:23 (NIV)

God has strong feelings and even stronger words to say about those who are callous and do nothing. The gentle Jesus who loved the little children, took *a whip* and drove the money changers out of the temple, because they were taking advantage of the weak and the poor. (See John 2:14.) The Bible doesn't say you shouldn't be angry, it says, "*Be ye angry, and sin not*"(Ephesians 4:26). Don't be resentful! It's *right* to feel *passionately* about a lost generation that's being destroyed by schools without discipline and homes without parents. When God's people get angry enough, things will begin to change. *But as long as you can tolerate it, you can never change it!* You are called to be salt and light. Salt *irritates* and light *reveals. Does that describe you?*

When Martin Luther saw Tetzel selling *indulgences* (the right to sin freely and without consequences)in the church, he rose up in righteous anger, and a reformation started that cleansed the church and changed it forever. Maybe you can't change history, but how about "brightening the corner where you are?" Listen: "The people of Zebulun risked their very lives" (Judges 5:18, NIV). That's why God cursed Meroz—*because they did nothing!* Child of God, get back to your post.

* * *

Put on your armor and take up your sword today, for the blessing and protection of the Lord belongs *only* to those who do. Think about it!

YOU NEED MORE FAITH!

* * *

Thy faith hath made thee whole.

Mark 5:34

In Mark 5, we read of a woman who was dying of an incurable disease. For twelve years she had gone from doctor to doctor until she spent all her money. One day she heard about *Jesus*. As she listened, faith began to grow in her heart, and she said to herself, "If I can touch His clothes, I will be made well." Then "she came behind Him . . . and touched His garment." When she did, "immediately the fountain of her blood was dried up." (See Mark 5:27-29, NKJV.)

Notice the progression: first, she *heard* something; second, she *said* something; third, she *did* something. She pushed her way through the crowd, overcoming every obstacle to get to Him. The moment she touched Him she was healed. Jesus turned and said, "Daughter, thy faith hath made thee whole" (Mark 5:34).

If faith can make you "whole," then what you need today is more faith. Get back into the *Word*. Bring others into your life who have faith, and who will speak "the Word of Faith" to you on a continuous basis. Paul said, "Above all, taking the shield of faith, wherewith ye shall be able to quench all the fiery darts of the wicked" (Ephesians 6:16).

* * *

Child of God, pick up the shield of faith use the sword of the Word, and watch God begin to give you victory over the things you're facing today.

GIVING AND RECEIVING

* * *

And whatsoever ye do in word or deed, do all in the name of the Lord Jesus.

Colossians 3:17

How do you give with joy, when you've been giving to the same ministry for years? There's only one way. You must give *as unto the Lord.* That means you don't give *to* that ministry, you give *through* that ministry and unto *Him.* If you keep Jesus clearly in view when it's time to give, you will always experience joy.

Expect to receive. Most of us have not been taught that, and some of us have a hard time trying to come to terms with it. But it's clearly the teaching of the Scriptures. Listen: "God is able to make it up to you by giving you everything you need *and more* so that there will not only *be enough for your own needs but plenty left over to give joyfully to others*" (2 Corinthians 9:8, TLB). When God gives you extra, it's not for *hoarding*, it's for *sowing* into the lives of others. By doing this, you live a lifestyle of sowing and reaping. By the way, the Bible says that God "supplies seed to the sower" (2 Corinthians 9:10, NKJV). Are you a sower?

* * *

When you can answer "yes" to this question, you can expect to live and walk in the blessing of God's provision.

WHY PRAY ANYWAY?

* * *

My prayer returned into mine own bosom.

Psalm 35:13

First, it makes us *slow down.* We run all over the place, we talk to everybody, and, finally, when all our options have been used up, we turn to God. Then, when we *get quiet* before the Lord, we start getting answers. His word to you today is, "Be still, and know that I am God" (Psalm 46:10).

Next, prayer makes us *God conscious.* Up until this point we have only been *problem conscious.* The disciples were like that when Jesus told them to feed the multitude with five loaves and two fish. They said, "What good will this be among such a crowd?" But look at the results. It's only when we realize the problem is too big and we put it into *His* hands that things begin to happen.

Finally, prayer keeps us *honest.* When we're speaking to others, we often only tell our side of the story. But when we're in the presence of God, we realize He knows our very thoughts. Three times, Jesus asked Peter, "Lovest thou me?" Peter finally looked at Him and said, "Lord, *thou knowest all things*; thou knowest that I love thee" (John 21:17). We can fool others, but we can't fool Him.

* * *

Child of God, those are three good reasons for you to make prayer a priority in your life today.

PRAYER IS MORE ABOUT RELATIONSHIP THAN WORDS

* * *

Before they call, I will answer; and while they are yet speaking, I will hear.

Isaiah 65:24

It's easy to talk to someone if you really love them. It's easier still when you know they love you too. There's no reluctance to pick up the phone and call them day or night. The thought of spending time with them is not a drudgery. The cry of the bridegroom in the Song of Solomon is, "Let me see your face, Let me hear your voice" (Song of Solomon 2:14, NKJV).

I remember a wonderful old hymn we used to sing when I was growing up: "Oh, the pure delight of a single hour, that before thy throne I spend; as I kneel in prayer, and with thee my God, I commune as friend with friend."

Unfaithfulness can hurt a relationship. Nothing can break a heart faster than when you would rather be intimate with someone else. Does that sound familiar? *Hours* spent with television, but *minutes* spent in prayer. You wouldn't dream of missing a day of work, but you'd let weeks go by without going to the house of God. A relationship has to be worked at continually. It must be a priority or other things will move in to take its place.

* * *

Maybe what you need today is to take some time out and work on your relationship with the Lord.

WHOSE REPORT WILL YOU BELIEVE?

* * *

Who hath believed our report? and to whom is the arm of the LORD revealed?

Isaiah 53:1

Every day you'll be faced with circumstances that call on you to choose what you believe. Will you choose what God says, or what someone else says? It can be difficult when those voices of doubt are coming from people who have loved you, stood by you, and given you good advice in other areas. It takes grace to love them and yet quietly move in a different direction because they don't *know* God's Word on the matter, or they don't have the faith to believe *with* you. Jesus said, "If any two of you shall agree as touching anything that they shall ask, it shall be done for them of my Father" (Matthew 18:19).

Child of God, whose report are you going to believe? Faith is a fight, and sometimes that battle can be long. Listen to the testimony of Eleazar, one of David's mighty men of valor: "*He arose, and smote the Philistines until his hand was weary, and his hand clave unto the sword: and the LORD wrought a great victory that day"* (2 Samuel 23:10). He became one with his sword, he stood his ground, and the Lord gave him great victory! Paul tells us to take the sword of the spirit, which is the word of God, and . . . stand! (See Ephesians 6:12-18.) When the battle is long, when the enemy keeps coming at you, when there's no end in sight—*stand your ground*!

* * *

Child of God, tighten your grip on the sword and aim it squarely at the devil, and declare that your day of victory is at hand!

STOP STRUGGLING AND START TRUSTING

* * *

He is able to save completely those who come to God through him.
Hebrews 7:25, (NKJV)

When I was a boy, I saved the life of a little girl who was drowning. She was caught in some deadly currents at the seaside, and when I tried to rescue her, she struggled so hard that she pulled us both under. I was scared and told her, "If you don't stop struggling, I'll have to leave you." She stopped struggling immediately and leaned back into my arms, and then it was easy to save her.

It's like that with salvation—the harder you try to save yourself, the faster you sink. You just need to lean back into the everlasting arms, trust Him and what He's done for you, and be saved. Paul said, "By grace are ye saved through faith . . . Not of works, lest any man should boast" (Ephesians 2:8-9). Salvation is not *probation* to see if you will keep all the rules and do all the right things, and then maybe you can go to heaven. Salvation is not *penance* to give you a chance to pay for your past sins and failures. No! When Jesus cried, "It is finished," He meant that He had paid *all* that will ever be required to save you and take you to heaven. *The moment you believe and trust in Him alone, you become His child.* No less will avail, and no more is needed.

* * *

Are you trusting in Him today as your Savior?

YOUR HABITS BECOME YOUR HABITATION

* * *

Be thou my strong habitation, whereunto I may continually resort.

Psalm 71:3

Recently, a man who had become ensnared in pornography confessed, "Little did I know twenty years ago, that when I looked at my first pornographic magazine, it would *only take me twenty minutes to look at it, but it would take me twenty years to forget it.*" What a sobering thought! What he saw was filed and recorded. Later, in an unguarded moment, the enemy stepped in, pulled that old file, blew it up larger than life, and projected it onto the screen of his imagination. Soon he was *driven* to do things he never thought he would do, and go places he never thought he would go. Child of God, stay alert, for it could happen to any of us.

If you keep taking liberties with the truth, you will reach the place where you're able to live comfortably in a house built of lies.

It's the same on the spiritual side—the more you pray, the more rewarding it becomes and the more you want to pray, or read the Word, or go to God's house. Someone has remarked, "A bad habit is like a warm bed: easy to get into, and hard to get out of."

* * *

Take an honest look into your heart today and ask God to show you the habits that need to be dealt with. Your destiny depends on it.

STANDING IN THE GAP

* * *

And I sought for a man among them, that should make up the hedge, and stand in the gap before me for the land.

Ezekiel 22:30

The gap is *the place between what is and what can be!* Your family may not be walking with God, but *you* can become the bridge between them and heaven; "Believe on the Lord Jesus Christ, and thou shalt be saved, and thy house" (Acts 16:31). When you see any area where the hedge of protection has been broken, and the devil has been given an entry point to come in, *then go stand in it.* Pray, using the name of Jesus, the power of the Blood, and the authority of the Word, and drive him out.

When some child of God fails, don't join the gossip circle—stand in the gap for them. First talk to God on their behalf and, if God tells you, speak to them in love and restoration: "Brethren, if a man be overtaken in a fault, ye which are spiritual, restore such an one" (Galatians 6:1). The only people likely to do this are *spiritual* people. The others will either stand by silently or dig the hole deeper.

And refuse to give your loved ones over to sickness and death, unless you've clearly heard from God that they've finished their course.

* * *

You don't have to go to Bible school or be ordained to do this. You can "stand in the gap" for *anyone, anywhere,* at *any time.*

DYING TO SELF

* * *

Except a corn of wheat fall into the ground and die, it abideth alone: but if it die, it bringeth forth much fruit.

John 12:24

Self-seeking, self-serving, self-centered—these words describe somebody: US! While we remain in this condition, we're prone to get depressed, insecure, fearful, defensive, or a lot of other negative things. So what's the answer? *Die!* Imagine how that sounds to someone who has spent most of his life searching for a bigger house, a better car, more money, or approval, and all the other things we pursue. Listen to the Word: "*He who has died* [to self] *is freed from sin*" (Romans 6:7, NASB). Sin appeals to your flesh, but when your flesh is crucified, you suddenly come to life spiritually and begin to walk on a new level of victory. The secret is, you have to die *daily*. (See 1 Corinthians 15:31.)

Jesus said, "Except a corn of wheat dies, it abides alone." But if it dies, it becomes *productive*. Loneliness is not the abscence of affection, it's the abscence of direction. *Find a cause bigger than yourself, and give your life to it!* Support a missionary; become a Sunday school teacher; *do something that's not for you—and watch what happens!*

* * *

Start today, and get ready to discover a joy you've never known.

ONE MORE TIME

* * *

Please strengthen me one more time.

Judges 16:28 (TLB)

Samson's disobedience cost him his sight, strength, usefulness, anointing, and his testimony. But don't count him out! God heard his cry for mercy and his hair began to grow again. His supernatural strength returned, and God gave him an opportunity to accomplish even more in his death, than he did in is life. Child of God, you may be hurting deeply today because of your failures. Legalistic Christians may have pointed their fingers and said you're not worthy to serve the Lord. Remember, that's *their* opinion, not *God's*! In spite of all that he had gone through, Samson finished his life victoriously, and is named among the heroes of faith in Hebrews 11.

There are two things you need to know about God. First, *His love will never let you off;* "Whom the Lord loveth He chasteneth" (Hebrews 12:6). Listen to these words: "Being punished isn't enjoyable while it is happening—it hurts! But afterwards we can see the result" (Hebrews 12:11, TLB). Second, *His love will never let you go.* When the Prodigal Son returned, his father was waiting for him. I have experienced that love in times of personal failure and despair. It's not a theory, it's a reality!

* * *

Don't give up. Look up and cry like Samson, "Touch me one more time!" I promise you, He'll do it.

DEALING WITH YOUR FLESH

* * *

Above all else, guard your affections. For they influence everything else in your life.

Proverbs 4:23 (TLB)

Every morning when you wake up, there are two forces that will immediately seek to control your life. They will speak to you, influence you, and try to direct your steps: *the flesh and the spirit.* Every day, including today, you'll have to make a choice between them.

When my carnal mind suggests, "Man that looks good, go for it," I know it's time to take control of that thought, before it takes control of me and gets me into trouble. I know about the pitfalls of life, because I've been in them, and I never want to go back there again. But I'll automatically *drift* that way if I don't decide to walk with God, live by the Word, and submit to the Spirit. How about you?

There is only *one* way to bring your carnal impulses into subjection, and that's to *declare* the Word over them. I literally say, "My body is the temple of the Holy Ghost, and I have been called to glorify God today in everything I do." (See 1 Corinthians 6:19.) Like any new habit, it takes *time* and *repeated effort* to become comfortable and consistent in it. But each time you bring yourself into alignment with the Word, your spirit becomes stronger and the flesh weaker.

* * *

Today, by God's help you can rule your affections.

TAKING THE HIGH ROAD

* * *

A gentle answer turns away wrath, but harsh words cause quarrels.
Proverbs 15:1 (TLB)

If you win an argument and lose a relationship, you haven't won anything. Speaking of the virtuous woman in Proverbs 31, Solomon says, "Kindness is the rule for everything she says" (Proverbs 31:26, TLB). Can you imagine what would happen if you operated by this principle?

It takes a lot of conflict and a lot of pain before most of us realize that taking the "short end of the stick" often means coming out on the right end of the deal. Today or tomorrow, you'll meet someone you can neither control, convince, or change. Instead of trying to win them over, why not just sow seeds of kindness.

What do you like about them? Surely there are things about them you can appreciate. Don't flatter them! Insincerity and manipulative words will do more harm than angry ones. *Ask yourself, how would God's love respond in this situation?*

Listen: "Hereby perceive we the love of God, because He laid down His life for us: and we ought to lay down our lives for the brethren" (1 John 3:16). God's love will cause you to lay down your own will, your own wants, and your own way, and reach out in kindness to others, even when it costs you.

* * *

This is what's called "taking the high road."

TAKING THE POTTAGE, OR WAITING FOR THE PROMISE

* * *

Then Jacob gave Esau . . . pottage . . . and he did eat . . . and went his way: thus Esau despised his birthright.

Genesis 25:34

What a price! Esau sold his birthright for a bowl of stew. The birthright meant twice as much of his father's possessions, and becoming head of the family. In those days it was a coveted position. In a moment of weakness, Esau gave it all away. Child of God, don't take the pottage—wait for the promise!

Some days it will seem like all hell has come against you and you don't think you can take another day of it. *When you reach your limits, you're on the verge of either a miracle or a mistake.* It's at those moments you must persist and endure. Listen to the Word: "He that shall endure unto the end, the same shall be saved" (Matthew 24:13). Paul said, "We must through much tribulation enter into the kingdom of God" (Acts 14:22). D. L. Moody once said, "Don't throw your ticket away when the train is in the middle of the tunnel." You are going to come through. *God has promised it!*

It's between the promise and the provision that we get tired and discouraged and want to give up. Don't do it! Don't sell your birthright for a *quick fix* or an *easy way out*!

* * *

Stand on His Word, claim His promise, and believe that He will take care of you.

PRISCILLA AND AQUILA

* * *

They . . . expounded unto him the way of God more perfectly.

Acts 18:26

Apollos had more to learn. So when he came to their town, Priscilla and Aquila took him aside and "expounded unto him the way of God more perfectly."

You'll notice some things about Priscilla and Aquila. First, *they knew the Word well enough to share it with others.* Whether it's a Jehovah Witness on your doorstep, or the person who lives two houses down the street, could you do what they did? Do you know the Word?

Next, *they discerned his spirit and knew he was open* to the truth. You can't graft a new idea into a closed mind. You need discernment to know if they are hungry and open.

Also, *they risked confronting him.* They didn't *put him down* because he didn't know as much as they did. Instead, they lovingly shared with him what they knew, and *God did the rest.*

Listen to what happened next in the life of Apollos: "He was greatly used of God to strengthen the church, for he powerfully refuted all the Jewish arguments in public debate, showing by the Scriptures that Jesus is indeed the Messiah [Christ]" (Acts 18:27-28, TLB).

* * *

Today, someone needs to know more about Jesus—are you ready to tell them?

THE HEART OPENER

* * *

As she listened to us, the Lord opened her heart.

Acts 16:14 (TLB)

In the beginning of my ministry, when I gave an invitation and no one responded, I felt like a defeated general. Then I came across these words, "*The Lord* opened her heart." Suddenly, I heard God say to me, "Do your part, but don't try to do *Mine*." What a reprieve! It was like getting out of prison. What perverse sense of responsibility or pride could have lead me to believe that I could either convince or convert anyone to Jesus. Listen to what He said: "No man can come to me, except the Father. . . draw him" (John 6:44).

Please note, *"As she listened . . ."* It's your job to tell the story. Never miss an opportunity, for someone may be hearing it for the *last* time. Peter said, "Be ready always to give an answer to every man" (1 Peter 3:15).

You don't have to be eloquent. Have you ever observed someone in love? You'll see it in their eyes, or hear it in the things they say. They'll always find a way to tell you about the person they love. Child of God, *if you're truly in love with Jesus, you'll find a way to talk about Him.* That's all *you* have to do! Then God takes over.

From Paul's first encounter with Lydia, a great church was born. What a harvest from one tiny seed!

* * *

Today, share the Word, and leave the rest to "The Heart Opener."

THE REAL QUESTION

* * *

Lovest thou me more than these?

John 21:15

This is the first time Peter had come face to face with Jesus since the night he denied Him. The weight of that awful failure must have been crushing. But what's amazing here is, Jesus *never* brought up Peter's past. He didn't ask, "How could you have turned your back on Me when I needed you most?" No, the only question He asked him was, "Do you really love Me?" That's the real question. Jesus asked it three times of Peter, and *He's asking it of you today.* Do you love Me? "Do you love Me *more* than anyone else, or anything else?" Peter's answer has to be your answer, too, "Lord, *you know* I love You. Others may doubt it—my weakness and failure may have convinced them of it, but *You know.*"

You see, you can be religious and not love Him. You can go to church and not love Him. You can give to the poor and not love Him. That night, Jesus looked into the heart of a man who was hurting beyond words, and saw a love that was true in spite of human frailty. Because of it, He restored him and sent him out to change the world.

* * *

Child of God, take a little time today and think about this question from the lips of Jesus, "Do you love Me?"

HAVE YOU BEEN WORRYING LATELY?

* * *

Do not be anxious about anything

Philippians 4:6 (NIV)

Leonard Thomas says, *"If you want to test your memory, try remembering what you were worrying about a year ago."* Paul said, "He who began a good work in you, will carry it on to completion"(Philippians 1:6, NIV). Notice, *we* didn't start this work—He did! He just gave us the privilege of being involved, but He never put us in charge. *He's* the captain of our salvation, and He's never lost a passenger. Sure there will be rough weather, and times when you'll feel "queasy". Jesus said, "In this world you will have trouble, but take heart! I have overcome the world" (John 16:33, NIV).

We're not hurt so much by what happens to us, *as by our opinion* of what happens to us. You can't control what happens *to* you, but with God's help you can control what happens *in* you. Remember the words, "Rejoice in the Lord always"(Philippians 4:4)? They were written from the worst prison you've ever seen. The secret was, Paul was in prison, but prison wasn't in Paul—the Kingdom of God was, and that equals righteousness, peace, and joy in the Holy Ghost. Did you hear that? *A right relationship* with God that gives you confidence; *a peace* that is not subject to your surroundings or other peoples actions; and *a joy* that works from the inside out.

* * *

Aren't you glad you're a Christian?

REPENTANCE

* * *

Then Peter said into them, "Repent."
Acts 2:38

Freud was right when he said guilt was the cause of most depression and neurosis. However, he was wrong when he attacked the *guilt* instead of the *cause* of the guilt: *Sin!* If we remove the guilt before the sin is removed, it's like relieving a headache caused by a brain tumor—the cancer grows undetected.

We are guilty, and it's right that we feel that guilt until we have been to the Cross. *I'm not OK, you're not OK!* We must go to the Cross for cleansing, deliverance, and healing.

The Holy Spirit came to *convict* us of sin. Listen: "And when He has come He will convince the world of its sin" (John 16:8, TLB). If you're not convicted of your sin, you're in a dangerous condition, but *if you feel pain and misery because of the way you're living, thank God and go to the Cross.* There you'll find peace.

When Jonathan Edwards delivered his famous sermon, *Sinners in the Hands of an Angry God,* people cried out, and some even fell to the floor under conviction. When Nathan exposed the sins of King David, David cried "I have sinned against the Lord."

If you don't know how to repent, turn to Psalm 51, get on your knees and make it your prayer: "Wash me thoroughly from mine iniquity, and cleanse me from my sin" (Psalm 51:2).

* * *

I promise you—He will!

TO BE NOTICED

* * *

Beware of practicing your righteousness
before men to be noticed by them;
otherwise you have no reward.
Matthew 6:1 (NASB)

Some of God's most devoted servants will have little or no reward, because they sought human recognition here on earth. When we do that, we receive our reward *in full* here.

If you're an intercessor, then listen: "Find a quiet, secluded place so that you won't be tempted to role play before God. Just be there as simply and honestly as you can manage. *The focus will shift from you to God,* and you will begin to sense His grace. This world is full of so-called prayer warriors, who are prayer ignorant. They're full of formula's and programs and advice, pedaling *techniques for getting what you want from God.* Don't fall for that nonsense. This is your Father you're dealing with, and He knows better than you what you need" (Matthew 6:5-6, TM).

I once had a dog who *was only loyal as long as you held him.* When you would put him down, he'd whine, and when you'd push him away, he'd take off looking for anyone else who would show him attention. Are you getting the idea? Ask God to reveal and then remove from your heart the need to be noticed.

* * *

Today, ask Him to make you more like Jesus, for He "made himself of no reputation" (Philippians 2:7).

YOU FIRST

* * *

Eat this scroll; then go and speak to the house of Israel.

Ezekiel 3:1 (NKJV)

The prophet was told to digest the message himself before he shared it with others. Until the Word is part of *you*, until it's been absorbed into your own life, it won't come out with power or authority, and it won't produce lasting fruit. What we feel compelled to share with others, is usually what the Lord is trying to say to us. Again Paul says, "I obtained mercy, that *in me first* Jesus Christ might show forth all longsuffering, for a pattern to them" (1 Timothy 1:16). Did you hear that? "Me first."

In Rome, there is a fountain where tourists throw coins into the water and make a wish. The water in the fountain pours from the mouths of two lions cast in stone. *They give it out—but they never taste it! It pours from their mouths, but they are not refreshed by it themselves.* Are you getting the idea? Jesus said out of "his innermost being shall flow rivers of living water" (John 7:38).

In ancient Israel, they had to gather fresh manna each day. If the manna was kept overnight it spoiled. Jesus must be new to you every morning. He must become your *daily* bread.

* * *

Have you eaten of that bread today?

BUILDING FOR 3 GENERATIONS

* * *

Do not forget the things your eyes have seen or let them slip from your heart as long as you live. Teach them to your children and to their children after them.

Deuteronomy 4:9 (NIV)

Recently, Chris Demetriou, who is building a great church in London, told me *"I'm not building this for myself, I'm building for 3 generations—for that's where God has placed His blessing."* Your influence should outlast your life span, and touch your children, and your children's children. Whatever you're building is not just for you, *it's for them.* If this is the standard by which your life is measured, how are you doing today? The son of a well-known missionary once confided, "My parents sure loved the heathen, but I'm not sure they ever loved me." Tragically, he rebelled against God, and everything they ever preached. *Their vision died with them! Law without love can cost you your family!*

Abraham *prayed* for everything he received, Isaac *inherited* it, and Jacob *schemed* and took shortcuts to it. But when trouble hit Isaac's life, he remembered and returned to his father's God. So did Jacob! (See Genesis 32:24-26.)

Cover your children and your grandchildren with prayer today, and every day. Sow the Word of God into their hearts. Don't just *talk* about it—*show* them! By the time your child is 12, he or she will have asked a half-million questions, and you'll have had a half-million opportunities to tell them what God has to say.

* * *

In other words, *when you go, make sure you leave the lights on!*

ONLY THE BROKEN BECOME MASTERS AT MENDING

* * *

With His stripes we are healed

Isaiah 53:5

In the place where you have been wounded and healed, you receive authority to bring healing to others. Even if you've been abused, you can bring healing to others who have been abused, too, for you remain sensitive in that area. That sensitivity will actually become *discernment*, so that you'll quickly recognize in others the same things you've suffered.

My father died when I was 12, and I became acquainted with poverty and fear. I've also walked through the fires of divorce and dealt with drug addiction. I've seen the grace of God work in every one of those situations.

One day my phone rang; it was my daughter. Sobbing, she told me that her husband of just seven months had just walked into the house and told her he was "gay." He asked her to leave, and, one week later, his male companion moved in to take her place. It took me a while, but I learned *a lot* about forgiveness. In time, I gained compassion for this young man. You see, he had married her hoping she could "fix him."

People all around you are hurting! It is out of brokenness and difficulty that you get the compassion, the discernment, and the power to minister to them.

* * *

Remember, God never wastes experience.

CHECK YOUR ATTITUDE TOWARD GOD

* * *

Great is His loving kindness toward those who fear Him

Psalm 103:11 (NASB)

Have you noticed lately that many of the promises we claim are conditional? They require *reverence and submission to God.* Could this be why, in spite of all the hours you've spent memorizing and quoting the Word, that you've seen no results? Listen: "*He will fulfill the desire of those who fear Him*" (Psalm 145:19, NASB). When you treat your relationship with Him as the most precious possession you have, then He will fulfill your desires. He must have first place!

Listen again: "*The fear of the LORD prolongs life*" (Proverbs 10:27, NASB). Reverence for God can *add years* to your life. Imagine what the lack of it can do! You can have a head full of knowledge and be *using* your faith, but until you learn to reverence God and keep His commandments, you'll get nowhere.

Finally, "*In the fear of the LORD there is strong confidence*" (Proverbs 14:26, NASB). When you live with a genuine *God-consciousness*, you can face anything life brings, for when you honor God, He'll honor you. When you put Him first in everything, He'll take care of anything that concerns you.

* * *

The question is, "Are you walking in the fear of the Lord?"

TAKE YOUR STAND

* * *

The righteous cannot be uprooted.

Proverbs 12:3 (NIV)

When Dr. Frances Kelsey joined the Food and Drug Administration in Washington, a pharmaceutical firm in Ohio applied for a license to market a new drug called *Kevadon*. It seemed to relieve nausea in early pregnancy, so it was given to millions of expectant women in Europe, Asia, and Africa. Although scientific studies revealed harmful side effects, the company exerted great pressure on Dr. Kelsey to give them approval. Repeatedly Dr. Kelsey said no; there were just too many unanswered questions. Even though it was popular and very profitable, she stood her ground. It wasn't easy!

After a fourteen month struggle, the company suddenly withdrew its application. *Kevadon was thalidomide*, and by that time, the horror of the "thalidomide babies" was shocking the world. It was a firm "no" by a courageous doctor who refused to give in, that spared agony to millions.

Joseph said to Potiphar's wife, "I cannot sin against the Lord." The three Hebrew children said to the king, "We will not bow down to your idols." Martin Luther said to the authorities, "Here I stand, I can do no other." Solomon said, "The righteous cannot be uprooted."

* * *

Ask God for the courage to a stand for what is right. If you're willing to, God will enable you to do it.

WALKING IN FAITH

* * *

Now unto him that is able to do exceeding abundantly above all that we ask or think.

Ephesians 3:20

A few years ago, God told me to send $2,000 to the family of a pastor who had died in the Oklahoma City bombing. At that time, I was $27,000 in debt. I argued with the Lord saying, "Couldn't I keep half and send half?" Have you ever tried to argue with God? Suddenly God spoke to me and said, "*Would you rather have what I've got in My hand, or what you've got in yours?*" I sent the money that day!

You say, "How did you feel?" My answer is, "Hopeful." I said to my wife, "I hope this works." Eight weeks later, I received a check from a lady in Australia for $23,000. She said God told her to send it. Twenty-four hours later, another check arrived for $5,000 from a couple in New York. In twenty-four hours, God wiped out my debt and stretched my faith to a new dimension.

When you walk in doubt, you're saying to God, "I've forgotten Your Word, I've forgotten Your faithfulness, I'm looking to something else as my source." *Is that where you are today.* God said to His people, "Prove me" (Malachi 3:10) and He's saying it to you, too.

* * *

Today, He longs to show you what He can do. Are you going to give Him the chance?

GET REAL!

* * *

Handle me, and see.

Luke 24:39

Jesus could say to Thomas, "Handle me and see—I'm real"! Can you say that? Do you dare let people get close enough to you to see your strengths *and* your weaknesses and to know that you're real? If we are the Body of Christ, *then we must let people in!* Take off the mask. Get rid of the ridiculous religious facade that hides our struggles, and shortcomings, and say to the world, "Come on, handle me and see—I'm real. I'm not perfect. I struggle with my kids. I battle with habits. I don't always read and pray as I should. But I'm a child of God. He has made a difference in my life, and He can do it for you, too!"

Ghandi once said, "If I could find Christians who were truly like Christ, I would be one too." Imagine having Ghandi on our team! The Christians he knew preached love, but practiced discrimination. They taught righteousness, but perpetuated a system that reinforced poverty and despair.

It's time to "get real!" Jesus was called the "Good Shepherd." The word "good" is translated *"winsome."* Are you winsome? When you arrive, what do you bring with you? Do you turn people *on* or *off*? It should be a crime worthy of prison—using Jesus to bore people. When you've had all the spiritual experiences you can have in church, how is your influence and your reputation in the marketplace of life? Can you look at those you live with and work with today and say, "Handle me and see"?

* * *

Ultimately, that's the scale on which we are all weighed!

DISCLOSURE

* * *

I will love him, and will disclose Myself to him.

John 14:21 (NASB*)*

For many of us, *what we know about God is only through the experience of others.* Sometimes our relationship with the Lord is like the one we have with our dentist, we only reach for him when a tooth aches. But Jesus said, "I will *reveal* Myself to [you]." This is an invitation to get personal with Him.

Yes, there's a price tag. Listen: "The one who *obeys* me, is the one who loves me . . . and I will reveal myself to him" (John 14:21, TLB). Are you walking in obedience? God cannot bless you beyond your last act of disobedience. Have you forgiven that one who hurt you? Have you paid that debt yet? Are you still living in disobedience where that relationship is concerned?

Jesus said, "If you ask Me anything in My name, I will do it. If you love Me, you will keep My commandments" (John 14:14-15, NASB). Do you see the connection? *Jesus will spontaneously answer your requests, when you instinctively obey Him.*

Has your obedience become mechanical and meaningless? If the answer is yes, you need to fall in love with Him all over again. Get into His presence and stay there until you've seen His face and heard His voice, and said "yes" to all He's asking.

* * *

He longs to "disclose" Himself to you.

HE STILL BELIEVES IN YOU

* * *

Now go and give this message to his disciples including Peter

Mark 16:7 (TLB)

In 1929, Georgia Tech played the University of California in the Rose Bowl. A California player called Roy Reigels, recovered a fumble, but made a mistake and ran *the wrong way.* One of his teammates tackled him just before he scored. He was devastated!

During halftime, the California players sat quietly, waiting to hear what the coach had to say. Coach Pierce looked at the team and said, "Men, the same team that played the first half, will start the second, *including Reigels.*" Roy Reigels responded, "I couldn't face that crowd in the stadium to save my life. I'll never play again!" Coach Pierce put his hand on Roy's shoulder and said, "Son, you made a mistake, but the game is only half over, and I need you to go out there and give me the best you've got." His team won in the second half, and Roy played like a hero. Later he told a friend, *"When I realized that my coach still believed in me, I could do nothing less than give him my best."*

Child of God, have you fumbled the ball? Have you run in the wrong direction? Do you feel like quitting? *Don't give up!* The coach still believes in you. The one who restored Peter after his weakness and denial, wants to put you back on His team and make you a winner.

* * *

Just give Him a chance today.

CHILDLIKE

* * *

Except ye . . . become as little children, ye shall not enter into the kingdom of Heaven

Matthew 18:2

What did Jesus mean when He said, "Become as little children?" He meant a child is *teachable*! David cried, "Give me understanding, that I may know thy testimonies" (Psalm 119:125). *If you're teachable, you're reachable.* If you're hungry for God's Word, you have a future.

A child is *dependent*! Jesus said in John 15:5, "Without me, ye can do nothing." We speak those words glibly, and then go out and *act* like it all depends on us. If we succeed, we become drunk on a success we had nothing to do with. If we fail, we fall apart under the weight of an assignment He never gave us to begin with. The truth is, you couldn't even get out of bed in the morning without Him. Right?

Notice, also, that a child is *trusting*! It never occurs to them to wonder if their needs will be met. They've learned to trust. Sadly, it's only after we have exhausted our own efforts, that we turn in desperation to God. Someone has said, "If we used God as a first resort, we wouldn't have to use Him as a last resort."

* * *

Today, you need to become as a little child—teachable, trusting, dependent, and obedient. Ask God to help you live that way!

SILENCE IN STRENGTH

* * *

Even a fool, when he holdeth his peace, is counted wise.

Proverbs 17:28

President Calvin Coolidge was a reserved man who spoke very little. One day a reporter attempted to interview him, and the conversation went as follows:

Reporter: "Do you wish to say anything about the war threat in Europe?"

Coolidge: "No."

Reporter: "About the strike in the clothing factories?"

Coolidge: "No."

Reporter: "About the farm production problem?"

Coolidge: "No."

As the reporter began to leave the room, Coolidge unexpectedly called him back and said, *"Don't quote me."*

Never let yourself be pressured into saying something when you don't feel like talking, or don't have an answer. Silence is not lack of communication, it's a very effective form of it. *What you don't say, you'll never have to explain.* Paul says, "Charity [love] suffereth long, and is kind" (1 Corinthians 13:4). All of us have certain people in our lives who irritate or provoke us, and the easy way is to react and tell them off. But what would Jesus do? The Bible says, "When He was reviled, He reviled not again" (1 Peter 2:23). *Make His way, your way.*

* * *

Ask God today to give you the grace to say nothing.

ENTERTAINMENT

* * *

While they were in high spirits, they shouted, "Bring out Samson to entertain us."
Judges 16:25 (NIV)

Samson once slew 1,000 Philistine soldiers single-handedly, reduced the harvest fields of his enemies to ashes, and picked up the gates of Gaza without assistance. Now he's doing the job of an ass, grinding corn. Sin cost him dearly. But there's something especially important in this story. One translation says, "And they brought him out of prison and he began to *entertain* them." Hear it, child of God! *When he lost his vision and his anointing, he began to entertain!* I believe the same thing is happening in the church today. We are seeing a generation of Christians that want to be entertained. Jesus became so disgusted with the *sign seekers* who just wanted to be *entertained,* that He refused to do one more miracle.

I believe in miracles. I thank God for the refreshing that is taking place in so many churches. But I feel an urgent need to sound a warning bell, lest we become caught up in *another form of entertainment*. Are we bored with Jesus? Is the *Word* a gold mine that we have exhausted? Are we running from place to place seeking the latest manifestation? If Satan can't drive us into disobedience, he'll drive us into self-centered experience, and take our focus off a hurting world.

* * *

Ask God to help you move from being entertained, to being intimate with Him!

LISTEN

* * *

If you want to know what God wants you to do, ask him, and he will gladly tell you.

James 1:5 (TLB)

Often we hear people say, "Only the Lord knows for sure." Yes, but don't stop there! He is willing to share with you what He knows. *He simply waits to be asked.* That's why He gave you His Word—to make you a success in every area of life. The other day, I read a slogan that said, *"When all else fails, read the instructions."* I smiled as I realized how often and how impulsively I rush into things, only to discover it's a lot easier to get *into* them, than it is to get *out* of them. Wrong moves can cost you dearly. Yet the solution is so simple. Listen again: "If you want to know what God wants you to do, ask Him, and He will gladly tell you."

If the answer doesn't come as quickly as you would like, there could be *other things* in your life that need to be dealt with first. Or it could be that He would just like to spend time with *you*. Not *asking*, just *adoring!* It's a lot easier to respond to someone who doesn't just show an interest in you when they *need something*.

* * *

Do you really trust Him? If you do, you'll wait, totally confident that He will direct you and take care of all that concerns you.

HE GIVES SEED TO . . . SOWERS!

* * *

For God . . . will give you more and more seed to plant, and will make it grow so that you can give away more and more.

2 Corinthians 9:10 (TLB)

The moment you start hoarding, your source will dry up. God won't violate His Word. Have you decided to withhold until you have more put aside for your retirement, or towards that new home or car? Listen: "All things come of thee, and of thine own have we given thee" (1 Chronicles 29:14). Everything you'll ever have comes from Him. You don't have a thing *He* didn't give you!

Paul said, in effect, "Take plenty of time to think it over, and make up your own mind how much you should give." (See 2 Corinthians 9:7.) Do you do that? When He tells you what to give, do you try to *bargain* with Him?

When God speaks to you about a *specific seed*, it's because He has a *specific harvest* in mind. The question is, are you listening, or are you afraid He'll ask you for something you would like to keep?

Move out of fear and into faith. God's saying to you today, "Test me . . . and see if I will not throw open the floodgates of heaven and pour out so much blessing that you will not have room enough for it" (Malachi 3:10, NIV).

* * *

Today, He wants you to have more than enough!

THE MOMENT OF TRUTH

* * *

Peter remembered the word of Jesus, . . .

And he went out, and wept bitterly.

Matthew 26:75

As the cock crowed, Peter remembered his words to Jesus, "If I die with you, I'll never disown you" (Mark 14:31, NIV). The moment of truth had come for Peter, and it will come for you, too. *Suddenly you start seeing things in yourself you never thought were there.* God permits the storm to blow away your cover and reveal your weakness, so you can begin to *deal with it.* Sometimes the very *point* where you thought you were strongest, is your point of hidden weakness. Sound familiar?

Maybe you were raised to always appear strong, and "have it together," but now God is permitting all that to be stripped away. Self-confidence is shattered! Ego is exposed! Paul says, "Have no confidence in the flesh" (Philippians 3:3). It's only when we reach this point that we can start laying a sure foundation, not with our pride or our ability, but His grace. Now we know we can do *nothing* of eternal value in our own ability. It's easy to *say,* but having that truth deeply rooted in our being is another matter. Peter was never the same after that night. He was humbled. Now he was a candidate for the grace of God. It was a lesson burned into his conscience. He wrote "*Be clothed with humility: for God resisteth the proud, and giveth grace to the humble*"(1 Peter 5:5).

* * *

Has God been doing this in your life lately?

WE NEED MORE KINGS

* * *

And hath made us kings and priests unto God

Revelation 1:6

My friend, Charles Neiman says, "Priests provide the *vision,* and kings provide the *pro-vision.* While the priests minister in the house of God, the kings go out and do battle, then bring back treasures into the house of God to fulfill the vision. What insight!

Christian businessman or woman, "You're a king!" You have a place in God's plan that's as important as that of any priest or prophet. If religion has convinced you that God is against wealth, or against doing things with excellence, listen: "I am the Lord . . . Which teacheth thee to profit"(Isaiah 48:17). David said, "The Lord shall increase you more and more, you and your children" (Psalm 115:15). God has increase on His mind, and He wants *you* to be like-minded. The New Testament believers were blamed for "turning the world upside-down," but there's something we often overlook—those who *owned houses* and *land,* sold them, brought the money from the sales and placed it at the apostles' feet. (See Acts 4:34-35.) It's time you started seeing "God's purpose" in your business and it's success.

There is no shortage of money—it's just in the hands of the wrong people! In the next 5 years, *history's biggest transfer of wealth* from one generation to the next will take place—*billions of dollars!*

* * *

I'm praying for an army of kings to go get it, and bring it into the kingdom of God, so that we can fulfill the vision of lifting up the name of Jesus on every continent under the sun.

YOUR POSITION AND YOUR CONDITION

* * *

These things have I written unto you . . .
that ye may know that ye have eternal life.
1 John 5:13

I was a guest speaker at a church when the pastor received a call to go to the hospital to attend a dying woman who had been a member of his church for forty years. When we got there, the doctor was leaving her room, very upset. He said to the pastor, "*Pastor, please teach your people how to die!*" and stalked off. Apparently she had died in torment, with no assurance of her salvation. The only gospel she had ever heard was *probation*, not *salvation.* She believed she could spend her life serving the Lord and still go to hell! She was taught you can never really be sure you're saved until you stand in heaven. How sad!

Listen: "These things were written that ye might *know* that ye have eternal life" (1 John 5:13). She didn't know the difference between her *position* and her *condition.* "If any man be in Christ, he is a new creature" (2 Corinthians 5:17). That's your *position*, but what about your faults? That's your *condition.* And that changes daily. Paul says, "It is God which worketh in you both to will and to do of his good pleasure" (Philippians 2:13).

* * *

The Holy Spirit is working in you to daily bring your condition up to par with your position! Aren't you glad?

HOW DO YOU HANDLE CRITICISM?

* * *

Faithful are the wounds of a friend.

Proverbs 27:6

When God sends someone to correct you, it's because He *loves* you. If you've never experienced His corrective hand, it's because you're not His child. Listen: "If you are not disciplined, then you are illegitimate children and not true sons" (Hebrews 12:8, NIV). Check your credentials! Maybe you've never had a legitimate birth into His family.

So how do you handle criticism? Do you, make sure that the one who brings correction never gets to do it again? Do you distance yourself from those who don't say what you want to hear? Do you point to your accomplishments and say, "Look what *I've* done for God—what have *you* done?" Do you give in to self-pity and say, "I'm just not understood or appreciated" or "The devil is attacking me"?

Peter needed correction from Paul. Joshua needed instructed from Moses! *Anybody who ever made a difference learned by taking advice and striving for excellence.* Solomon says, "As iron sharpens iron, so one man sharpens another" (Proverbs 27:17, NIV). That's God's way!

* * *

Today keep you eyes and your ears open, *for God wants to sharpen you up, and He'll use "true friends" to do it!*

A SEASON IN DRY DOCK

* * *

Examine yourselves, whether ye be in the faith.

2 Corinthians 13:5

My grandfather worked in the Belfast Shipyard where the Titanic was built. In those days, ocean liners often came there to be serviced in dry dock. Often a ship that could do forty knots, carry tons of cargo, and make great profit, would suddenly start losing power, and money. When this happened, the trouble was usually *under the water line* where the eye couldn't see. The problem: *barnacles*—big outcroppings of coral and sludge clinging to the sides and robbing the ship of her power. So it had to be taken out of service while the hindering barnacles were stripped off. (See Hebrews 12:1, TLB.)

Have you noticed a loss of power in your life lately? *The solution could be a season in dry dock!* All of us need it. David said, "Search me, O God, and know my heart" (Psalm 139:23). Paul says, "Examine yourselves" (2 Corinthians 13:5). It could be a critical spirit, an attitude of self pity and blaming others, or a life that has become self-centered. One thing is certain, you will never know until you get into God's presence and let Him reveal what is *under the water line* in your life. A little time now will save you a lot of time later.

* * *

It's only when He reveals and removes it, that you can be everything He has called you to be.

HEALING FOR A WOUNDED PAST

* * *

I will heal thee of thy wounds, saith the LORD; because they called thee an Outcast.

Jeremiah 30:17

When Jim Bakker first came out of prison, he was so fragile. One day, he looked at me in tears and said, *"I know who I used to be, but I don't know who I am anymore."* My heart ached. When your circumstances change, do you? Are you less than you used to be? Who says so? Is their verdict final? Is their opinion based on the Word?

God told Jeremiah to go down to the house of the potter and watch as he took a vessel that was broken and marred, and made it over again. Then God asked Jeremiah a question that you need to ponder, too: "Can't I do to *you* as this potter has done to this clay?"(Jeremiah 18:5, TLB). Have you been broken on the wheel of life? Have you been through experiences that have left you marred and feeling like an outcast? Don't give up child of God, *the Potter wants to put you back together again!*

Jeremiah found healing in the potter's house, and you will too! At one of the worst times in their history, God spoke to His people and said, "I will bring you home again. I will restore your fortunes. I will multiply you and make you great and honored. Your children will prosper. I will punish anyone who hurts you. You will be my people and I will be your God." (See Jeremiah 30:18-22.)

* * *

Child of God, this is His word to you today. He's not through with you! He didn't bring you this far to leave you!

A KEY TO ANSWERED PRAYER

* * *

And when ye stand praying, forgive . . . if ye do not forgive, neither will your Father which is in heaven forgive your trespasses.

Mark 11:24

This verse was spoken to *disciples*. You ask, "Is it possible that someone like that could harbor resentment?" Yes! I have, and God has dealt with me concerning it. How about you?

Smith Wigglesworth once refused to pray for a lady in one of his meetings. When she asked him why, he said, "You have bitterness in your heart toward another sister in this service." Reluctantly, she went back to the lady and gave her a cold, formal handshake. Wigglesworth shouted back to her, "Lady, you will die of your sickness, if you don't repent and make things right." As five thousand people looked on, she put her head on the lady's shoulder and began to sob and ask for her forgiveness. The other lady did the same. Suddenly, it started to *spread through the crowd*, and people began to forgive one another of old resentments and unresolved issues. Wigglesworth shouted, "Now, come up and I will pray for you!" "*You don't have to*," she said, *"God just healed me!"*

Could this be the key to unanswered prayer in your life? Take some time today and think carefully about it. Read Mark 11:22 *through* 11:26.

* * *

When you forgive, it positions you to receive all God has for you.

GOD IS YOUR SOURCE

* * *

Everything we have has come from you,
and we only give you what is yours
already!

1 Chronicles 29:14 (TLB)

Sometimes we forget that, and act like our employer or somebody else is our source. No! They may be the *instrument*, but God alone is the *source.* Listen: "Everything . . . has come from you." He holds the title and deed to absolutely everything we have.

An old lady in Ireland, hadn't eaten for days and was praying for bread. Two boys heard her praying, ran to the store, bought a loaf of bread, then climbed up on her roof and dropped it down her chimney. The old lady was thrilled, gave thanks, and began to eat. The boys knocked on the door and asked her what had happened. She told them how she had been praying for bread and God had sent a loaf down the chimney. They laughed and said, "*We* heard you praying, *we* bought the bread and *we* put it down your chimney. Now what do you think?" She replied, *"The devil may have delivered it, but God still sent it!"*

Today, the fact is, even if God has to turn the devil into His errand boy, *He will come through for you!* David said, "I was young and now I am old, yet I have never seen the righteous forsaken or their children begging bread" (Psalm 37:25, NIV). Have you?

* * *

Remember, God is your source!

RECEIVING—SEARCHING—BELIEVING

* * *

They received the word with all readiness of mind, and searched the scriptures daily, whether those things were so. Therefore many of them believed.

Acts 17:11

What a testimony! The new Berean Christians were so hungry for God, that they received the Word with a *ready mind*, then took it home and studied it for themselves to see if the things they heard were really so. What a contrast they were to the Athenians, who "spent their time in nothing else, but either to tell, or to hear some new thing" (Acts 17:21).

We are living in such an age today! Many are searching for *something new* to interest them, move them, or entertain them. Recently someone said to me, "What has God been saying to you?" I replied, "The same thing He's been saying to me for a long time, and I've got the feeling He's going to *keep* saying it until I do something about it."

Child of God, do you want to succeed? Listen to the Lord's formula for a happy and successful life: "This book of the law shall not depart out of thy mouth; but thou shalt meditate therein day and night, that thou mayest observe to do according to all that is written therein: for then thou shalt make thy way prosperous, and then shalt thou have good success" (Joshua 1:8). This formula will work for you, if you make it part of your life each day.

* * *

Get into the Word and watch the difference it makes in your life.

PASSIONLESS RELIGION

* * *

Woe to you who are complacent in Zion.

Amos 6:1 (NIV)

American rock star, Kurt Cobain, took his own life, and shocked thousands of his followers. When they were asked why they loved him so much, many of them replied, "His music stirred something inside us, it had *passion*." Think about that.

A pastor friend of mine, whose son is a professional rock musician, told me that when he invited him to go to church he refused. This man has a close and loving relationship with his son, so he asked, "Why won't you come?" His son replied, "*Because there's no passion.* People just sit there like bumps on a log."

How can we be born-again and filled with the Spirit of God, and just sit there and show no excitement and no emotion. Something is wrong! In the New Testament church they were blamed for being *drunk* and *turning the world upside down.* Today, the world hardly notices we're around. John Wesley said, "If Christians would get on fire, the world would come to watch us burn." A religion that costs you nothing, is worth nothing. If your experience with God doesn't excite you—it won't attract anybody else.

* * *

Today, get into God's presence and ask Him to give you a passion for Christ that sets you on fire.

THE FRIEND OF SINNERS

* * *

This man receiveth sinners, and eateth with them.

Luke 15:2

One of the greatest compliments His enemies ever paid to Jesus was when they called Him "a friend of... sinners!" (Luke 7:34). *Could you be accused of that?* In the story of the Good Samaritan, Jesus taught us how *religion* treats hurting people, and how *He* treats them. Religion passed right by the injured man, and refused to get involved. Why would a church turn it's back on the very people who need it most?—people with AIDS; people who've had abortions; people struggling with alcohol and drugs; people in prison. Could it be concern over their *image?* Or over their *financial support*? Jesus ate with sinners, spent endless hours talking with them, and even accepted invitations to stay as a guest in their home.

He said that the Good Samaritan showed compassion, not contempt. He went out of His way to show the love of God to this man who had taken the wrong road, and even paid the cost to make him whole again. Then Jesus said, *"Go, and do thou likewise"* (Luke 10:37). He's saying that to you, too! Most folks think a good sermon is one that goes over their head, and hits their neighbor right between the eyes. Not so! *You* have been called to be His hand extended to those who've lost their way.

* * *

The friend of sinners is calling you today to go and show His love to a hurting world. What's your answer?

THE OLD-FASHIONED WAY

* * *

Ask for the old paths, where is the good way.

Jeremiah 6:16

Jeremiah is speaking about the things that never go out-of-date—things like *loyalty!* Solomon says, "Never abandon a friend" (Proverbs 27:10, TLB). In the Book of Ruth, when famine and trouble came, Naomi's two daughters-in-law reacted in totally different ways—Orpah kissed her *and left her*, but Ruth stood by her and said, *"Whither thou goest, I will go"* (Ruth 11:16). Thank God for the friend who stands by you.

How about old-fashioned *courtesy*? How you treat the elderly says a great deal about your character. The Word says, "Rise in the presence of the aged, show respect for the elderly" (Leviticus 19:32, NIV). This can lengthen or shorten your life. Listen: "Honour thy father and mother . . . that it may be well with thee, and thou mayest live long on the earth" (Ephesians 6:2-3). That's serious stuff!

How about old-fashioned *honesty?* Do you remember when a man's word was his bond, and a handshake meant more than a roomful of lawyers? Listen to the Word: "In all things [be] willing to live honestly" (Hebrews 13:18). Whether you're the farmer putting his best apples on the top of the barrel, or the pastor exaggerating the size of his congregation, Paul says, "Provide things honest in the sight of all men" (Romans 12:17).

* * *

Child of God, it's time to go back to the "old paths" again.

LIVING FOR OTHERS

* * *

He never thought of doing a kindness.

Psalm 109:16 (NIV)

Make sure that what you're most concerned about, is what God's most concerned about, otherwise you'll have eternity to wish you had done things differently. What a testimony these people had! The King James Version says, "He remembered not to show mercy." Could that charge be laid at your door? You're ambitious, you're hard working, and you're responsible, but have you forgotten to show mercy—especially to those who seem to deserve it the least? David said, "With the merciful thou wilt show thyself merciful" (Psalm 18:25).

Listen to this moving story:

When the British government sought to reward General Gordon for his brilliant service in China, he declined all money and titles, but accepted a gold medal inscribed with the record of his 33 engagements. It was his most prized possession. But after his death the medal could not be found. Eventually it was learned that he had sent it to Manchester during a severe famine, directing that it should be melted down and used to buy bread for the poor. Under the date of its sending, these words were found written in his dairy: *"The last earthly thing I had in this world that I valued, I have given to the Lord Jesus Christ."*

* * *

The truth is *there is no way to live for Jesus without living for others!* Think about it!

GOD WILL USE WHATEVER YOU'VE GOT!

* * *

What is that in thine hand?

Exodus 4:2

When God asked Moses, "What is that in thine hand?" you can almost hear the discouragement in his reply, "A rod." Just a walking stick. *But it was what came naturally to him!* Today the Lord wants you to know that He'll use what comes naturally to you! The secret is to put what you've got into His hands. Make it available to Him. When Samson faced a thousand Philistines, he had nothing to fight with but the jaw bone of an ass. *It was what was available to him!* It was enough! Reverently speaking, God could have used a daffodil, if that was all Samson had.

When my friend, Ray Bevin, from Wales, preached recently on this thought, a church secretary came to him in tears and said "I see it. All my life I've felt inadequate and inferior because I wasn't talented like other people. I never thought God could use me, but today I see *God has been using me for years*. Every time I sit down at my word processor and type 90 words a minute, *that's God using my gift!*"

Stop trying to be someone else—and discover who you are. *Instead of trying to compare yourself with others, or change what God has made you, recognize the gifts and strengths you've got, and start building on them.*

* * *

You'll be amazed what God can do with them!

HAVE YOUR DISCOVERED YOUR "GIFTS"?

* * *

For God's gifts and his call are irrevocable.

Romans 11:29

The Greek word translated repentance in this verse means "irrevocable." Samson's gift finally destroyed him, but he never lost it. Even if you've never discovered your gift, or you've been running from it—it's still there! *That means you can choose to do something with it beginning right now.* God's gifts are never loans, they are always deposits. As such, they are never used up or depleted. The more you use them, the stronger they get. Paul told Timothy, "Stir up the gift that is within you"(2 Timothy 1:6).

John Mason says, "You were born an original, don't die a copy!" Discover your gift! In the time of famine, Elijah asked his servant to go and look at the horizon and come back and tell him what he saw. He said, "I see a little cloud the size of a man's hand"(1 Kings 18:44). But that little cloud was the beginning of a *downpour* and the *end of a drought. Don't despise your small beginnings.* Walt Disney told people, "This whole thing began with a mouse."

In the New Testament, they started with 120 against the might of pagan Rome, but they ended up changing the world. There are people waiting to be, reached, saved, and blessed by what God has placed within you.

* * *

Ask Him to help you discover it, unlock it, and offer it to Him.

BANG! BANG! YOU'RE DEAD!

* * *

Except a corn of wheat fall into the ground and die, it abideth alone: but if it die, it bringeth forth much fruit.

John 12:24

A man I know tells of receiving a telephone call. When he answered it, a voice on the other end said, "Bang! Bang! You're dead!" Then he recognized the familiar voice of a friend saying, *"John I was just calling to remind you, that we all need to die to ourselves every day."* That's hard to remember! Paul says, "For we know that our old self was crucified with Him, so that the body of sin might be rendered powerless"(Romans 6:5). Some days my "old man" is anything but dead. I'm aware of it—when someone "steps on my toes," or I don't get the appreciation I think I deserve, self-pity rises to sit on the throne. I'm sure you know what I mean!

The Christian life is so opposite to the way of the world. You can't *rule* unless you're willing to *serve.* You can't *receive* unless you're willing to *give.* You can't *live* unless you're willing *to die* to self.

Jesus said unless you die to self and sow your life into the lives of others, you'll always be "alone". Here's the answer to loneliness! *Find a need that no one else is meeting, and sow your life like a seed into it.* Jesus said, "He that is greatest among you shall be your servant"(Matthew 23:11).

* * *

The old saying is still true: "The way to the throne room is through the servants' quarters." Think about it today.

CONSIDER THE BIRDS

* * *

Live in harmony with one another; be sympathetic, love as brothers, be compassionate and humble.

1 Peter 3:8 (NIV)

Have you ever seen a flock of geese flying in a "V" formation? What a lesson for you and me. When a goose gets sick or wounded, it never falls from the formation by itself. Two other geese fall out of formation with it, and follow the ailing bird to the ground. One of them is usually the mate of the wounded bird, since geese mate for life and are extremely loyal. Once on the ground, the healthy birds protect him and care for him as much as possible, even to the point of throwing themselves between the wounded bird and any predator. They stay there until he is either able to fly again, or until he dies. Only then do they leave and rejoin the flock.

That's what the family of God should be like. Listen again to these words: "Live in harmony; be sympathetic, love as brothers." Have you ever seen brotherly love in action? My brother and I fought often when we were growing up. But if someone else touched one of us, they ended up fighting *both of us!*

When you don't agree with your brother, don't tear him down—pray for him; and if he fails, pick him up! Let the world see how much we love one another. (See John 13:35.)

* * *

God help you and I to develop this kind of love and care for each other.

DON'T GET SPREAD OUT TOO THIN

* * *

Little by little . . . until you have increased enough to take possession of the land.

Exodus 23:30 (NIV)

Listen to what God told His people about possessing the land, for it's the same thing He's saying to you today: "I will not drive them out in a single year, because the land will become desolate and the wild animals too numerous for you. Little by little I will drive them out before you, until you have increased enough to take possession of the land" (Exodus 23: 29-30, NIV). *God knows when you're ready and, in His mercy, He won't give it to you before then.* He'll give it to you "little by little" as you mature in character and discernment. He'll also check to see how your relationship with Him is. If all these things line up correctly, He'll give you *more*. Ministries have failed and good men have finished up under a crushing yoke of debt and despair, because they failed to discern God's plan or couldn't *wait* for His timing.

God knew there were too many enemies to handle at one time, and if they tried to inhabit all the cities at once, they'd be "spread out too thin" and the enemy could defeat them easily. One of Satan's oldest strategies is getting you to reach for "too much, too soon" and get you "spread out too thin." Sound familiar?

We want to go by "leaps and bounds," but He's saying "little by little . . . Until you have increased enough to take possession of the land."

* * *

Remember, that is His way and it's always best!

THREE KINDS OF PEOPLE

* * *

A friend loveth at all times.

Proverbs 17:17

Experience has taught me that there are three kinds of people in my life—and in yours.

First, the *critical* people. Basically they're *users*, because they reach for your strength but run from your weakness. When you're in trouble they hold you at arm's length, lest they become tainted by association. Sadly, you'll find them in the church as well as the world.

Second, there's the *cautious* crowd. They won't criticize you, but when you're in trouble, they'll wait to see if you make it through the tunnel, and even when you come out, they'll wait further to see how others treat you. If it's *safe*, they'll reach for you again. They're *fair weather* friends.

Third, is the *committed* one—a friend who loves at *all* times. Though he hears the *worst*, he still believes the *best*. Others may leave, he stays! When the critics tear you down, and the cautious folks stand silently by, he'll speak up for you. Paul said about a friend, "The Lord give mercy unto the house of Onesiphorus; for he oft refreshed me, and was not ashamed of my chain" (2 Timothy 1:16). Jonathan loved David and stood by him, even when it could have cost him his life. Don't you think we need more people like these?

* * *

If you agree, then ask God to make you that kind of friend to someone today.

TAKE THE BRAKES OFF!

* * *

They . . . would not put their shoulders to the work.

Nehemiah 3:5 (NIV)

Against all odds, they rebuilt the walls of Jerusalem, but sadly, some of them would not put their shoulders to the work! Could that be said of you?

I'm reminded of the two Irishmen riding their tandem up a hill. When they finally reached the top, exhausted, the one on the back seat said "Man, you're lucky, if I hadn't kept the brakes on, we'd have slid back down the hill again!" *You may smile, but a lot of God's people live with the brakes on.* They speak of being "balanced" or "prudent" or "not making waves." The truth is they don't even make an impact at all!

On the summit of Mt. Everest there's a marker in memory of one of the oldest climbers ever to attempt to scale the mountain. It reads simply: *"He died climbing!"* Child of God, make that your testimony! Harold Kushner says, *"Our souls are not hungry for fame, comfort, wealth, or power. Those rewards create almost as many problems as they solve. Our souls are hungry for meaning, so that our lives matter, and the world will at least be a little bit better for our having passed through it."*

* * *

Whatever God has called you to do,—build cathedrals or sweep streets—when you find God's purpose for your life—*take the brakes off*, and give it everything you've got—starting right now!

THE SCULPTOR

* * *

I will pour my spirit upon thy seed, and my blessing upon thine offspring.

Isaiah 44:3

Listen:

I took a piece of living clay, and gently formed it day by day;

And molded with my power and art, a young child's soft and yielding heart.

I came again when years were gone, it was a man I looked upon;

He still that early impress bore, *and I could change it nevermore.*

Nothing so totally changes your life as children do. They'll keep you on your toes most of the time, and on your knees the rest of it. If you think having a baby will solve your problems, think again! If you think life will be easier when they reach their teens, you're dreaming! The first time they take the family car or go on a date, you'll pray that the values you taught them will guide them and bring them home safe.

If you were raised without words of love, make sure your children are! Tell them often you love them—it's the basis of their self-worth. Plant the Word deep in their hearts.Give them an anchor, because life will give them lots of storms. Cover them with the prayer daily. Expect God to bless them for He promised, "I will pour out my spirit upon thy seed."

* * *

That's the word for today for you and your family.

THE REASON WHY

* * *

Great is the mystery of godliness: God was manifest in the flesh.

1 Timothy 3:16

In his book, *The Reason Why*, Robert Laidlaw tells of two friends who went to law school. One became a judge, but the other squandered his life, broke the law, and finished up in court. Sitting in the judge's seat was his old friend. Everyone there wondered what kind of sentence he would pass. To their surprise, he demanded the full penalty of the law. No sooner had he passed sentence, however, than he stepped from the seat of judgment, took off his robes, walked over to the dock where his old friend stood, put his arm around him and gently said, "Let it be recorded today, not only have I passed sentence upon him, *but I will stand chargeable with all his debts."* In that moment, his *judge* became his *redeemer.*

Christmas is the story of the day God took off the robes of deity and put on the garments of humanity. He left a palace to come to a stable because He loved *you.* Listen to the poet:

> The Maker of the universe,
> as man for man was made a curse.
> The claims of law that he had made,
> unto the uttermost He paid.

Did you hear that? *He* paid! Had you been the *only* sinner who ever lived, He would have *come*, He would have *died,* and He would have *paid* the price just for you.

* * *

That's a fact you must deal with now—or someday.

ENOUGH IS ENOUGH!

* * *

Shamgar . . . killed six hundred Philistines with an ox goad, thereby saving Israel.

Judges 3:31(TLB)

The Philistines had been running roughshod through the land. They were bullying God's people, and Shamgar wasn't taking any more. Maybe he was like us. He was waiting for *God* to do something about it. But, God was waiting for *Him* to do something about it. All God needs is a vessel He can use.

Shamgar discovered he had *rights*. He had the right to *own*. He had the right to *defend*. He had the right to *win*. Child of God, do you know your rights today? Listen: "Keep the charge of the LORD thy God, to walk in his ways, to keep his statutes, . . . that thou mayest prosper in all that thou doest" (1 Kings 2:3). You have the right to succeed! After all, look who your Father is!

You also have the right to *defend* what God has given you. Don't surrender your family to the devil. Sure, he may be working on some of them; but remember, God keeps His promises, "All thy children shall be taught of the LORD; and great shall be the peace of thy children" (Isaiah 54:13). *Shamgar wasn't talented, he was just determined!* God honored that determination, and he not only slew six-hundred Philistines, he delivered an entire nation.

* * *

Today, it's time for you to rise up in the name of Jesus and tell the devil, "Enough is enough!"

BEING IN "THAT PLACE"

* * *

Then the LORD said, "There is a place near me where you may stand."
Exodus 33:21 (NIV)

Opinion polls are fickle! The children of Israel forgot in forty days all God had done for them in forty years. While Moses was at the top of the mountain with God, they were at the bottom worshipping a golden calf. If you seek to do anything significant for God, then here's a lesson you must learn: Love the people and lead them, but listen to God only!

God told Moses, "There is a place near me where you may stand." *That should be the goal and passion of your life, to find "that place" and stay in it.* When Moses was there, he could handle anything. He received revelation, built a relationship with God, and got clear guidance on how to lead the people to their inheritance. *But out of "that place" he was no different from the crowd—(neither are you!)*

If God has called you—find "that place." Minister out of "that place," and relate to those around you out of "that place." Do business out of "that place." Raise your family out of "that place." Remember, this is not just *any* place, it's the place beside Him!

* * *

Nothing in your life is more important than being there!

REBUILD YOUR ALTAR

* * *

Then he restored the altar of the LORD

2 Chronicles 33:16 (NIV)

Just about anybody who has ever made a difference in the Bible built an altar unto the Lord. Abraham built seven during his lifetime. In this story, Manasseh turns back to God. Listen: "In his distress he sought the favor of the LORD his God and humbled himself greatly before the God of his fathers (2 Chronicles 33:12, NIV). Few have fallen lower than this man. He promoted witchcraft, practiced human sacrifice, and even put a huge idol into the temple. Yet, in a Babylonian prison, he turned to God, and the One whose "compassions fail not" reached him, restored him, and gave him another chance and *He'll do it for you, too!* Nehemiah says, "Thou art a God ready to pardon" (Nehemiah 9:17). Did you hear that? God is ready when you are—all you have to do is come.

Manasseh rebuilt his altar, and so must you. An altar is a place of *cleansing*; and today you need to allow the blood of Jesus to cleanse you from those attitudes and actions that rob you of your fellowship with Him. An altar is also a place of *sacrifice*. Ask Abraham! It's here that God asks you for your *first*, your *only*, your *best,* and your *all.*

* * *

If you're not giving it to Him, then you need to re-examine your life, put first things first, and rebuild your altar. That's His word to you today.

ANYONE INTERESTED IN FASTING?

* * *

Is not this the fast that I have chosen?

Isaiah 58:6

Some things only happen when we add fasting *to our prayers*! It's not some ritualistic thing that very spiritual people do. No, it's about *focus*. For a time you're saying "No" to self and focusing on the Lord. *That creates intimacy.* Jesus did it before He entered His ministry and Paul did it often.

One day, a man brought his deranged son to Jesus and said, "I brought him to your disciples, but they couldn't cure him" (Matthew 17:16, TLB). *I wonder how often the world has said that about us?* If you're facing a situation like that today, there's something *more* you can do. After Jesus had cast the evil spirit out of the boy, the disciples asked Him why *they* couldn't do it. Listen to His answer—it's a *key* for someone reading this page: "If you have faith . . . nothing shall be impossible unto you. Howbeit this kind goeth not out but by prayer *and fasting*" (Matthew 17:20-21).

If nothing worked for you, *this* may be the situation in which you need to *pray and fast*. Together, they'll bring you to a new level of faith and boldness and that's what brings results. Listen again: "Is not this the fast that *I* have chosen? to loose the bands of wickedness, to undo the heavy burdens, and to let the oppressed go free, and that ye *break every yoke?"* (Isaiah 58:6).

* * *

Prayer and fasting are the keys, use them!

STAYING FRESH

* * *

I shall be anointed with fresh oil.

Psalm 92:10

Your experience with God should be *new every morning,* otherwise you'll become spiritually dull and rigid. God was able to bring His people *out* of Egypt, but He couldn't bring them *into* the Promised Land because of their *attitude.* They had become hardhearted.

When I'm confronted with this, I usuallydeny it. But in the honesty of my own heart, I know it's becoming harder to pray, harder to go to church, and harder to give. Next, I resist anything new, especially any experience *I've* never had, or any truth that hasn't been revealed to *me.*

This morning, I found myself asking God to forgive me for attitudes I've had and words I've spoken concerning things I had little understanding of. It's hard to rejoice when *others* seem to be having an experience with God I haven't had. Children don't like to feel left out!

Rick Joyner says, "The first dangerous illusion is for us to think that *we* would never oppose a true move of God. That great saint, Andrew Murray, *failed to recognize the very revival for which he spent his life praying.* Though he earnestly desired to see the release of spiritual gifts he was *offended by the package they arrived in.*" Sound familiar?

* * *

Ask God to give you fresh insights into His Word and a heart that's always *open* to His spirit. He'll do it!

COME TO JESUS

* * *

Are you tired? Worn out? Burned out on religion? Come to me, I won't lay anything heavy or ill fitting on you. Keep company with me and you'll learn to live.

Matthew 11:28-29 (TM)

Why do we continue preaching a God who cannot be approached to people who have spent most of their lives hiding from Him? Their concept of God is all wrong. Some have said to me, "God's too holy, I can't measure up." Your acceptance is not based on His *holiness*, it's based on His *love. God* thinks you're worth saving so He redeems you by His love. His *standards* never change, but neither does His *compassion.* Listen: "His compassions fail not. They are new every morning" (Lamentations 3:22-23). Without that, none of us have hope.

The basis of any relationship must be *trust.* We can talk to *anyone* about our successes, but we need someone we can talk to about our failures. We have to know for sure, that they understand the *worst* about us and still believe the *best.* If you want someone to love you completely, then they must *know* you completely, for only then will their love satisfy you. That's why Jesus said, "Come to me." You have nothing to fear when you tell it to Jesus, for you're not telling Him anything He doesn't already know. Even before you approach Him today, He has already made up His mind about you.

* * *

You're loved. You're secure. You're His. What more do you need?

OTHER TEACHING MATERIALS BY BOB GASS

For a free catalogue and teaching materials please write to:

Bob Gass Ministries
P.O. Box 2140
Stone Mountain, Georgia 30086

Sources

I'd like to gratefully acknowledge the inspiration I've drawn from different sources in the writing of this book. Much that is rich and original has been gleaned from the following books and authors. I highly recommend them to you.

The Exceeding Greatness of His Power by Rick Joyner
(Morningstar Publications)
God's Little Devotional Book
(Honor Books)
The Place of Immunity by Frances Frangapane
(Arrow Publications)
Naked and Not Ashamed by T.D. Jakes
(Treasure House)
Even Eagles Need a Push by David McNalley
(Dell Publications)
Spiritual Burnout by Malcolm Smith
(Honor Books)
The Message by Eugene H. Peterson
(NavPress)
Wisdom for Winning by Dr. Mike Murdock
(Wisdom International, Inc.)
An Enemy Called Average by John Mason
(Harrison House).
Ladder to the Top by Sherman Owens
(Leadership Publishing)

Topical Index